WHY I HATE CANADIANS

. . . .

Will Ferguson

WHY I HATE
CANADIANS

Happy Birthday Daniel
Enjoy!   Love Mom & Dad

May 11/2009

Douglas & McIntyre
VANCOUVER/TORONTO/BERKELEY

Copyright © 1997, 2007 by William Stener Ferguson

07 08 09 10 11   5 4 3 2

Douglas & McIntyre Ltd.
2323 Quebec Street, Suite 201
Vancouver, British Columbia
Canada v5T 4S7
www.douglas-mcintyre.com

Library and Archives Canada Cataloguing in Publication
Ferguson, Will
Why I hate Canadians / Will Ferguson. — 10th anniversary ed.

ISBN 978-1-55365-279-3

1. Canada—Humor. 2. National characteristics, Canadian—Humor.
3. Canadian wit and humor (English). I. Title.
FC173.F47 2007   C818'.5402   C2007-900291-9

Editing by Saeko Usukawa
Cover design by Naomi MacDougall & Peter Cocking
Cover illustration by Ryan Heshka
Interior design by Peter Cocking
Printed and bound in Canada by Friesens
Printed on acid-free paper
Distributed in the U.S. by Publishers Group West

We gratefully acknowledge the financial support of the Canada
Council for the Arts, the British Columbia Arts Council, the Province of
British Columbia through the Book Publishing Tax Credit,
and the Government of Canada through the Book Publishing Industry
Development Program (BPIDP) for our publishing activities.

CONTENTS

. . . .

PREFACE

. . . .

I WOULD LIKE TO THANK my agent, Carolyn Swayze, for leading me through my first book auction with a minimum of casualties—and I congratulate Douglas & McIntyre for putting together the winning offer.

Teena and Bruce Spencer read most of this manuscript as it was being prepared and offered much-needed words of encouragement and support. It was Teena's enthusiasm right at the start that first got me going.

I should also point out that the views presented in *Why I Hate Canadians* are not those of the publisher. Any errors, omissions or oversights are the sole responsibility of, oh, I don't know. Somebody, I suppose. Not me.

INTRODUCTION TO
THE 10TH
ANNIVERSARY EDITION

. . . .

*D*ANY LAFERRIÈRE's wonderful debut novel, *Comment faire l'amour avec un nègre sans se fatiguer* (translated into English as *How to Make Love to a Negro,* the coda "without getting tired" having been discreetly dropped) was a tale of Haitian exiles in the francophone ghettos of Montreal. As might be imagined, it caused quite a stir, not the least of which was over Laferrière's choice of a title.

The novel quickly became a bestseller, was made into a film and thrust Laferrière headlong into literary notoriety. Looking back at the experience, he mused, "My first novel. The gods could have at least waited for the third before hitting me. The first shot. Bull's-eye. Not even the first novel. The first novel's title."

3

I know how he feels. On a different scale, of course, but still. Naming your first book *Why I Hate Canadians* is a feat of cunning strategy, an act of self-sabotage or simply a case of dumb luck. Much as I would like to ascribe my choice to sheer cunning, I'm afraid a good deal of it was luck, though more naive than dumb.

The title was so obviously tongue-in-cheek, so clearly exaggerated for effect—sort of like "Why I Hate Bambi's Mother"—that I was, and still am, amazed by the number of people who have taken it literally. Among certain types, being offended is a popular pastime.

Why I Hate Canadians was originally entitled "So This Is Paradise," which caused no end of punctuationally induced angst on my part ("So . . . This Is Paradise?" "So, *This* Is Paradise!"). I was going to subtitle it "a collection of essays" but was dissuaded from this on the warning that putting either the word "collection" or the word "essays" on the cover was the kiss of death when it came to sales. Apparently, upon seeing those words, especially in close proximity, readers would fling said book aside and run shrieking in the opposite direction. (Which is actually how a lot of reviewers reacted, now that I think about it.)

Still, I do regret not signalling the anthological aspect of this book better, if only to prepare readers for the "laundry-strung-on-a-line" nature of the pieces it contains. Although essentially a tale of reverse culture shock, of coming home and not recognizing the place—or rather, seeing it in a new and often unflattering light, sort of like trying on a swim-suit from summers past under the sickly green glare of fluorescent lights—this is still a "collection" of "essays" (cue shrieks) and is meant to be read as such. There is a larger narrative arc to it, from the initial jolt of culture shock to an understanding of one's place within that same culture, but *Why I Hate Canadians* is still something of a grab bag, as all collections are.

At the time I wrote these pieces, I was working at a travel company in P.E.I. selling *Anne of Green Gables* sightseeing packages to Japanese tourists during the day, while struggling by night to become a successful freelance journalist (an occupation I now realize is about as economically viable in today's world as chimney sweep or purveyor of fine whalebone corsets). My only attempt at a canny career move was to treat *Why I Hate Canadians* as a portfolio. I was still hoping to get lucrative writing assignments from Canada's many lavishly funded regional newspapers, and in *Why I Hate Canadians* I wanted to showcase my abilities (or lack thereof, unwittingly). Which is why this book contains as wide a range of styles as possible: sports writing, history, political essays, travel writing, satire, spoofs and personal memoir. It was meant to be a romp of sorts, one that readers would find enlivening, whether they agreed with me or not. I like books that both engage and enrage, ones that make your head buzz as though filled with bees by the time you're done, ones that make you want to scribble angry retorts in the margins. And though I didn't quite capture that "bees-in-the-cranium" effect I was looking for, I like to think I came close.

My single greatest regret with *Why I Hate Canadians* is that my wife is nowhere to be seen among its pages, even though she had an enormous impact on the book. While I was living in Japan, I married a lady named Terumi from southern Kumamoto. Terumi moved to Canada with me, and a good deal of my homecoming was seen through her eyes. You never realize how odd your own country is until you try to explain it to someone else. Terumi was with me when I suffered urban amnesia in Fredericton. (Or was it Saint John?) And it was Terumi who made me realize the power that lies beneath the cornball kitsch of our national myths. The book ends with a performance by a theatre troupe of young Canadians, on Canada Day no less, as they sing out—youthful, hopeful, multiculturally aware— "I want to be . . . Canadian!" I turned to Terumi and was about to apologize for this, for the awful sincerity of it all, when I saw that she had tears in her eyes.

Why I Hate Canadians leads up to that moment. The book was meant to move from surface to depth, from the silly accruements of popular culture to the wellspring of emotions and identity that lies below.

Unfortunately, when I told Terumi the catchy new title I'd come up with for my proposed book she was— well, horrified is not too strong a word. "Most people will get that it's a joke," I said. "It's like calling it 'Why I Hate Bambi's Mother.'" "You hate Bambi's mother?" "No, no, it's just, well—"

Turns out, my wife most assuredly did *not* want to appear in any book about her newly adopted homeland that contained the word "Hate" in the title. And so, in the end, I was forced to go through and remove all references to her, much in the manner of a Soviet historian erasing certain salient facts. The book is weaker for not having Terumi's views counterpointed to mine, but no amount of pleading and cajolery would budge her from her insistence she be excused from something so public, so potentially misguided.

Fortunately, *Why I Hate Canadians* did not blow up, trick cigar style, in my face. It sold out the first week and went immediately into a second print run. Then a third. Then a fourth. And a fifth. At last count, there have been over a dozen printings, with more than 50,000 copies sold. Even better, it allowed me to quit my day job and concentrate purely on writing books, something that has caused certain reviewers no end of anguish.

The response to the book abroad was even more revealing. Other nationalities couldn't quite get their minds around the concept of anyone "hating Canadians." (Which was sort of the point, but never mind.) The publisher of my Japanese travel guide caught what he considered an obvious mistake in my author bio and ran it through a spell-checker in order to "fix" the error. That is why, even now, the back cover of *The Hitchhiker's Guide to Japan* lists my previous books as including *Why I Hate Comedians*. Which does make me sound a bit sour, no? *Bloody comedians, think they're so funny*. . . And when I was interviewed live on *Australia Today,* the tag they ran on the screen below read: "Will Ferguson, author of *Why I Don't Like Canadians.*" Even the Australians couldn't do it.

Reaction in Canada, meanwhile, ranged from "Why I Hate THIS BOOK"–type articles to "Why I Hate Will Ferguson!!!!!" (responses so completely predictable I had actually referred to them within the book itself—an irony lost on most of my critics). One intensely focussed fellow cornered me at a book signing—armed with flip charts and pie diagrams, as I seem to recall—to explain at great length that the character in the cartoon kicking Uncle Sam's ass was NOT Johnny Canuck, as I had so erroneously stated, but was in fact a prototypical forerunner of the aforementioned character. (Since corrected.)

I do regret singling out Associate Professors as being standard-bearers of the Canadian Dream, if only for the endless letters and open hostility I received in return. I imagine some of those letters were written without the need of hands, the pens clenched tightly in the anuses of the people who sent them. Certainly, I could have papered my walls with the messages I received from people wanting to know "just exactly" who I thought I was. (I'm assuming the question is rhetorical and not existential, though you never can tell with these academic types.) So let me just say, for the record, that I consider Associate Professors to be the height of humanly perfection, both intellectually and physically. Known for their fine creative minds, their sexual prowess and undeniable charisma, their excellent penmanship and good posture, Associate Professors represent the very pinnacle of the apex of the acme of what we might all become. Likewise my views on suburbia. More than one critic has argued that the burbs are in fact vibrant, close-knit, passionate communities. I stand corrected. Apologies all 'round.

Part Four ("Sex in a Canoe") remains my personal favourite in *Why I Hate Canadians,* and was in fact what I'd planned to open with, to establish both the tone and the humour (or lack thereof) contained within. My publisher, however, felt I should first establish what little credentials I had (mainly as the recovering participant of sundry and assorted youth volunteer programs) before I plunged too deeply into humour. But I'm still tempted to advise readers to skip ahead and start with "Sex in a Canoe." (Not literally, of course, though they may want to do that as well. I'll keep my eyes peeled for news stories with the lead-in: LITERAL-MINDED CANADIANS FOUND BUCK-NAKED BESIDE OVERTURNED CANOES. AUTHOR BLAMED.)

If nothing else, Part Four contains a succinct summation of the typical Canadian career path:

1. Hating Toronto
2. Moving to Toronto
3. Wishing you could move to Vancouver
4. Staying in Toronto
5. Hating Vancouver

(Though, with the current boom in which Calgary is basking, I imagine you could probably change "Toronto" to "Calgary" and it would read just as well.)

The anger in *Why I Hate Canadians* comes from a specific political context. This book was written both as a response to, and in the aftermath of, the 1995 referendum, wherein Canadians allowed one segment, in one province, to try to vote an entire country out of existence through a fucking *plebiscite*. It was the sort of process usually reserved for rezoning school playgrounds. Ending Canada with a show of hands is the political equivalent of making an elephant disappear through a massive act of misdirection, aided with copious amounts of smoke and mirrors. Canada's near-death experience in 1995 would prove to be a formative moment for an entire generation of young Canadians. Whenever I speak to people younger than me—which is a disconcertingly larger and larger segment of the population—I am struck by what a vivid, cold-water splash to the face that referendum really was.

Let's face it: the nineties were a hellish decade for Canadian unity, a time of wrenching debates and constitutional turmoil that solved nothing—absolutely nothing—while the country staggered, punch-drunk, from one artificially induced national crisis to another, beginning with Meech Lake and ending with a Clarity Act that outlined the very terms of Canada's future surrender.

Ironically, while all this was going on, the rest of the world was curled up in sleepy PJs. *Why I Hate Canadians* was written during that Great Lull, in the time between the Fall of the Berlin Wall—when democracy seemed ascendant, triumphant, inevitable—and the horrific crash of the Twin Towers on September 11. My reference to "democracy breaking out all over" and how "things couldn't be better" may seem pointed now, but I assure you, when I wrote that, it was not meant to be the least bit ironic or wry. It was a time when the end of history seemed quite plausible. And desirably so.

Why I Hate Canadians was published on the very day that Lady Diana died. Remember the mounds of flowers and waves of grief? A good time to launch a humour book, that, especially one that went out of its way *to poke fun at Lady Di*. The next print run was hastily amended. So if you own a copy of the original version of this book with a reference to a "publicity-hungry divorcee," you've got yourself a (minor) collectible.

The big "marshmallow" alluded to in the White House is, of course, Bill Clinton. It was a pre-Google, pre-Internet age. Back in 1997, the "World Wide Web," as they were calling it, was still very much a novelty, and references in this book to me phoning newspaper editors at great cost instead of doing a simple search/mass e-mail seem almost quaint ten years after the fact. And in our current gynecologically revealing age of cyber porn, references to the black stickers that were legally required to cover up the naughty bits in Canadian nudie magazines now seem downright prudish, in the most charming sense of the term. In the same way that we chuckle over Victorians hiding piano legs with skirts, future generations will surely marvel at the idea of anything less than full-blown anatomical spelunking being considered the norm.

Still, the portents are there. References to *American Gladiators* presage the current Andy Warhol allotment of fame given to everyone under the auspices of Reality TV. And Farley Mowat's blocked entry to the U.S. in the Reagan era—on info fed to the Americans by our own RCMP— eerily foreshadows what would later happen to Maher Arar. (In this case, history appears *first* as farce and then as tragedy.)

The Three Great Themes of Canadian History, as outlined in this book, are with us still. Native issues barely register on the Canadian consciousness—unless the people involved block a road or go toe-to-toe with the police— and the shadow of the Almighty U.S. still looms, large as ever. The Hudson's Bay Company has been bought out by the Americans, which is, in some ways, apt. It began as a colonial enterprise, and it ended as one.

The separatists are still as wonky as ever. Just recently, they denounced playwright Michel Tremblay as a "traitor" for expressing the mildest of doubts about the sovereignty project. The attack on Tremblay was swift and virulent, and Tremblay, backpedalling like mad, quickly recanted.

His apostasy was forgiven, with penance due, but still. If there was any doubt that separatism in Québec has become a fundamentalist religion, as surely as have Marxism and certain brands of Islam and Christianity, there's your proof.

At the same time that Tremblay was being denounced as a Judas to the cause, an educational guidebook was being prepared by the Council for Québec Sovereignty. It contained a wealth of helpful suggestions for teachers on everything from preschool colouring books to music classes to college curriculum—all of it with a separatist bent. The guidebook even featured an illustration of a Canadian flag ripped in half and included arithmetic problems that asked students to calculate such things as how much "federalist intrusions" on Québec sovereignty were costing them. It was reminiscent of North Korean textbooks that famously asked questions like, "If one hand grenade can kill six American soldiers, how many American soldiers can *three* hand grenades kill?"

It gets better. The company that published this guide—one aimed at undermining Canadian federalism, remember—was generously funded by, you guessed it, a grant from the Canada Council for the Arts, courtesy of the federal government. So don't imagine for a moment that the examples of separatist silliness given in *Why I Hate Canadians* are in any way dated. They aren't.

Meanwhile, on the non-separatist side of the ledger, Canada's self-congratulatory parade rolls on. Consider the November 20, 2006, issue of *Maclean's* with its self-generated "news" story, complete with bannered headline, on the front cover: "Exclusive International Poll: WHY THE

WORLD LOVES CANADA... more than the Americans, and more than just about everyone else."

Plus ça change...

Looking back, ten years later, I retain a certain nostalgic affection for *Why I Hate Canadians,* it being my first book and all, even if I scarcely recognize the person writing it at times. For the tenth anniversary, I considered updating certain references—changing Preston Manning to Stephen Harper, Lucien Bouchard to Gilles Duceppe, that sort of thing—but who knows how long Harper or Duceppe will be around.

Canada, once at the forefront of peacekeeping, now ranks fifty-ninth in its contributions. The Canadians in Afghanistan are serving in a war zone, as combatants, and my chapter on peacekeeping and the call for a UN standing army now belongs to another era—almost another world.

Ralf the Porcupine, who appears in the chapter on Sudbury, has since gone on to that Great Quill Forest in the Sky. Pierre Berton is no longer with us, nor is Pierre Trudeau, and Conrad Black is, um, not quite the formidable presence he was in 1997. Terumi and I have left the Loyalist loveliness of St. Andrews, New Brunswick, and moved west, to the architectural Etch A Sketch that is Calgary. And Canada stumbles onward, as always, not so much walking as maintaining a fall.

WILL FERGUSON
2007

Part One

MADE

IN CANADA

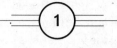

1

SO THIS IS PARADISE:
A TRAVELLER RETURNS

. . . .

*I*T BEGINS on an airplane, high above
the Pacific.

The moon is down and the night is as black as print-
er's ink. I am surrounded by the sound of strangers sleeping, amid the hiss and sigh of compression and the smell
of recycled air. It feels as though we are flying through
a tunnel.

It begins on an airplane, because this is a tale of return.

I am returning to Canada after five years in exile, 1990
to 1995. Half a decade. When I left, Canada was mired in
the muck of Meech Lake. Remember Meech Lake? That
was several crises, a referendum, a failed Accord and the
collapse of the Conservative Party ago. In 1990 the nation

17

was charged with portents of doom. In 1990 we were careening pell-mell into the future, head first, hands on the dash, foot pumping the brake. It was a good time to leave.

I had once been a rising star in the Struggle for Canadian Unity, working in youth projects, overseas programs and cultural exchanges with Québec. But my early idealism soured and my work in the Third World undermined my faith in nationalism. Then came Meech Lake, renewed separatism, the rise of the Reform Party and yet another angst-ridden Constitutional debate.

I was tired of being Canadian. Tired of the endless dialogues, the countless "blueprints for change," the innumerable "calls to action." There is a weariness in being Canadian, and with it comes an opposing force: the desire to escape. In Canada, it seems that you are either mindlessly optimistic or depressingly realistic. Having swung from one end to the other, I finally decided to bail out. I ran away, as far away as I could go, and for this I apologize. While the rest of you were manning the ramparts and penning heartfelt letters to the editor and attending Citizens' Action Forum Unity Committees for a Brighter Tomorrow, I was in Asia ingesting questionable quantities of local inspiration and attempting to induce post-traumatic amnesia.

More than anything, I wanted to forget I was ever Canadian. I wanted to be reborn without nationality.

Unfortunately, forgetting about Canada proved as impossible as forgetting your first love—the one who broke your heart, the one who first held your hand, the one rejected in all the others that followed. For a while I managed to submerge myself in Zen studies and cheap beer, but the only thing I learned was this: when it comes to clearing your mind of earthly illusions, cheap beer works better than Zen meditation.

Beer asks no questions. But Zen poses *koans,* riddles unanswerable that are meant to snap your mind free like an overextended rubber band. What is the sound of one hand clapping? What did your face look like before your ancestors were born? Can a dog have the Buddha nature? But for all my Zen musings, I never heard a single koan that tormented me as much as the one of my own making: *Canada? What does it mean?*

In *Touch the Dragon,* Karen Connelly, a fellow Canadian in exile, writes: *Canada? Even the name is a question.*

Like so many things in life, I gave up on Zen. Or rather, Zen gave up on me. The fact that I kept giggling during the most solemn of moments didn't help, nor did my Gen X attention span. It didn't matter. I was living on the Amakusa Islands, south of Nagasaki. There were palm trees in the yard and the winds were always warm. Canada started to dissolve. I hitchhiked across Japan and wrote a guidebook for freeloaders. I backpacked through southeast Asia and I made my way across China, but for all my Jack Kerouac pretensions, I wasn't really drifting. I was turning, like a dog on a tether, around and around that central, three-syllable hole in my identity: *Canada.*

Occasionally, at the back of an Asian newspaper, I'd find a teeny tiny article on Canada, hidden in among the sumo standings and GNP updates. The headline was always the same: CANADA: GOING TO HELL IN A HANDBASKET. And, a few weeks later, CANADA: *STILL* GOING TO HELL IN A HANDBASKET.

Meech Lake and the Charlottetown Accord. Mulroney tossing the keys to the motor home over to Kim just as it went under the ice. The rise of Peg-Leg Pete and the Bloc Québécois. The tragicomedy that is Canada just seemed to go on and on and on, like one of those old Hollywood serials that left the heroine hanging from a tree root at the end of every episode.

Meanwhile, back in Asia, no one gave a damn.

My initial euphoria over escaping Canada subsided. I began to crave information. It became obsessive. I started sending wads of high-powered Japanese yen back to friends and siblings, wheedling, whining and cajoling them into sending me articles and books on Canada. I read and learned and fretted more over Canada after I left than I ever did while I was home. I absorbed everything I could on topics that ranged from folklore to history to political manifestos. I gave presentations on "Understanding Canadian Culture" to polite but impassive Japanese audiences at the Ministry of Education. ("Does Canada *have* a culture?" was the usual, devastating response.) I provided research for the now defunct Japan-Canada Alliance. I ranted and raved and seethed about things beyond my control. In short, I acted like a Canadian.

Among the various things I read, one book stopped me cold. It was by a right-wing, ex–South African slogan-maker from Ontario, and the title said it all: *Only YOU Can Save Canada.*

Who *me?*

Yes, me. And so it was, I decided to return to Canada and save the nation.

Which is how I came to be here, on a plane high above the Pacific, my head lolling drunkenly, eyes as glazed as a

Tim Hortons doughnut, drool dribbling from the side of my mouth, a hardcover book open on my lap: *Canadian Constitutional Frameworks for Unity and Challenges of Regionalism in a Political Structure of International Economics Including Simply Reams of Footnotes and Endless Qualifying Statements All of Which Is Guaranteed To Make Your Eyes Glaze Over and Your Head Begin To Loll.*

I kept reading the same page over and over, but none of it was registering. It was one of those books that put you to sleep before you finish the title page. And no wonder, it was written by a world authority on management and organizational something-or-other.

That's the problem with most of these books—they are written by experts, people who have studied a subject for so long they have gone stark raving mad. You remember those really boring professors at university? The ones who could describe a train wreck and still make it seem dull? ("A pair of metal-wheeled vehicular transports came into physical conflict such that both occupied the same space or 'proximity' due to the apparent—or, more precisely, *assumed*—intoxication of the individual located at the front of the train.") Well guess what, these people are now writing books about the Canadian social-political situation. This may be one of the reasons we are in such a mess. I struggled through a few more chapters before I gave up. As near as I can figure, the message was basically: CANADA: GOING TO HELL IN A HANDBASKET.

The nice thing about reading sombre, densely written, mind-numbing books is that they help make a long flight seem that much longer. I buzzed the flight attendant and she came around with some honey-roasted peanuts (peanuts per package: four).

"You shouldn't eat nuts late at night," she said. "They are hard to digest. You may have trouble sleeping."

But I didn't want to sleep. I wanted to be home, awake, ready to face the future. Peanuts pass right through you, in much the same way that I had passed through Asia. Undigested. Hard. And now I was returning, to be among my own: hardheaded peanut-brained nationalists and kernel corn Québécois, stubbornly undigested in the Great Colon that is Canadian Society. Everything engendered metaphors. The air-sickness bags of separatism. The plastic tube earphones of federalism. Canada! *Mon pays!* I was coming home.

It used to be that travellers had weeks on the open sea to muse about their homecoming, to muse and reflect and write florid, quill-and-ink journals.

I had only nine hours and an inflight movie to mentally prepare, to decompress and—figuratively speaking—to brace for impact. *Roger, Houston. Prepare for re-entry.*

The truth be told, I was sick of Japan. I was sick of being stared at. I was sick of eating rice. I was sick of being drunk all the time. And I was really sick of taking my shoes off at the door. I wanted to track filth through the house with impunity. I longed for a more open and tolerant land. I missed Mounties and malls and Moosehead beer and Molson Canadian. I missed hockey. I missed snow. I missed *slush,* for God's sake, that's how far gone I was. I call it Expatriate's Amnesia: the ability to idealize whatever patch of sod you came from and elevate it above whatever patch of sod you now happen to be occupying. Nationalists can do this without even leaving, a remarkable trait and one of the things that keeps them so proudly uninformed about the world beyond their borders.

Canada was Camelot to me. Paradise Lost. A land of opportunity. A model for the world! (Actually, the rest of the world is barely *aware* of Canada, let alone studying it as a role model, but none of that stopped my glorification of the Great White North.) Canada: where everyone is happy and kind, where children—all the colours of the rainbow—play in multiracial harmony, where the moose and the black bear frolic, where the Mighty Beaver stands majestically atop a rugged pine tree in Georgian Bay overlooking the vast Rockies.

Alas, as any tree-climbing beaver knows, the higher you climb, the farther you fall. After working my fantasy of Canada up to the heights of Heaven on Earth, I had nowhere to go but down.

"Going home?" It was the woman two seats down.

"Yes!" I said.

"You must be very glad to be going back."

"Absolutely."

"Well," she said. "Personally, *I* couldn't stand Japan. I have been to Europe and France and America and whenever I go away I always appreciate Canada much more when I return. Why, I practically kiss the ground when I get back."

"Then why bother travelling at all? It would be cheaper just to sit at home and feel good about yourself."

"You sound like you don't even like Canada."

I shrugged. "Canada is alright."

"*Alright?* Canada is the best country in the world! The United Nations even said that, they did. You can look it up."

"And the year before they picked Japan. Next year it'll be Australia. It doesn't mean a thing."

"Well," she said. "Personally, I think we are lucky to live in Canada."

"And Japanese people feel they are lucky to live in Japan. Japan is safer, richer, more cohesive than Canada. And the Americans think they are lucky to live in the States, because they have more money and lots of nukes. The British have more castles. The Chinese have more history. The Dutch have more tulips. Don't you find it funny how people always admire whatever their particular speciality is?"

"Well," she said, straightening herself. "In Canada we may not be the strongest or the richest or the best, but we are—*nice.*"

"Nice?"

"Yes. Canadians are nice."

"That's it? *Nice?*"

"That," she assured me, "is more than enough. Good night." And with a final hallumph she rolled herself over and angrily feigned sleep.

There you have it. The blandest adjective in the English language, and we have claimed it proudly as our own. Canadians are nice. I was never more depressed.

The plane landed in the early dawn, and as we filed groggily through customs the young officer who greeted us—bright of eye and bushy of tail—was impossibly, annoyingly friendly. I was used to being searched and intimidated by customs officers. In Korea, I had to pay a bribe just to *leave* their damn country, but here I was given the world's most cheerful interrogation. "Returning, are we?" Big smile. "You must be glad to be back."

I stumbled through the foyer, watched the sun rise across the parking lot. Newsstands were running recycled headlines. Regionalism. Deficit. Separatists. Referendums. Renewed Federalism. Letters to the editor explaining why Canada is the best country in the world. Editorials congratulating ourselves on being so self-deprecating. Editorials denouncing intolerance in the most vehement terms. More letters to the editor. More recycled air. It was 1990 all over again.

I had left Canada under the cloud of Meech Lake; I came back just in time for the 1995 Referendum. Five years had passed and the headlines had barely changed. In my journal, I wrote: *Canada is still Canada. Only more so.* And Canadians—the doe-eyed, soft-spoken, tolerant Canadians I had created in my mind—were nowhere to be seen. Everyone was so loud, so impatient, so self-obsessed, so exclamatory, so—so much like *me*. It was all I could do not to get on the first plane out.

The Pacific Ocean is one of the world's great divides. The Atlantic joins, but the Pacific separates. When you travel eastward across the Atlantic, the world changes by slow degrees: North and South America connect with their European roots; Europe blends into Turkey; Turkey into India; India into Southeast Asia; Southeast Asia into China; China into Japan. But when you go the other way, when you cross the Pacific, you make the great jump from Occident to Orient with no steps in between. Canada to Japan is a leap, not so much of faith as of imagination.

If you could look up Canada in the Dictionary of Life, it would say *ant: see Japan.* Canada and Japan are opposites in virtually every category you care to name. Japan is the most homogeneous nation on earth. Canada is fast becoming the most heterogenous. Ninety-eight per cent of Japanese people belong to a single ethnic group: Japanese. Ninety-eight per cent of Canadians have ancestors From Away. Japan is a long, thin, heavily populated nation. Canada is mainly tundra. Much of Japan is lush, green, and mountainous. Almost 50 per cent of Canada is permanently frozen.

Japan is a high-context society: what you say is not nearly as important as how you say it and in what situation. Canada (like most immigrant nations) is low-context. There is little subtext. We say whatever IS ON OUR MIND even when nothing is. Especially when nothing is. The Japanese value *enryo,* imperfectly translated as "restraint." Canadians have no restraint. Canadians will tell you, within five minutes of your having met, about their job, their family history, their marital status and how their father is an alcoholic and their mother is on Prozac and how they thought they had bowel cancer last year but it just turned out they had been eating too many peanuts. In Japan, you might work with someone for years—as I did—and never know whether or not he was married or even what his first name was.

Japan is a (relatively) ancient nation. Canada is (relatively) young, but neither society is as ancient nor as young as it would like to believe. Canada has been a democracy from day one. Canada was *created* as a democracy. Japan has been a democracy for barely fifty years, and even then it had to be A-bombed into submission first. The Japanese were the bully-boys of World War II. Canadians were the good guys. (Abroad at least; at home it was another story.) Japan was—and essentially still is—an insular, xenophobic society. Canadians are tolerant to the point of allowing people dedicated to destroying the very country to be sworn into public office.

The Japanese don't work hard, but they do work long. Canadians avoid both. The Japanese take immense pride in the company they work for and, by extension, the nation they belong to. Canada is a plurality. Japan is a unity.

Yet, for all their differences, the good citizens of Canada and Japan share one overriding, all-important characteristic. They both have an obsessive fascination with themselves. There is a constant search for identity—or at the very least, cultural tics. Whether we say *zee* or *zed, jam* or *jelly*. Whether Japan has four seasons or whether foreigners can eat raw fish.

Tell the average Japanese person that countries all around the world have four seasons and that Korean cherry blossoms are every bit as beautiful as Japanese ones, and you will break his heart. Or piss him off. Or both. Tell the average Canadian—well, that is the whole point of this book.

This is a book born of reverse culture shock. It was much harder than I ever imagined readjusting to life back in Canada, and from my journals and notes over the last two years comes this book. As well as seeking to tip over as many sleeping sacred cows as possible, it also attempts to answer three (3) fundamental questions:

1. Are Canadians really as nice as they think they are?
2. If so, when exactly did this happen? When did we become so darn nice?
3. And is nice necessarily a good thing?

Some people build sandcastles in the sky. Others come and kick them over. I am of the sandcastle-kicking variety. But before you dismiss me as some sour-pussed, misanthropic know-it-all, let me assure you that I am in fact a *well-qualified* sourpussed, misanthropic know-it-all. My credentials are impeccable: I have *never* held public office. I have no string of postgraduate abbreviations cluttering up my name, and not only have I never taught economics at McGill—I actively avoid the subject. Simply put: You can't blame me for anything. I have never sat on any Committee or Subcommittee or Royal Commission, and I have never inflicted my social/political theories on Canada. Until now.

I was once a foot soldier in the Struggle for Canadian Independence, and I speak with the wisdom of the walking wounded. During the 1980s I was at the forefront of no less than *three* misguided attempts at fostering "the Canadian Spirit." Namely: Canada World Youth (an overseas volunteer corps brimming with earnest, young, publicly funded Canadians); Katimavik (a national volunteer corps brimming with earnest, young, publicly funded Canadians); and the long-forgotten Project Megapôle (a Québec volunteer corps brimming with earnest, young, publicly funded Canadians).

These programs were dedicated to instilling an *esprit de canadien*. Their aim was nothing less than the capture and taming of the elusive Canadian Soul. Alas, it proved about as effective as buying a lamp and then going out to search for a genie.

When I was young I believed in many things. I believed that Wayne Gretzky was God, that Ben Johnson was the fastest man alive, and that Canada was a good idea. I still do. Unfortunately, I also believed in us. In Canadians. In our desire to Do Good. I believed—*I truly believed*—that if we just wished for something hard enough, if we closed our eyes and hugged ourselves really, really hard, we could save Canada. I believed in magical gestures. I believed in the future.

My disillusionment didn't happen overnight. There were many hints and premonitions along the way. As I set out to travel the world, I was assured by countless fellow Canadians that everybody simply loves Canadians. After all, how could anyone not love such a modest, restrained, swell bunch of people like us? Just sew a maple leaf on your backpack, my boy, and when the terrorists storm the bus they'll be offering you tea and crumpets while the Americans, Israelis and Brits are being lined up against a wall and shot. Wear a maple leaf on your backpack, my son, and people will run up to shake your hand, they will give you wholesale, they will ask you to marry their sister. They will thank you for being a model of tolerance and goodwill.

This "maple leaf on the backpack" myth was the first to die. The truth is, people do not treat you better when they know you are Canadian; they simply treat you less bad because they know you are not an American. This is something even the Americans have picked up on. The January 1997 issue of *Escape: the Global Guide for the Adventurous Traveler* assures readers that tours of Iran are possible, but adds, "even so, a little extra precaution can't hurt—a Canadian flag perhaps. Don't leave home without it, eh?"

The Japanese can't tell us apart. The Iranians can't tell us apart. *And even Canadians have trouble telling the difference.* I was sitting in a sidewalk café in Paris when a bunch of gum-chewing, camera-wielding, brightly bedecked tourists came in, hooting and hollering and making loud, public statements like "YOU SIT HERE. I'LL GO LOOK FOR A TOILET!" I sighed and muttered "Damn Yankees" under my breath. My travel companion agreed. Then these same brightly coloured tourists began comparing the prices in France with those back home—in Canada.

Canadians are the second-loudest people on earth. Unfortunately, Americans are the loudest, and because we live next door to them we never realize how much we SHOUT. It's like sharing a duplex with Def Leppard; your own stereo seems quiet in comparison.

But so what? So we're a little LOUD! Who cares, right? My real awakening came when I gave the students in my Japanese adult English class a reading assignment: a book called *My Canada*. This is a very patriotic book, published in 1984 in the wake of the *first* referendum. It was dedicated to the memory of Terry Fox. I had a whole box-load of these books sent to me in Japan and I went around handing them out at random, much like a Jehovah's Witness peddling the Word of God. *My Canada* is a compilation of short essays by all kinds of Canadians: young Canadians, old Canadians, famous Canadians, not-so-famous Canadians, smart Canadians, dumb Canadians, demographically varied Canadians, all writing down their feelings about what it means to be—you guessed it—Canadian.

I'd read *My Canada* in high school, and though I hadn't reread it since, I remembered it as a stirring work, sure to inspire my Japanese students. I knew something was wrong when the first student began to giggle. Then the next. Soon they were all laughing. They began to make up their own "My Canada" essays. The formula was simple enough to follow, and they soon had it down pat: "Canada is the best country in the world. We are not Americans. Canada has beautiful countryside. We are very lucky to be Canadians."

That's the problem with nationalism. It's like body odour and beer farts; everyone else's always seem much worse than your own. In fact, much like body odour and beer farts, you secretly kind of *enjoy* your own version of it. Some nationalism is violent and dark, some is self-congratulatory, but all nationalism—in its purest form—is fundamentally irrational. Nationalism asks you to believe that the country you happen to live in, by amazing coincidence, also happens to be the greatest country in the world. What luck! That Canadian nationalism is so innocuous doesn't make it any better. In some ways, it makes it worse.

We boast about the Great Canadian Inferiority Complex (what other nation would dare call its inferiority complex "great?") and we compliment ourselves incessantly on being so very, very nice. What we fail to realize is that self-conscious niceness is not niceness at all; it is a form of smugness. Is there anything more insufferable than someone saying, "Gosh, I sure am a sweet person, don'tcha think? Couldn't you just hug me to pieces?"

My first few days back in Canada were difficult. I had some painful adjustments to make. Mark Messier is in New York? *Florida now has two hockey teams?!* I had been gone a long time. When I left, Edmonton was still winning hockey games, that's how long it had been. Hockey is the heartbeat of Canada, and everywhere I saw dark omens and ominous parallels. There were new teams on the block. The Sharks? The Bloc Québécois. The Mighty Duck? Preston Manning. The Senators? Asleep as usual. I read the paper and I rolled my eyes so often people thought I was having epileptic fits.

I began to make lists:

- The Canadian gymnastic event is the balancing beam.
- The favourite colour? Plaid.
- The musical note is sustained. Barely.
- The verb tense is conditional.
- The kiss is French, but the position is missionary.
- The food is porridge. The cheese is whiz.
- If Canada were a coffee, it would be decaf espresso.
- If it were an actor, it would be described as having "bland good looks." Canadians: the Mark Harmon of Nations.

My friends and family became exasperated. "Why do you hate Canada so much?" I was taken aback by the question. I don't hate Canada. Canada is pretty good as far as countries go. In many ways it is superb—even great. The question that was gnawing away at me was this: Do we, as Canadians, *deserve* Canada?

One of the most annoying Canadians to lurch into view during my absence was, in my opinion, William D. Gairdner, who wrote a best-selling book entitled *What's Wrong with Canada*. To me, reading Gairdner is like being trapped in an elevator with Grandpa. "Let me tell you, sonny boy, in my day the immigrants knew their place, women stayed at home, and everybody went to Church." A social revolution is sweeping the globe, the world is changing as we speak, and Grandpa Gairdner—it seems to me—is clinging to Depression-era slogans. His premise is simple: there are serious flaws in the structure of modern Canadian society; we need to go back to older, simpler times. You see this assumption in the works of others, such as David Frum, Conrad Black and Premier Mike Harris of Ontario.

But was yesterday all that sweet and nice? And is today's Canada all that bad? Our institutions have produced a social structure and material lifestyle second to none. Canada, on a grand scale, has never been better. What if the problem is not Canada? What if the problem is *us*? Our insecurities, our self-delusions, our suburban world view, our shopping mall mentality, our insistence on taking the edge off of everything, of pulling our punches, of avoiding the issue, of diluting even rage—all those bovine qualities that make us seem dull and whiny, quick to complain but slow to act. Perhaps Gairdner is mistaken. Perhaps the question is not "What's wrong with Canada?" but "What's wrong with Canadians?"

The title of this book raised some eyebrows among my friends. "How can you hate Canadians?" was a common question. "It's like hating Bambi's mother."

More than one person warned me that newspapers would be flooded with letters to the editor enumerating the reasons "Why I Hate Will Ferguson." Which actually buoyed my spirits. It's wonderful to live in a country where the worst a writer has to face is an angry epistle from Upper Rubber Boot, Saskatchewan, explaining why they think you are a jerk. There are no assassins and political gulags in Canada. Were I to write a similar book in Japan, the ominous black buses of the right wing party would pull up and *yakuza* thugs would have me beaten to a pulp. I repeat: Canada is an excellent country, politically, socially, and even—how we hate to admit it—economically. It is the inhabitants that make one pause to wonder.

It was once said of Voltaire that he loved humanity, but couldn't stand people. I found myself in a similar situation. I loved Canada—but Canadians?

So we aren't perfect. Who cares? After all, we have so much *potential*. Gobs of potential. It oozes out of our pores, it drips from the end of our nose. We are young. Free. True. North. Strong. And we are brimming with potential energy.

Potential energy is a funny thing. Not "ha-ha" funny, but more "oxymoronically funny." It's a contradiction in terms, no? A bit like talking about passive action, intellectual nationalist, or Progressive Conservative. Canadians are masters of the oxymoron. Maybe it has something to do with our need to transcend the opposites inherent in our society (French/English, East/West). After all, Canadians are also acknowledged masters of irony, and oxymorons and irony spring from the same source: dilemmas that can't be solved, yet can't be ignored. But I suspect the Canadian love of oxymoron is less complex. It has little to do with transcending dilemmas. We just don't think things through. *Intellectual nationalist?* This is an oxymoron of the first degree.

In Canada, the intellectuals are nationalist, the conservatives are progressive, and the energy is potential. Potential energy exists in springs compressed, in rocks poised at the edge of a cliff, and even in someone slouched in front of a television set who *intends* to get up and do something. They all contain potential. They all contain energy. Whether anything comes of it is another thing entirely.

Being described as having "potential" is the booby prize of compliments. It's like being told you're a lousy poet, but you have good penmanship. It doesn't stir the blood. Dreams deferred to a later date never do.

What an impotent battle cry: *Rah Rah Canada! We could probably do a lot more if we really tried!*

Canadians don't try harder. We hardly try at all. This is one of our most endearing qualities; we are a nation that talks a good revolution but still hasn't gotten around to mowing the lawn or fixing the fence or signing that what-do-you-call-it Constitution thing.

At times it seems Canada has the potential energy not of a spring, nor of a body at rest, but of a boulder at the edge of a cliff. And the best we can hope for is that the ledge doesn't crumble too quickly.

THE 1995 REFERENDUM was slipping away. Lucien and the boys were about to push Confederation over the edge and everybody was, well, edgy. I flew in to Fredericton just days before the referendum, and tensions were high. I had been hired to write a piece on Canada's current turmoil, and—being an astute journalist—I decided to take the Pulse of the Nation.

"I'll tell you what I think," said the cab driver, as he pounded the dash for emphasis. (Cab drivers are the source of all great journalistic insights.) "Canada is the best country in the world! The United Nations even said so. It's true. You can look it up." The driver was a young and very animated student from UNB. He was in poli-sci. He aspired to the position of Associate Professor, but for now he was driving cabs, overcharging tourists, taking scenic routes and solving the world's problems in his spare time—as is the prerogative of cabbies the world over. He was definitely in favour of Canada.

"I don't want to see Canada destroyed," he said. "I'm even thinking about going to that rally in Montréal, you know, to show the people of Québec that the rest of

Canada cares. To show them that we can all live together, regardless of our differences."

"I hope it works," I said. "The separatists seem pretty intent on breaking up this country."

"Yeah," he said. "Fucking French-Canadian bastards. I tell you."

Québec is breaking New Brunswick's heart. If Québec goes, it will strand the Acadian and Brayon nations in an understandably hostile, Anglo-dominated country. New Brunswick is the one province where bilingualism actually works—despite the best intentions of the provincial government—and anything that can survive the best intentions of the government deserves our praise. (This is why Native Canadians are so praiseworthy; they have survived more good intentions than anyone.)

So I decided to go. A bunch of people were heading up from Saint John by Super Express Discount Unity Bus. I expected the bus to be filled with either drunken party-goers looking for an excuse to vomit on Québec territory, or with fervent nationalists breaking into song every couple of miles—"*Land of the Silver Birch!* Everybody!" But I was wrong. The people who boarded the bus were not boors. Nor were they zealous. They were very sincere and very worried. Canadians *talk* a good revolution, but when the time comes to storm the palace gates, this is what we get; a bus filled with good intentions. I got off. Couldn't do it.

It didn't matter. We were all there, on that bus. All of us, in heart and soul. It was an all-Canadian pilgrimage, and the frightening thing is: it worked. If the polls are to be believed, the Unity Rally helped boost the *non* side by a half a percentage point, and on October 30 that's what it came down to. A stunning, inspirational 1.2 per cent victory for Team Canada. What the hell, a miss was as good as a mile, and the sedition of Bouchard and the PQ was staved off yet again, like a vampire with a clove of garlic.

Thousands upon thousands crowded into Place du Canada. There were banners and hugs and lots of people saying "excuse me." There were speeches, interchangeable. And rhetoric, incomprehensible. Abstract nouns were batted about like balloons. Faces were painted. Songs were sung. And then, like an eclipse, the Canadian flag uncurled above the crowd. Nothing had changed. Here it was, that same stubborn belief in magical gestures, that Peter Pan faith that if we just wish for something hard enough it will come true.

Canadian nationalism, like all nationalism, is a talisman against thought. Amid the biggest demonstration of self-love in our nation's history, all I could feel was numb. In Canada, we talk a good revolution, but when the time comes we will die in our sleep, holding onto talismans, waiting for the magic to work.

PROJECT MEGAPÔLE:
QUÉBEC IS A JOKE, CANADA
IS THE PUNCH LINE

. . . .

*M*Y FIRST great love affair was in Québec and with Québec.

I was nineteen years old and smitten with a girl from Lévis. Her name was Marie-Claire, and she was beautiful. She never wore make-up, she never wore a bra, and she never bothered to scrape the hair from her legs—it was blonde and soft as down. She knew how to make love, she understood jazz, she knew all the best cafés, and she hated heavy-handed gestures and romantic pretensions. (Which was a shame, because heavy-handed gestures were all I knew; it was kind of my forte.)

We first met in a group work camp in British Columbia, and over the next few years our lives kept intersecting and crisscrossing like twin jet trails, until we finally came together in Old Québec. I had hitchhiked across the Canadian Shield to reach her, and I arrived with fifty dollars in my pocket.

It was the best summer of my life. And the worst. Looking back, I find it hard to separate the streets of Old Québec from the woman Marie-Claire; the two seemed to be manifestations of the same spirit. Québec was charged with a certain nocturnal, subterranean vitality. History. Hashish. Jazz. It had everything I could possibly want. In the rain it was better than Paris; it was how we imagine Paris to be. The outdoor coffee shops, the youth hostel rapport, the Nostradamus Café, the crêperies with menus written on the walls, the rain along Terrace Dufferin, and the alleyways of the Latin Quarter, as small and narrow as secret love affairs. It was a city of sidewalk painters and music and midnight rambling monologues. It was like nothing I had ever seen before.

Marie-Claire lived across the seaway in Lévis, atop a cliffside flight of stairs that seemed to grow longer and steeper with every climb. From Marie-Claire's window, we could see the Château Frontenac lit up like a castle keep, the Old City shimmering in wet reflection on the waters of the St. Lawrence.

We caught the last ferry home every night, running to make it and arriving in ever decreasing increments of time until we made it by a heartbeat, then by an eyelash flutter and then—we missed it. As the night ferry slipped away, I threw down my jacket in an impotent rage (impotent rage also being one of my fortes). But Marie-Claire just laughed. "Life," she said without judgement or sentiment, and off we went to find lodging. I have never lived quite like that before and I doubt I will ever live like that again. In some ways, I have spent the last ten years trying to recapture that summer, but in all my travels and blind-end blunders, I never found it.

Do you remember the Leonard Cohen album cover on *Songs from a Room?* Do you remember the photograph on the back? For one short summer in Québec, I lived that photograph.

Like most aching teenage love stories, the Ballad of Billy and Marie-Claire ended somewhere between comedy and farce. I was clingy. Hopelessly infatuated. Hopelessly unilingual. She was always translating for me and halfheartedly apologizing to her friends. My gestures became heavier and heavier, until one day another boy arrived in the room. I left the apartment in Lévis, and I have never been back.

Oh woe to be nineteen and heartbroken. Forget world peace, the rain forests or the plight of our nation's homeless, nothing mattered more than my own bruised throbbing heart. I wandered through Old Québec, collar up like James Dean, wishing it would rain. I drank *café au lait* alone and wrote long self-pitying poems. Smoked a lot of cigarettes. Finished off the hash. And then, as I was coming out of a coffee shop, I caught my reflection in a storefront window and, suddenly, I was aware of myself in a scene. This is the moment you grow up, and nothing is ever the same afterwards. I have never lived completely spontaneously since. I am always aware of myself as if from distance, as if in the third person.

Through a friend of Marie-Claire's, I joined a theatre troupe. It was part of Megapôle, a project created to commemorate the International Year of Youth. Megapôle brought young people together from across Canada with the goal of spending a lot of money making symbolic gestures. (It was the '80s; there was money to burn.) Among our "achievements": we helped put a time capsule atop some remote snowy mountain renamed Mont Jeunesse (Mountain of Youth), and we later released ten thousand balloons into the air, each balloon containing the wish of a young Canadian solicited from elementary schools and youth organizations across the country. The dreams and wishes of children sent out into the world! It was a minor media event. Very minor.

Later, I learned that helium balloons, untethered, will rise and rise, higher and higher and higher. . . until they deflate and fall to earth like withered condoms, littering the woods and waters and choking sea birds. Which was a very apt metaphor for Project Megapôle.

I didn't fit in with Megapôle. I clashed with the organizers, a bunch of bearded Baby Boomers who saw everything as a morality play. I remember one chap named Claude who described with intense eyes his lifelong dream: to travel around in a big school bus, "Just like the Partridge family."

Not that the youth participants were any less flaky. One young man from Saint Something-or-Other, Québec, was a follower of a church that worshipped extraterrestrials. He wore a pendant that incorporated a swastika in a Star of David. I asked him if that might be a little insensitive, and he said with the utmost innocence, "Why would it be?"

We were billeted in the wind-tunnel sterility of Laval University, a million miles from Old Québec and a million more from Marie-Claire. Project Megapôle was like being transported back in time, to a more politicized, simplistic past, and it reminded me how deeply thankful I am to have missed the '60s. God, what an insufferable decade that was. Unfortunately, in Canada, volunteer youth projects are where old hippies go to die, and Project Megapôle was chock-a-block full of them. We were supposed to write, stage and perform an outdoor cavalcade of Canadiana, but it was Theatre by Committee, with all that that implies. Federally funded counterculture: a paradox anywhere else, but fairly common in Canada. (In the leadup to the 1995 referendum, the Parti Québécois commissioned a poem to be written by a committee. The committee consisted of the following: two lawyers, a journalist, a sociologist and a separatist folk singer. The results, needless to say, were underwhelming.) The results of Project Megapôle's own Theatre by Committee were equally as dismal. Our "outdoor cavalcade" was all message and no brain, as subtle as a grand piano dropped from the fourteenth floor. It opened with two grunting cavemen coming out on stage and smearing blood over a balloon-ball of the planet Earth. And it just went downhill from there.

As opening night approached, tensions were deepening between myself and Claude. The entire mess was being paid for by the federal government with the intent of promoting trans-Canadian unity, but a hidden agenda soon emerged. In one scene an English-speaking boss (me in an ill-fitting suit, looking like a kid in an eighth grade production of *Under the Yum-Yum Tree*) all but spat on a folk-singing French-Canadian type girl. This was to symbolize the historic humiliations that Québec has suffered at the hands of *les maudits anglais*. Subtle, eh?

Then came the poster incident, or as it is better known, The Poster Incident.

"Why are our posters only in French?" I asked. And verily, the room did chill.

"Because we are in Québec."

"So?"

"Québec is a French province. We speak French in Québec and the signs are in French and so our poster will be in French. That's it. There is nothing to discuss."

"But the performers are from all across Canada."

"Yes, but the show is in Québec and Québec is a French province and the signs are in French and—"

"But the show itself is bilingual."

"Yes, but the show is in Québec and Québec is—"

"But Ottawa is paying for this, and it's supposed to represent all of Canada."

Other participants, both from Québec and beyond, began calling out, "Yeah! Why can't we have French *and* English!" Claude denounced me as a troublemaker, the meeting degenerated into name-calling and flailing arm gestures, and I found myself "deselected" from Project Megapôle, to use the proper bureaucratic term.

It was only years later, after reading Milan Kundera's *The Joke,* that I realized what I had come up against: ideology, pure and simple. Québec, which came of age in the Quiet Revolution, is a product of the '60s. (During the 1995 Referendum, OUI posters featured flowers and peace signs and other '60s relics.) And the '60s were marked and marred by ideology.

Ideology is a comforting but dangerous thing. And it is dangerous because it is so comforting. It simplifies the world. It supplies a set view, and in doing so it relieves you of critical case-by-case thinking. Whether it be communism, feminism or religious fundamentalism, ideology provides a Procrustean solution; everything is interpreted to fit and support the ideology. Life is reduced to class conflict or gender roles or sin or whatever your particular bent is. Canada, thankfully, is mostly free of ideology, but pockets do exist: in our universities, in the West and in Québec—where nationalism has become a religion of sorts. Project Megapôle taught me more about Québec than I wanted to know.

My departure from Megapôle, just days before the opening night, turned out to be a godsend. Not only did it save me the embarrassment of actually appearing on stage enunciating lines like "Violence is a Circle! We must break the Circle!" But it left me free to sign on with Canada World Youth—another earnest, federally funded youth project. I called Marie-Claire to give her the news, and she said, and I quote, "Bye." Then, after she thought for a moment: "Good luck."

I hitchhiked down to Montréal and stayed with Aline Johnson, a friend of my father's, who, despite her English surname, is very much a "dyed in the wool" *pure laine* Québécois. By this point I was an emotional wreck, flat broke and utterly confused. Aline took me out for dinner and some sympathy. When I told her what I had been through, she shrugged. "This is Québec," she said. "Québec is Québec. You can't understand it. Don't try."

WHEN THEATRE DIRECTOR Robert Lepage launched a production of *Romeo and Juliet,* he chose a typically Canadian way to separate the two star-crossed lovers; he used language. The Capulets spoke English and the Montagues, French.

This male/female imagery runs through the Canadian psyche. Even Hugh MacLennan's famous description of Canada as "Two Solitudes" is from a description of romantic love penned by the poet Rainer Maria Rilke, who spoke of "the love that consists in this, that two solitudes protect and touch and greet each other."

Canada is a linguistically estranged nation featuring the world's longest unconsummated divorce, a lovers' spat maintained for so long it has become habit, or maybe hobby. The historian Abbé Groulx (one of my favourite fascists) called Canada a marriage of convenience, though personally I would describe it as a marriage of *in*convenience.

A marriage, even a bad marriage—*especially* a bad marriage—changes your life. No matter how much Québec separatists and Reform Party collaborators hate to admit it, both solitudes are irrevocably entwined.

"The two identities have been related for more than two hundred years," writes professor Christian Dufour in his book *Le défi québécois*. "They have penetrated each other, are present in each other's core."

It's embedded in our psyche, it's hidden in our national flag like an ink blot test: the image of two faces arguing. Cover the bottom half of the maple leaf and you'll see it, a pair of bickering profiles that have been named—what else?—John and Jacques. It might more accurately have been John and Yvette.

Canada reminds me of a forty-year-old accountant married to a twenty-year-old go-go dancer. As Québec skips off to the discotheque, Canada waits by the window, wondering if she will ever return. But perhaps go-go dancer is not the right image. Perhaps a better parallel is that of a moody adolescent stomping about the house, slamming doors and throwing tantrums. The refrain is remarkably familiar: "I hate you, I hate you, I hate you."

The saddest disillusionment English Canadians have had to face in the last few years is not that so many Québécois want out, but that they are so petty about it. We always looked up to the Québécois; they were the coolest kids on the playground. They drank more, sang louder, laughed longer, dressed better, kissed deeper. They enjoyed life more than the rest of us. Alas, as we have come to know them better, this myth has crumbled. The Québécois nationalists have revealed themselves and the society they represent as being petulant, ethnically obsessed and—saddest of all—small-minded. This has been the biggest disappointment of all. Not that they are worse than the rest of us, but that they are no better.

Canada, we are told, is a binary code. Either/or. English/French. But like any set paradigm, this excludes as much as it explains. Natives, for one, are omitted from the formula, as are other ethnic groups—*including francophones outside of Québec*. Our on-going Cold War with Québec has been narrowed down from a French/English conflict to one between French Québec and the Rest of Canada—which Québécois nationalists erroneously assume to be some kind of homogeneous block. We understand each other so little, and it just might be the death of us.

The problem with any either/or thinking is that, much like a referendum question, it excludes any compromise or synthesis of options. It forces you into extremes. Black or white. One or the other. An example: the separatists have been blowing it in our face for years that Québécois identify themselves with Québec more than with Canada. This is true. But the same polls tell us that over 60 per cent have an attachment to Canada as well. It is not an either/or choice, no matter how much the separatists insist. The Québécois put Québec ahead of Canada, but it does not follow from this that they have automatically rejected Canada. The logic is sloppy and the intent is insidious. It is an attempt to portray separation as inevitable, as though the battle has already been won. In this, then, thinking in opposites is a kind of ideological tool, one that the separatists have learned to use well.

The binary code has failed us as of late. It used to be so simple: the Americans bullied English Canadians, English Canadians bullied French Canadians, and everybody crapped on the Indians. Alas, those halcyon days have passed. English Canada, as in "Englishman," has lost its majority status. Queen Victoria is dead, the Boer War is over, the First Nations are with us still, and we are fast becoming a nation of mongrels and misfits. That is the good news.

The bad news is that someone has to convince Québec. It is all very well for Canada to decide it has become a multicultural nation, but Québec is still locked into the old familiar two-step. The New! Improved! Multicultural Canada forgets that the francophones are more than just another minority group; they are one of our founding nations. They supplied the dowry. Any vision of a united Canada must accept the importance of the French Fact; it is that simple.

Trudeau tried to set the framework for a multicultural nation within the boundaries of official bilingualism. This was loudly opposed by regionalist thinkers across Canada who refused to see the nation as anything beyond a collection of provinces. In Alberta, they argued, French is well below German and Ukrainian as a second language. But what these deep thinkers failed to recognize was that the law was a *national* law and so—reasonably—*national* demographics and *national* history should take precedence. If 30 per cent of the Canadian population speaks French, and if being a Canadian citizen is to have any meaning whatsoever, then it doesn't matter where those 30 per cent live, whether it is scattered evenly across the country or concentrated entirely on Baffin Island. They are still entitled to national access to services in French. But try explaining that to someone in Vegreville.

Growing up as I did, in Alberta (which I hope to some day overcome), I was constantly hearing about That Damned Trudeau. So often, in fact, that I began to suspect Damned was his first name. It was fortunate I never met the man. "Ah, Mr. Trudeau. Or may I call you Damned?" The constant refrain, accompanied by much coffee-counter slapping and head-nodding, was that Trudeau "is shoving French down our throats." I heard this tired old bleat so often that at one point I resolved to punch the very next person who said it. Unfortunately, the very next person was a very large person—red of neck, thick of chest—and I decided that discretion being the better part of valour etc. etc.

The point is the world didn't end, the commies didn't take over, and—son-of-a-bitch!—Canadians started to learn French. The number of francophones who consider themselves bilingual is still twice the number of anglophones who do, but the gap is closing. English Canadians are enrolling in French immersion classes and pursuing second-language studies at a rate now higher than that of Québécois. But just as Canada was finally beginning to accept the idea of a bilingual nation, Québec set about to become officially *unilingual.* It's maddening. We keep just missing each other, like characters in a play by Chekhov.

Yes, it wasn't enough to *promote* French, and it wasn't enough to encourage *le visage français,* Québec went that extra step and outlawed English. Now, English is a big language, it spans the globe and bullies other languages into submission; it will certainly survive Québec's language laws. But the reputation of the Québécois may not. The French-only laws quickly became exercises in silliness that have greatly damaged Québec's relentless boast at being a hip, happenin', cosmopolitan place. In an odd way, it was almost comforting at first to know the coolest clique in Canada could prove just as provincial and shrill as the rest of us. Now it's just tedious.

Here is just one celebrated example from many: On a cold grey morning, Montréal police make a surprise raid and confiscate 15,000—*what?* (A) bags of cocaine, (B) automatic rifles, (C) hard-core video tapes, or (D) Dunkin' Donut bags. The answer of course is (D). Not only did the Dunkin' Donut bags *not* contain a French translation, they were barely English.

And if there is any doubt that Québec was acting like a second-rate banana republic, consider this item from the bulging files of Language Crimes: Del Monte ships bananas around the world with that little Del Monte sticker that kids take off and stick on their foreheads. If you look closely, however, you will find below the company name, less than one-eighth of an inch high, the word "quality." *Mon Dieu!* An English word! The Surveillance Commission of *L'Office de la langue française* (otherwise known as the Language Police) was outraged and insisted that the stickers be replaced with ones that read *"qualité."* It was the difference of a single letter: changing *y* to *é*. Sensing the harmful effects that English bananas might have on the fragile French language, the commission announced that it would levy fines against any supermarket in Québec caught importing the offensively stickered fruit.

What the language issue in Québec comes down to, beyond police raids of Dunkin' Donut bags, is a fundamental conflict between individual and collective rights. Even as it pursues banana boats and leads campaigns against enemy stop signs, the language war leads us back to some hard, cold questions. What is the foundation of society? What is the final court of appeal? Is it to be the state, the family, the ethnic collective or the individual?

The individual, myths to the contrary, does not have absolute freedom in any society. No one stands alone. We all belong to collectives, and we are all a part of some minority and some majority. I am a white, Protestant, male (the crowds boo), but I am also from a poor but proud single-parent family that was mightily oppressed by the Euro-centric patriarchal system (the crowds cheer, my credentials have been restored). In Canada, English speakers are the majority. In the province of Québec, French speakers are in the majority. In Montréal, it depends on which neighbourhood you live in. Boxes within boxes. Islands within lakes, and lakes within islands.

Where does it end?

The answer is enshrined in the Canadian Charter of Rights, which invests the individual with final value. That is, in the conflict between individual and collective, the individual takes precedence.

So far, so good. But what if a collective fears for its survival? Are they allowed to supersede the rights of the individual? Well, they are in Québec.

When Québec Premier Robert Bourassa brought in Bill 178, which outlawed English signs, he declared with great pride, "Never before in the history of Québec has a government suspended fundamental liberties to protect the French language and culture."

Québec's intellectual nationalists define the state on ethnic grounds: a common race, ancestry, language, history. Theirs is a vision of a *nation-state,* defined by the tribe.

Canada, however, is conceived as multinational state. That is, a *territorial* nation, a pluralistic society unified by common values and common policies. The important thing to note is that while the Québec definition of state cannot include Canada, the Canadian definition of state *can* include Québec, and any other number of nations within its territory.

Québec's leaders have declared that Canada is not a nation at all, but is merely a state. This is true only if you accept their definition of nation-state prior to discussion. When Lucien Bouchard says "Canada is divisible because Canada is not a real country," he has assumed his own premise and is simply begging the question. He is also pissing off a lot of people.

The paradox that Québec nationalists face is this: Why stop at Québec? Why not surrender entirely to centrifugal forces? There will always be more ethnic groups and racial/linguistic/historical nations than there are states. Are all of them to be granted sovereignty? If Québec can separate from Canada, why can't the anglophone West Island of Montreal separate as well? If Canada is divisible, why not Québec?

But Québec's intellectual separatists refuse to consider any partition of Québec. They are adamant; territorial boundaries of their would-be state cannot be altered to fit minority groups. After all, they can't allow every ragged ethnic group to separate, can they? Suddenly Québec has become a *territorial* entity whose borders cannot be violated along ethnic lines. Truly an amazing sleight of mind.

What does Québec want? asks the accountant as his go-go girl stands on the threshold, bags packed but not quite able to leave.

What does Québec want? ask the tormented Old School nationalists, who are at an utter loss when it comes to Québec. It is all very good and well to boldly proclaim "My Canada includes Québec!" but if Québec doesn't reciprocate, you might just as well declare "My Canada includes the Moon!"

What does Québec want? They want out of Canada—by a slim margin. And they want to stay in Canada—by a slim margin. It all depends on how you tally the votes.

What does Québec want? Comedian Yvon Deschamps called out for *"un Québec indépendant dans un Canada uni!"* (An independent Québec within a united Canada!)

He was making a joke, of course. A zinger. A yuk-yuk. A send-up. But as Terence Corcoran reported in the *Globe and Mail,* the Parti Québécois missed the point. In their 1995 Referendum Blueprint, they adopted Deschamps's description as an official party slogan. Incredible, unbelievable, but true.

"A Yes vote means wanting sovereign Québec in a strong partnership with Canada. And it means proving that Yvon Deschamps was essentially right."

It's a scene right out of Milan Kundera. A joke has been enshrined as political doctrine. And Canada, if not the punch line, is certainly the brunt.

YOU MAY HAVE noticed something. We have been talking about Québec and Canada as if the two were already separate entities, as though Canada did not include Québec. To speak this way is to concede defeat, and we are all guilty of this.

Some commentators have begun using the terms Québec and the ROC (the Rest of Canada), an approach popularized by Mordecai Richler. This is an improvement on Canada/Québec, but it is also Québec-centric, as though only Québec matters, as though anything else is simply happening "out there." If this were true, we would have to accept it, but it isn't. Québec is not the centre of Canada. Québec is simply a large, lively and very troublesome tribe contained within certain provincial boundaries. They may set the agenda, but they are not the future of Canada.

It is out here in the other provinces that the real battles are being fought and won, where the world is being redefined. Québec can stagnate in its ethnic nationalism if it wants, but they will be left behind. It is here, outside of

Québec, that life is lived on the cutting edge. Here in the RC. The Real Canada.

Let us serve notice that the term ROC, as well as being inaccurate, is also insulting. Let us use instead the RC (like the cola but less effervescent), a nation bound not by bloodlines and language but by an idea: Canada. (Insisting on calling it the RC may seem picky, but what the hell, if Québec nationalists can get upset about a single letter, so can we.)

The RC is where all the action is. It is a polyglot, mix-and-match, jumbled jigsaw-puzzle culture, and we have a lot to sort out. If we are going to make it through the next millennium, we are going to have to start looking outward, not inward.

Some marriages are not worth saving. Some marriages can be reconciled. Some marriages are doomed from the start. Some are shotgun affairs. Some can be annulled. But Canada, for all the imagery, is not a marriage. We may have begun as a pact between two founding peoples, but we have evolved into something far grander. Canada today is not a choice between opposites, it is an opportunity for *embracing* opposites. We in the RC are in the process of transcending our colonial past, of reinventing ourselves as a postmodern nation.

The question is not whether Québec will separate, but whether she will ever finally *join* us.

CANADA

WORLD YOUTH

. . . .

*T*HE MEMORIES come back in vignettes: small moments, odd angles. Indian women in panama hats. Songs of sweat and sugar cane. Burros twisting and braying under heavy loads. Valleys so deep they collect clouds. And buses, gaudy as any rooster, careening down mountain-ridge roads, passing on corners, flirting with death.

Those buses, painted red and purple, dancing the high wire—that is my metaphor for Ecuador and the time I spent there. We crowded inside, we hung out the door, we rode on top like wind-surfers, shirts billowing in the South American air. The bus speedometers were always broken, buried at zero like an Einstein equation, and the dash-boards were decorated with statuettes of the Virgin Mary,

Mother of Mercy. I remember wondering if there was a connection between the two, the broken speedometer and the appeal to Mercy. I remember the Spanish voices. I remember how the air tasted. I would give anything to be back there, riding those buses, defying gravity. From the intense claustrophobia of Québec to a wider world, from one love affair to another. I turned twenty in South America: not yet an adult, but more than a teenager. I would give anything to be back there.

Today, in Indonesian villages and Nepalese schools, in Thailand and Honduras, in Uruguay and Egypt, in India and Ecuador, you will find them: young Canadians, noses sunburnt and shoulders sore, working alongside other young people from the host nation, speaking in local dialect, uncertain English, broken French. The term "global village" was coined by Marshall McLuhan, a Canadian media guru. *The global village.* As a Third World exchange program, Canada World Youth accepts this not as an end point but as a point of departure. We live in a global village, and it's time to meet the neighbours.

Canada World Youth stages a dozen or so working exchanges every year, bringing together over five hundred volunteers from across Canada and the Third World, with work time divided between the two—usually just under a year—and all for the cost per volunteer of less than it takes to train a soldier to march and salute.

Who benefits the most from Canada World Youth? The question is unanswerable, but I won't let that stop me. The Canadians gain a sudden insight into the realities of life in a Third World nation, but I suspect the volunteers from the host countries are affected even more. Many of them are from privileged classes (CWY tries its best to discourage this, but participant selection is each nation's prerogative), many are the sons and daughters of government ministers and most are from urban centres. The urban/rural division is far more decisive in developing countries than it is in Canada, and the Malaysian and Senegalese and Filipino participants suffer a culture shock within their own countries. The program shakes them up. And let's face it, real reforms are not going to be implemented by a bunch of Canadian teenagers descending on a village for four months. The real changes are going to be made by the people who live there.

Like Project Megapôle, Canada World Youth was idealistic and politically correct. I had a hard time fitting in. There was a tightlipped, humourless sincerity about the program—our group leader for one was so utterly sincere it was all I could do not to slap her in the head—but in the end, the program managed to rise above its own good intentions.

The Canadians in my group included participants from Toronto, Montréal, rural Québec, Parry Sound, Longueuil and the Annapolis valley of Nova Scotia. We were joined by an equal number of Ecuadorians, and our multilingual, multiethnic, multicultural group was then shipped off to New Liskeard, Ontario. What this pleasant little town ever did to deserve us, I am not sure. But it must have been something really bad.

Ecuador, home of the Galápagos Islands, is a small, proud nation wedged in between Peru and Colombia. I envied the Ecuadorians their ease and friendly openness. Victor, straw-thin and wide of grin, decided that our group needed a name and he came up with *Pamasitos,* a contraction of *papasito* and *mamasita* which mean "little papa and mama" but—in Ecuador anyway—carries the nuance of Stud and Babe. We had Pamasito T-shirts and everything. The other CWY groups were jealous, you could tell.

When the Pamasitos hit the streets, there was electricity in the air. I remember Pierre from Montréal. (We carried our place of origin with us like a medieval surname. Jon from Parry Sound, Peter of Twickingham, that kind of thing.) I liked Pierre from Montréal because he was the only person I have ever met who had *more* raging hormones than I. Pierre and I considered ourselves to be God's gift to the women of New Liskeard. Slick and Dude, that's what they called us, until our notable lack of success inspired some wit to change it, and we became instead Slack and Dud. I hate nicknames.

In Canada World Youth, participants are usually paired and billeted with local families. My partner was a university student from Quito named Nicholas Travez. Nick was a Marxist revolutionary who played a passionate guitar and wrote songs that started with lines like *"Mi pueblo es pobre, no tenemos pan"* (My village is poor, we have no bread). It was only when we went to Ecuador that I discovered Nick was from a very rich family. They had a maid, a guard dog, a cook and a terribly posh house. By contrast, the modest Canadian home we stayed in must have been a bit like roughing it in the woods for Nick.

In New Liskeard, Nick and I worked at an experimental farm, shoveling cow shit, horse shit, sheep shit and sometimes—just for a change of pace—pig shit. We helped out in crop experiments as well, and we once helped deliver a calf, which was even gooier and ickier than you can imagine.

At work, Nick and I got along wonderfully. After work, it was a little more volatile. We argued about politics incessantly, flinging out words and slogans and resolving nothing. For instance, Nick was adamant that people in the Soviet Union were happier and more fulfilled than those in America. When I asked him why hundreds of people were willing to risk execution and imprisonment trying to escape this socialist paradise, Nick said, "Because capitalism is a mirage." (He always had great aphorisms.) Years later, when the Soviet Union imploded and East Germany rushed out of the dust and paternalism of communism like fresh air into a vacuum, I thought of Nick. Not maliciously. I missed him. I missed his eloquence, his sincerity, his theories so finely woven that neither facts nor reality could penetrate them. I wondered if he still had a maid.

That Nick and I eventually became friends was more a credit to him. I kept bringing up points of debate long after the argument had ended, only to be slapped down by another one of Nick's aphorisms. Still, we enjoyed each other's company and we even began collaborating as songwriters. Simon and Garfunkel we were not. Most of our songs were lust-filled ballads with political overtones (guess who supplied what?), but they were kind of catchy: *"Your breasts rise up / like workers united / in a common cause."* As well, in the spirit of co-operation, Nick and I managed to completely bury our room under our dirty clothes and assorted debris. Our host family was quite impressed by our efforts: wall to wall disorder, beneath which—this is true—Nick and I succeeded in submerging not one but *two* beds.

Call it critical mess, but we were proud of what we had wrought. It happened in the otherwise tidy home of Candy Keith and Graham Gambles, an eccentric, possibly mad, couple who took Nick and me in during our sojourn in the New Liskeard area. Candy and Graham were full of surprises; they lynched their neighbour's pink flamingo one dark night, and the evening before our departure, the four of us—Candy, Graham, Nick and myself—sat around drinking hot chocolate and making moose-shit necklaces. Honest. In autumn, Graham explained, moose subsist almost entirely on branches and bark, and their droppings come out as little more than pressed pellets of wood, dry, odour-free and handy for making decorative jewellery. All they needed were some holes drilled in them and a bit of varnish. Nick was nonplussed.

In the Third World, North America is either glorified or vilified. We are either glamorous millionaires or capitalist vampires. In the same way, in North America, the suffering of the Third World is written off as something on the periphery, an object of charity and pity. Canada World Youth brings the two sides face to face, and few myths survive the contact. Consider it a principle of human interaction: it is very hard to hate—or idolize—someone with whom you have made moose-shit necklaces.

It snowed the day we left for Ecuador, great big storybook flakes fluttering down and feathering the lake. "I imagined Canada in the snow," said Nick, "with tall buildings and people walking at night under street lamps." It was the only time he ever showed a soft or romantic spot for Canada, and even today whenever I pass by a street lamp when the snow is falling, I think of Nick.

We left the snow and cold behind and arrived in the dry heat of Ecuador, where we were met by waiting parents and relentless Latin hospitality. Ecuador is named after the equator, which runs through it, and Nick and his father took me out to the line itself so I could stand on one foot in both hemispheres, caught in shaky posture between both. (More metaphors.)

Then, with Nick's twelve-year-old sister in tow, they took me on a tour of Quito City, the capital. It was, how shall I say, a memorable drive. Nick and his father clearly had different agendas, and I found myself caught in the crossfire of both a generation *and* a political gap. "Over there you can see the modern tunnels that are being built for our new superhighway," Nick's father would say proudly, and then Nick would cut in with, "And over there is where the government fired tear gas on protestors during a general strike last year." His father: "Here is the palace of the third vice-president, a great Ecuadorian hero." Nick: "Over there is the office of the People's Press which was burned to the ground by government troops last month." Back and forth it went: the air fair sizzled with tension. I realized that they were talking *through* me, sparring with each other over my head, and I'm sure I could have snuck out at a stoplight and the conversation would have continued unchanged. "Over here is one of Ecuador's many modern factories—" "Where the workers are paid pennies and forced to work twenty hours a day." On and on it when. Then, from the back seat, Nick's little sister piped up, and for once Nick and his father agreed on something; they both rolled their eyes.

"What is it?" I asked. Nick sighed. "Nothing." But his little sister persisted, and finally Nick said, "She wants me to tell you that the building we just passed is where Menudo played when they came to Quito." (Menudo is a teeny-bopper band made up of prepubescent boys. In Latin America they are superstars.) Nick's little sister smiled and settled back, satisfied that she had contributed to my education.

Our CWY group went south to Malacatos, a village hidden in the Andes not far from the Peruvian border. We took the Bus of Death to get there, past adobe villages and sugar cane fields. We were riding a continental divide, between the Amazon River basin and the sweeping lowlands of the coast.

Canada World Youth is funded through CIDA (the Canadian International Development Agency). Unfortunately, CIDA is also a homonym for the Spanish word for AIDS, and when we went around thrusting our hands at villagers telling them *"Hola! Yo estoy con CIDA!"* (Hi! I am with AIDS!), we got some terrified looks. There were rumours that we had been chased out of our home country because we had AIDS, but this matter was eventually settled. Though it did make it hard for us to get dates.

Nick and I were billeted with the family of Don Francisco across from the church and the public square. The Franciscos welcomed Nick and me into their home like long-lost sons, and after a first-night celebration and a dinner of roast guinea pig (an Ecuadorian specialty), we were no longer strangers. Don Francisco was a quiet man; his wife was anything but. When I complained about the heat, she poured water over my head. And laughed. When I became too pink from the sun, she dusted me with flour "to whiten me up again." And when we said goodbye, she cried and cried. For me, the Third World is Ecuador, Ecuador is Malacatos, and Malacatos is the Francisco family.

Our group tackled a number of projects; we worked at schools and on farms, we even painted cartoon figures on the kindergarten walls. With the extra paint, we decided to update a globe of the world, three metres high and made of cement, which stood beside the village church. The globe was faded and still contained pre-World War I boundaries: Austro-Hungarian Empire, Abyssinia, Siam, and so on. Needless to say, when we repainted it, we made Canada *really* big, so that even today in a small village in the Andes highlands of Ecuador, travellers are surprised to discover that Canada has surreptitiously conquered most of New England, all of Oregon, much of Montana and a good deal of Alaska. We cackled to ourselves as we did it. It was a typically Canadian act of defiance: sneaky, clever and completely ineffectual.

The people of Malacatos were keen to know more about Canada, but when we compared the Ecuadorian songs and folk dances and tight sense of community to our own, Canadian culture seemed ephemeral. Our lack of folk culture was acutely embarrassing. What is a Canadian traditional dance? Or even a song that we can all get through? The suburbs don't engender a sense of community, and hanging out at the mall is difficult to convey in a dance.

Never let it be said that our group let Canada down. We carried the banner high, and when asked to perform a Canadian dance for the town, we did what any true-blooded Canadian would have done—we made one up. Call it the Pamasito Stomp: a group dance involving much arm swingin' and hand-clappin' and which might, to someone who didn't know better, have resembled a square dance. Unfortunately, none of us knew a do-si-do from an allemande-left, so instead we performed set manoeuvres and just yelled out whatever came into mind. Pierre from Montréal, the most unabashed, became our caller, lapsing into gibberish and e.e.cummings—not a big step, granted—as the rest of us lunged about the stage, hissing frantic instructions to each other. It amused the Ecuadorians to no end. "Do your dance again!" they'd say and then laugh hysterically.

But hey, what we lacked in finesse we made up in volume. Pierre was particularly gifted when it came to hollering loudly in a square-dance rhythm. *"Everyone lived in a little how town. A bicycle up and a bicycle down. Grab yer partner like a bell. One-two-three, Now yell like hell!"* (Everybody: "Yee-haw.") We must have performed that dance a dozen times to bemused audiences throughout the valley, and I like to think we left a little bit of Canada behind us wherever we went. Yee-haw.

I remember the man who so desperately wanted me to marry his daughter. He had worked his hands into leather and still could not feed his children. We drank sugar-cane tequila, called *agua-ardiente*—literally "hot water"—an alcohol so pure and refined it appears on some Periodic Tables. He asked me if I was rich. I said no. He asked me if my family had a car. I said yes. He said, "Well then, you are richer than I." Then we agreed that his daughter was beautiful, and we drank some more and clasped hands and swore undying friendship. That man hated me. It was palpable. So we laughed and drank and laughed some more. His youngest child came toddling over and smiled up at me. "Go on," he said, "pick her up. Soon she will be your niece. Soon we'll all be family!" More strained smiles. I didn't pick the little girl up. "Go on," he said, but I didn't, because there is nothing more frightening, more terrible, more pornographic, than brittle limbs and a swollen belly.

I wanted to run away, to yell over my shoulder as I ran, "I'm poor! I'm poor as well."

Only in Canada is my family poor. Ecuador knocked that particular chip off my shoulder in a hurry.

Returning to Canada after a season in South America was like re-entering a Platonic cave and trying to explain to others a world beyond the shadows. "You must be glad to be back." That's what everyone said. *You must be glad to be back.* And I was, but not in the way they insinuated. I was glad to be back, not because Canada was better or richer or safer, but because it was lazier. It is possible to live an incredibly lazy life in Canada, far from the life-and-death questions that other humans have to face daily. Our preoccupations suddenly seemed so trite. How could I still call myself a Canadian nationalist, when Canada itself seemed as unsubstantial as cotton candy?

On my first day back, I remember walking through Toronto's Eaton Centre in a daze, past shop after shop of perfumes and shoes and cameras and fashion statements and electric can-openers, and I realized nothing would ever look quite the same again. Our horn of plenty is full of trinkets and distractions, our shopping malls are not a triumph but a symptom. Consumption has become an end in itself.

The lesson learned in Canada World Youth is a simple one: *local actions have global repercussions.* The good news: this isn't necessarily a bad thing. The village work projects, the friendships that span cultures and oceans, the small victories: these too have global repercussions.

Canada World Youth did not make me a good person—that would be asking too much—but it did make me a *better* person, and for that I will always be grateful. The

Pamasitos have long since drifted apart, I have lost touch with Nick, and I imagine that if Pierre and I were ever to run into each other, we wouldn't have much to say. But there was a time, somewhere between being a grownup and being a child, that our lives intersected. And that, as Robert Frost would say, has made all the difference.

4

THE KATIMAVIK
GENERATION

. . . . . .

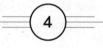ATIMAVIK WAS going to save Canada. That was the goal, that was the mission, that was the whole idea. By bringing young Canadians together and forcing them to eat granola and dig ditches and sing songs, Katimavik was going to create a sense of national cama-raderie. Thousands of us took part every year. Our work ranged from outdoor conservation to soup kitchens. The salary: a dollar a day. We called ourselves "Katima-victims."

I joined Katimavik as a stopgap measure, in lieu of attending college, and it was a good thing I did. When I began Katimavik, I was planning to major in Political Science. By the time I was finished, I was so thoroughly disgusted with politicians—and one politician in par-ticular—that I decided to switch to Fine Arts. From a financial point of view this was a dismal decision. But from a not-selling-your-soul-to-the-devil point of view, it was the right move.

Katimavik was Canada in miniature. The same ratio of francophone to anglophone, urban to rural, middle class to working class, male to female, and region to region that existed in Canada was represented in each Katimavik group. And thus, the same linguistic and regional divisions that torment the nation as a whole were enshrined in every project. The results were predictable. We were rolling caravans of self-sustaining tension. We fought and cursed and learned to swear in both official languages.

My group included Eric, a reform school dropout from Toronto who had a knack for carpentry; François, an intensely focussed law student from Montréal; Sara, a green-haired, nose-ringed Doukhobor from Delta, B.C. (in this case, *Before Common Sense*); Lise, from Québec City, a person of endless enthusiasm, the Energizer Rabbit of the Group; Josée from Trois-Rivières, the daughter of a government cheese inspector and now a theatrical designer of note; and Duncan, a rotund, affable chap from outport Newfoundland, the Slowest Man Alive, our version of the Energizer Turtle.

We travelled from the interior of British Columbia to small-town Ontario to the farmlands of rural Québec. We lived in converted barns and suburban bungalows. We restored Native graveyards and built outdoor nature trails. We worked with senior citizens and handicapped children. We studied wilderness survival and sensual massage. We were young, we were Canadian, and we were growing up in the shadow of the Baby Boomers.

We managed our own budgets and schedules, and we prepared our own meals. We baked our own bread and we bred our own yogurt. We ate a lot of granola.

Once every rotation, the group split up to live with local families for two or three weeks. The families were even more eclectic than the group itself. They included Québécois farmers, Okanagan wine-makers, ex-hippies, Mormons, magicians, shopkeepers and a pair of New Age accountants who read our palms.

Katimavik was the most ambitious attempt ever made at fostering a sense of national unity among Canadians. The program had roots in 1,360 communities across Canada and was actively supported in every province and territory. Over 20,000 young Canadians volunteered for nine-month stints with Katimavik.

Add to that the 20,000 families of these participants. Add to that 60,000 short-term host families. (Every Katimavik participant was billeted with local families *three times* during a tour of duty.)

Add to that the over 3,000 group leaders and regional co-ordinators and their families. Add to that the tens of thousands of work supervisors, community leaders and co-workers who were involved with Katimavik groups at the local level.

Add also the families of the elderly, the disabled and all those whose lives were touched by Katimavik. Add to that the Indian bands across Canada that supported the program from the start. And the youth clubs and the group homes.

Consider all the people who were a part of it. An independent study estimates that the number of people who had direct and personal experience with Katimavik is in the *hundreds of thousands*. For better or worse, Katimavik helped shape an entire generation.

Jacques Hébert, the program's founder, called Katimavik "an apprenticeship for life." He was convinced that young Canadians, through communal living and community service, would help forge a sense of national and personal identity. The word *katimavik* itself is from the Inuktitut for "meeting place."

Hébert, as you may have guessed, is an idealist. An author, publisher and Third World activist, he is also a world traveller of note. In his youth he backpacked through Communist China with Pierre Trudeau, and they wrote a book about their experiences, *Deux innocents en Chine rouge (Two Innocents in Red China)*.

Hébert believed that you could take young Canadians from all walks of life and disparate regions and bring them together, and that we would somehow like each other. This assumes a homogeneity of values. It also relies on a certain Peter Pan faith. That is, if we all just wish hard enough, we can make Canada a better place.

Jacques Hébert is Canada's most indefatigable Peter Pan, and Katimavik was the epitome of everything he believed in. It struck me then, as it does now, just how purely *Canadian* Katimavik was: it was painfully well-intentioned, resolutely optimistic, vaguely socialistic, very idealistic and publicly funded. National brotherhood by bureaucratic mandate. Remarkable, really.

Even more remarkable: it worked.

Great Britain, New York City, India and Australia all modelled youth volunteer corps directly on Katimavik.

The Business Council on National Issues, an organization upon which the federal government bases much of its economic policies, hailed Katimavik as a success and urged that the program be expanded. In the words of the council, Katimavik had reached the "social conscience" of Canada. And when the Business Council starts talking about "social consciences," you know you have something unusual on your hands.

Katimavik was also remarkably cost-efficient. The program paid participants who completed the full nine months a $1,000 bursary, and together with the regular dollar a day, this worked out to a wage of less than $35 a week.

What did Canada get in return? A study by Econosult-Lavalin, an independent firm, found that every dollar the government spent on Katimavik generated $2.43 in the Canadian economy, and that two thirds of all the money spent went directly into the communities involved.

In 1985, Katimavik was awarded a medal by the United Nations Environmental Program.

And in 1986, Katimavik was cancelled.

Brian Mulroney, our very own bush-league Margaret Thatcher (but without Thatcher's virility), cancelled the program. And then, almost in the same breath, he announced that Canada would invest some six million dollars colour-coding the uniforms of our armed forces; a sum which just happened to be the amount saved by cancelling Katimavik. The government's priorities were clear.

The Conservative government of Brian Mulroney killed Katimavik abruptly and without public debate, and just days before a nonpartisan Senate study was about to be released. The study recommended *expanding* the program, but by then it was too late.

Katimavik had actually been on the chopping block since 1985, but one of Mr. Mulroney's advisors had pointed out that 1985 was also the International Year of Youth and that closing down Canada's only national youth program might perhaps send the wrong message. The government waited just a month after the Year of Youth had ended and then pulled the plug.

The cancellation of Katimavik in the spring of 1986 launched one of the most extraordinary political protests in Canadian history. Jacques Hébert, age sixty-two and by that time a Senator, went on a hunger strike in the foyer of the Upper House.

Hébert was protesting not only the end of Katimavik but also the government's apparent disregard for an estimated 600,000 young Canadians out of work at the time. In Senate debates and newspaper interviews, Hébert warned of a Lost Generation, one trailing the Baby Boomers, a generation without a sense of direction or even identity. Senator Hébert's warning has since proven all too accurate. Today, this lost generation has a name: simply, X.

In fact we have lost even this designation; Generation X has slid down a notch and is increasingly used for the kids just now coming of age: our self-confident, ill-mannered, skate-boarding, backward-hat-wearing younger siblings.

Somewhere between Baby Boomer and Generation X, neither fish nor fowl, an entire group of Canadians exists on the cusp between worlds.

"We were the Middle Child Generation," says my brother Ian. "We got lost along the way."

I FIRST MET Jacques Hébert in August 1984, when I was chosen as a participant representative on the Katimavik national planning committee in a conference outside of Montréal. Hébert and the other directors were in attendance, and together we reviewed the program and drew up a plan that was meant to extend Katimavik well into the 1990s. Hébert envisioned a day when every young Canadian would have the chance to spend a year as a cross-Canada volunteer, with college credit given for the life experience gained. Not military service, but *community* service.

The meetings were filled with this high-pitched energy, this sense that anything was possible. A year later, Mulroney was at the helm, Katimavik was gone, and Hébert was on a hunger strike.

I went to see Jacques again in the spring of 1986. By then he had gone almost three weeks without food and with nothing more substantial to drink than mineral water. He was gaunt and becoming weak, but still as stubborn as always.

In Montréal, ex-Katimavik participants staged a rally. It was the first and only protest march I have ever attended, and if you have never been to one, let me tell you, they are pretty silly: walking around in circles, waving signs, yelling for the cameras. Still, we had a cool chant: *"Brian, Brian, don't be a prick! Give us back Katimavik!"* How the prime minister could fail to be swayed by such an argument is beyond me.

Senator Hébert's hunger strike lasted twenty-one days and ended only when Jean Chrétien and an *ad hoc* coalition of private citizens intervened to help organize private and municipal funding to continue many of the volunteer projects. But in the end, Katimavik was gone.

And the Lost Generation has since grown up.

Katimavik participants were between the ages of seventeen and twenty-one. Most Katima-victims are now in their early thirties, and a few of the original participants are pushing forty. For most of us, Katimavik was the central experience of our youth.

A follow-up Gallup poll has demonstrated that ex-participants are twice as likely to be gainfully employed as other members of their age group. They are also more keenly aware of themselves as "Canadian" than almost any other segment of society.

You see, we were never really lost. We just weren't sure where we were going.

5

DISCO NATIONALISM

. . . .

*T*HE BEST thing about spending five years in Asia was this: I missed the entire Grunge Era. The ratty hair, the incomprehensible guitar riffs, the postpunk ennui: I missed it all. When I left, no one had heard of Kurt Cobain and fortunately, by the time I came back, he had already committed suicide. Grunge came and went, and I was out of the country. That alone was worth going into exile.

I was in the airport lobby in Vancouver, still groggy with jet lag, when through my mental fog I noticed a young lady smiling at me. She was a clerk at a magazine stand. She was pretty, friendly and apparently interested in me. So I sauntered over in a confident yet casual manner, and using one of those epigrams that have made me famous on four continents, I said, "Hello, there."

"You have a goatee," she said.

"Pardon?" said I.

"A goatee," said she. "You have one."

And so began one of the most surreal conversations of my life.

"A goatee?" I preferred to call it an Understated Yet Virile He-Man Beard, but if she insisted, sure, I suppose it was a goatee.

"I like goatees. A lot of women don't, but I do."

"Ah, thanks."

"Makes you look like a barenaked lady."

"Huh?"

You must realize that although the Barenaked Ladies were then a top concert band, I had never heard of them, nor did I know that several of the band members sported goatees at the time, or that I happened to look a lot like one of them. All I knew was that this otherwise seemingly sane woman—a complete stranger—was comparing my fuzzy triangular beard to a naked lady.

It got worse.

Her voice dropped to a stage whisper. "You aren't are you?"

I was baffled. "Aren't what?"

"A barenaked lady."

"No!" I sputtered. "Why would you say such a thing?"

"Because you kind of looked like a barenaked—"

"Because of the beard?" I said, still aghast, my brain not fully computing what my ears were hearing.

"Yes."

"I am not a naked woman!"

"Lady," she corrected. "You aren't a barenaked lady. I didn't think so. It's just that with the beard you sort of look like one."

I fled the shop in confusion and the conversation haunted me for days. It was only when I related it to my brothers that they cleared it up. The Barenaked Ladies, it turned out, were performing in Vancouver that weekend. I'm just thankful their name wasn't Complete Doofus or there might have been fisticuffs between me and that shop clerk.

The point of this anecdote is that in just five years I had been left behind. Fashion, in clothes, music—or ideas—is like a great debris-choked wave sweeping you along, or under, as it goes.

Modern Canadian nationalism was born on just such a wave in 1967. Expo. Man and His World. Canada's Centennial. The nation's coming out party. Expo '67 has been immortalized as a climactic moment in the story of Canada. I guess you had to be there. I was only two and a half years old at the time, so it didn't have much of an impact on me.

It was held on a man-made island, and you can still see the geodesic dome, a golf ball of the gods, in all its rusting glory across the water from Old Montréal. Big. Hairy. Deal. It was just a fair. It's finished, alright? It's been finished for thirty years—*get over it!* I know I sound callous, but I'm getting more than a little tired of hearing about that damn Expo. It's not like it was the 1972 Russia-Canada hockey series. Now THAT was a high point in Canadian history! (See Chapter 8.)

In *Mondo Canuck,* Geoff Pevere and Greig Dymond examine the Expo '67 Phenomenon and the impact it had on an entire generation. "Expo '67 was Canada's Summer of Love . . . After Expo, there wasn't anything we couldn't do."

Even Peter C. Newman found deliverance in a fairground. "This was the greatest thing we have ever done as a nation."

The *Montreal Star* went one better, calling it "the most staggering Canadian achievement since this vast land was finally linked by a transcontinental railway."

Today, like most artificially induced high points in life (high school proms, wedding ceremonies, etc.), Expo '67 lingers in the memory, at once nostalgic and melancholy. After all, high points also mark the beginning of the end; there is nowhere to go but down.

Expo coincided with our Centennial, and 1967 marked the first stirrings of modern Canadian nationalism. Everybody sing: *It's the hundredth anniversary of Confederation!*

The Baby Boomers led the way. They came of age in the 1960s amid wealth and indulgence, not so much the Age of Aquarius as the Age of Adolescence. It was an ideological time, very earnest, very sincere and utterly lacking the redeeming quality of irony or even humour. I don't mean they were—as a group—humourless, but their vision of Canada certainly was. It was a mishmash of Romanticism, nineteenth-century nationalism, suburban rebellion and a self-love so strong it bordered on masturbatory. Like those grating student-council types at a pep rally, they were forever trying to stroke up some school spirit. "Come on everybody!" "Unite!" "Stand up for Canada!" "Down with Mom, Dad and the U.S.A.!"

It was a time of slogans and set phrases, of dire predictions and self-righteous youth. It was a time of clichés.

A good deal of the new nationalism focussed on anti-American sentiment and the Vietnam War. In the midst of all this, Mel Hurtig, the Don Quixote of Canadian nationalism, published an entire book on Canadian views of America, entitled *The New Romans*. The list of contributors reads like a Who's Who of Canadian writers: Margaret Atwood, Earle Birney, George Woodcock, Mordecai Richler, George Grant, Al Purdy, Margaret Laurence, Michael Ondaatje, Robert Fulford, John Robert Colombo, Irving Layton and Farley Mowat.

Vietnam was the focal point and rallying cry, but my own recollections of that war are vague. We were living in a farmhouse near Regina while my father was finishing his M.Ed. It was the only time we ever lived within driving distance of the United States, but I was only five or six at the time and wasn't much aware of *nations* let alone the concept of nationality. My parents were part of the clandestine underground railroad, a chain of safe houses that helped smuggle American draft dodgers into Canada, and my memory of the war is a series of nervous young men with strange accents coming through our house.

I remember one tall, lanky boy who liked to make us laugh. He was spinning my little sister Lorna around and around and around, when suddenly her elbow was pulled out and dislocated. There was an instant commotion, with tears and stammered apologies and a frantic trip to the hospital. I suppose, in a way, that has always been my image of America: a clumsy young man knocking over furniture and hurting people and then awkwardly apologizing.

The Vietnam War was the ultimate spectator's sport. Many Canadians crossed the border going the other way, to *volunteer* to fight, but in essence it was always a foreign conflict. In it, our sense of moral superiority hardened and the Myth of Nice—as contrasted to Americans—took firm root. The *New Romans* is replete with such anti-American sentiments. One particularly subtle poem in the anthology begins "America you bastard, murderer of dreams." And the next poem—*the very next poem*—begins "Canada my beauty, everybody's love." There you have it: America you bastard, Canada my beauty.

True, there were other, less outrageous items in the book, but it is the anti-Americanism that concerns us here. It was added, like a layer of *papier-mâché,* onto the older, staid nationalism of the Mountie and Moose School, creating a bizarre collage of ideology and folksy affectation.

The rhetoric of the 1960s lives on. Our faults are projected outwards, our insecurities and failures are blamed on social conspiracies and bad childhoods. In a recently revised *Take Back the Nation,* Maude Barlow and Bruce Campbell, like most social commentators, find the roots of the crisis everywhere but in the mirror. Our national woes are blamed on government policies, Free Trade, the United States, and even on an ominous "alliance of corporate leaders and politicians."

At the same time, every year brings us a crop of "Why I Love Canada" books aimed at rallying the troops, my favourite being one by former Prime Minister Joe Clark, entitled *A Nation Too Good To Lose.* If anyone should know about losing, it's Joe. There is even a book of *child* nationalism, *Dear Canada/Cher Canada,* produced by Ben Wicks & Associates during the lead-up to the 1995 Referendum. It's a revealing book; the kids have learned to mimic the self-conscious nationalism of their Baby Boomer parents and teachers quite well. The following is by a six-year-old boy from B.C. (original spelling intact):

> I am varry prowd to be a Canadian. And so I am prowd
> to live in Canada. Eavn tthow we have probblms we
> solve them with no vilnts or wors! Thaits wout I think
> about Canada. Yey CANADA!!!

Clean up the spelling, add a few footnotes and a reference to unity, and you have *A Nation Too Good To Lose*. Yey Canada!!

A young girl from Nova Scotia, at the tender age of nine, has already grasped the very essence of Canadian nationalism:

> If you were visiting Canada,
> you'd know it was Canada
> because we're just . . . nice.

There it is, the N-word. In children, a degree of naivety is very cute, but when adults are still walking around starry-eyed and brimming with bromides, you know it's time for a change.

From George Grant to the perpetually peeved Farley Mowat, the 1960s bred an entire generation of muddled Romantics responsible for the shape of Canadian nationalism today. And why not? Somebody has to take the blame.

What happened to the '60s? They led to the '70s.

In the 1970s, the self-indulgence that was such an integral part of the '60s consciousness came to the forefront.

Folk music turned into disco. Free love turned into one-night stands. Cotton turned into polyester, and primary colours ruled. Protest songs were replaced with Patsy Gallant, and political and spiritual pretensions hardened into plastic, all shine and brittle gloss.

Modern Canadian nationalism was born in the '60s, but it came of age in the '70s, and the result is Disco Nationalism, a synthesizer drumbeat repeated ad nauseam, like a mantra. Like an ode to arrested development. It was the '60s without the rhythm. Disco Nationalism was passion by rote. Petulant clichés became internalized and Canadian nationalism became a caricature, as predictable and relentless as disco music—and as embarrassing as big floppy hats and platform shoes. I remember seeing photographs of my older brother in a fuzzy Afro and a baby-blue leisure suit with the cuffs flipped up, and I asked him, "What the hell were you thinking?" He shrugged and said, "Hey, it was hip at the time." And then, even more chilling: "You know, disco is making a comeback."

Give me grunge, give me punk, give me country-and-western. Anything, but spare me the posture-pose dancing and plastic appeal of disco.

For those of us who came of age in the 1980s, after disco and just as the Baby Boomers discovered greed (not that any of it trickled down to us), Disco Nationalism now holds very little appeal. What we need is not modern Canadian nationalism, but *postmodern* nationalism: one that is eclectic, wry, unpretentious and untainted by ideology. The time has come for the Baby Boomers to get off the dance floor and make room for someone else.

Booma-chuka-booma-chuka.

Part Two

PADDLES, PUCKS AND PEACEKEEPERS:

THE EVOLUTION OF NICE

. . . .

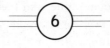

VOYAGEURS
AND HABITANTS

. . . .

*I*N THE FAR WOODS of northern Alberta the people are Cree, the language is English, but the names are French: Lizotte, Boyer, Lambert, Beaulieu.

This swath of French surnames runs halfway across Canada. It follows the waterways of the Great Lakes and the Canadian Shield, cutting an arc through the tribal lands of the Ojibwa, the Slavey and the Cree. It traces a trade route centuries old: the trail of the Frenchmen who first ventured into the interior, the *coureurs de bois,* or "runners of the woods," and the company men who followed in their wake, the *voyageurs.*

The lumberjack and the voyageur are quintessential Canadian protagonists: one chopping down trees as he sings a rustic woodland tune, and the other paddling his canoe full of furs over rapids as he sings equally rustic French-Canadian tunes. But unlike the apocryphal "singing lumberjack" of Monty Python fame, the voyageurs really *did* sing. The songs, with their measured beat and cadence, set the rhythm of the paddles and helped relieve the fatigue and boredom of long journeys. Like so much of the voyageur legend, it is surprisingly true to form.

The life of a voyageur was romantic mainly from the sidelines. The American writer Washington Irving may have called them "Sinbads of the Wilderness," but he didn't have to paddle halfway across a continent.

Aching arm sockets, long hours, stingy bosses, finicky company regulations and binding contracts: in some ways the voyageurs were more "hewers of wood and drawers of water" than the *habitants* of New France who watched the voyageurs pass by their waterfront farms every spring. The Canadian character was set by these two figures: the voyageur and the habitant, the traveller and the settler.

Images to the contrary, the habitants enjoyed a good deal of freedom in their lives, far more than the peasants of France or the crofters of Scotland. The voyageurs, on the other hand, were company employees, hired labourers, human mule trains.

For all that, the voyageurs were a breed apart. Their story captivates us because it is an epic writ small, a saga of the common man set against a vast and indifferent landscape. The voyageur is as Canadian as a gunslinger is American or a samurai is Japanese.

Almost from the beginning there were woodsmen. Samuel de Champlain, the Father of New France, knew that the ornate courts of France wanted more than land and Christian converts; they wanted furs. Champlain was also well aware that he shared the continent with Native people, whom he had a habit of shooting. When he realized that there were too many to shoot, Champlain decided to send young men into the *pays d'en haut,* the "upper country" beyond Montréal, to live with the Natives and to learn their customs and languages.

Through these original *coureurs de bois,* Champlain extended his network of trade and alliances deep into the Great Lakes interior. Although originally an offshoot of the codfish and whaling industries, the fur trade soon became the central source of wealth, and in 1670 this wealth attracted an English outfit, the Company of Adventurers, better known as the Hudson's Bay Company.

Unable to wrestle the English away from the coast of Hudson Bay, the French instead sought to cut them off from the interior by building a string of forts along the river routes to intercept the Native suppliers. The HBC was caught napping as they "slept at the edge of a frozen sea."

And frozen it was. Then as now, the entire bay, 1500 by 830 kilometres, froze solid to the centre every winter, from shore to shore. The HBC's ships slipped in and out ahead of the ice, leaving behind a small crew to man the forts: the loneliest posts on the continent. With the Indians bringing furs to them every spring, the traders of the HBC had grown lax, lazy. Unimaginative.

After Britain's conquest of New France in 1763, the Hudson's Bay Company assumed that the competition was gone forever. They were sadly mistaken. The newly arrived Scottish merchants in Montréal simply took over the

French trade system, including their line of forts, and they began competing even harder than the French had, much to the chagrin of the HBC. Rogue traders joined forces with the Highlanders and freelance voyageurs, and this loose coalition eventually amalgamated in 1783 into the North West Company.

In response, the HBC was forced deeper inland, and various forts were built by both sides, as they hopscotched down the waterways, trying to intercept each other's supply lines. The two rival companies even took to waylaying Indian canoes bound for the competition and forcing the Indians to trade with them instead.

In the midst of all this, the voyageur was in his glory. Every spring, as the snows melted and the ice broke, flotillas of transport canoes would leave Lachine, west of Montréal, loaded down with trade goods. These impressive craft, the *canots de maître,* were 10 metres or more in length and powered by a dozen or so voyageurs. These canoes were the freight trucks of their day, capable of holding an incredible four tonnes of supplies each. They were light on the water, bobbing over rapids and bouncing off river banks, and when damaged, they were easily patched up on shore with spruce gum and pine tar.

The voyageurs pushed themselves to the limit of endurance. They paddled upstream along the Ottawa River and then downstream to Georgian Bay, scrambling to portage past the white-water rapids at Sault Ste. Marie. Then, onto the oceanlike expanse of Lake Superior, with its terrifying walls of waves and sudden squalls. They pushed on every day until dark and longer still when the moon was full, spending as much as twenty hours a day in their canoes. They even slept under them, surrounded by smudges of wet moss to drive away the hordes of mosquitoes and blackflies, and with the first wash of dawn, it began again.

When the water broke over rocks too jagged and into currents too strong, the men unloaded their tonnage and with "tump lines" taut around their foreheads and hundreds of pounds of supplies wedged against their backs, they carried their cargo and canoes through forest-cut paths that were almost as treacherous as the rapids they bypassed. Portages, it was said, killed more voyageurs than any rapids. They certainly crippled more.

At the end of Lake Superior was *le Grand Portage,* an ordeal over 14 kilometres long, deemed too difficult for horses, but not voyageurs. Each man was expected to haul at least four loads of 80 kilograms each. At the end of the Grand Portage, the Montréal men rendezvoused with the even more rugged *les hommes du nord,* "the men of the north."

Long-haired, dark, dressed in buckskins and standing tall, *les hommes du nord* revelled in their own image, and they looked down on the voyageurs from Montréal, who hurried home for the winter. They sneered at the Montréal men, calling them *mangeurs de lard,* "pork-eaters," who lived on bacon fat and flour, while the north men ate wild rice and animal hearts. This really annoyed the Montréal men, who, after a gruelling six-week journey, had to sit around and listen to the north men thump their chests and declare, *"Je suis un HOMME DU NORD!"* There were a lot of fist-fights over this.

Grand Portage was the halfway point, where furs gathered in the interior were exchanged for trade goods. As the crossroads of a frontier caravan route, this sprawling, palisaded post was a ragged, frenetic place, full of sin and vice, with its "harlot's tavern" and endless rounds of rum, late-night revelries and Métis girls, all followed by the inevitable fist-fights.

After a grudging farewell, the Montréal men and *les hommes du nord* went their separate ways. The Montréal men returned home in canoes weighted down with furs. The north men in their lighter, quicker canoes, loaded up with supplies and trade items, set out, battling the current out of Grand Portage for several days until they reached the height of land. From there, they paddled downstream into the breaking waters of the Winnipeg River with its countless portages and dangerous rapids. Then, into another inland sea, Lake Winnipeg.

From Lake Winnipeg, the various brigades would fan out, down smaller rivers, over sandbars and muskeg, and even descending cliff faces in tense detours. Eventually, often just as the first winter chill was in the air, they would arrive at their respective, isolated posts. They were home.

The intermarriage of wintering north men and Native women may sound romantic, and at times it was, but many young girls were more or less sold by their fathers to curry favour with the traders, and many a wife and child were abandoned at the end of a contract. The voyageurs left the woods scattered with broken hearts. Some, however, formed allegiances that would last a lifetime. It was from these trysts and unconsecrated marriages—some dysfunctional, and some not—that the Métis nation and half my home town would descend.

The promise of sex was a prime motivational factor, as much as the furs, in luring young men into the woods, especially in the early years, when the balance of men to women in New France was about seven to one. Lonely young men often sought companionship *en pays d'haut*. Sex, therefore, played a small but important part in the development of Canada, though I mention this only to keep your attention by gratuitously mentioning the word *sex*.

The interaction, amorous and otherwise, between the First Nations and the fur traders is also credited with creating a certain stability along the Canadian frontier. The trade and intermarriage, though limited in scope, provided a basis for further co-operation, which later arrivals—the Mounted Police, the railway and the settlers—were able to take advantage of.

Without their French-Canadian voyageurs and Native guides, the Scottish traders and explorers would never have made it inland, let alone be able to leave their own swath of surnames across the Northwest, as they did. Scottish schemes, voyageur muscle and Native knowledge were the three keys to the success of the North West Company, even if posterity tends to remember only the first two.

Especially important was Native technology, from lightweight canoes to preventative medicines for scurvy, from weight-distributing snowshoes to pemmican, a dried mix of pounded meat, fat and berries that powered the voyageurs along their way. Pemmican played a critical role in opening up the Northwest, and one writer made the intriguing comparison between it and the dried foodstuffs used by twentieth-century astronauts.

As for the position of the First Nations in the fur trade, an odd and persistent belief has them as passive, innocent people, taken advantage of at every turn as they naively handed over fortunes in furs for a handful of beads. Interestingly enough, this "Indian as patsy" canard is promoted by both ends of the spectrum, by those who see the

European expansion into the New World as not only inevitable but for the best, and by those who see the New World as some sort of mythical Paradise Lost. This only underlines the basic agreement in attitude between neo-conservatives and the politically correct: they both look down on Natives, one in contempt, and the other in condescension. I'm not sure which is worse.

In fact, the Natives were aggressive bargainers who well understood the use of trade monopolies, middlemen and comparative shopping. The fur trade did have an enormous impact on Native society, especially in the east, where fishing tribes became trappers, and along the Great Lakes, where one band of Ojibwa even began specializing in the production of canoes. Whether this is necessarily a bad thing is debatable. Human societies along trade routes are always transformed, and the notion that Native societies should exist in some kind of perpetual pastoral stasis smacks of wish fulfilment. Kettles, rifles, traps and woven fabrics *did* make the Indians dependent on white trade, but they also made life much easier and far more interesting. For the most part, it was not luxuries that the Natives were trading for, and it certainly wasn't the case of "trinkets for furs," as commentators like Pat Bird have written.

At Fort Edmonton, I remember watching an Indian woman, all wrinkles and smiles, demonstrate beadwork. She was decorating a pair of moccasins with flowing shapes of wild roses set among interlocking patterns of blue and green in soft aromatic leather, the scent of which is impossible to describe. Our tour guide sombrely intoned, "Here we see a Native woman demonstrating an ancient, traditional art of her peoples, from long before the time of the white man." Everyone nodded thoughtfully. Except that beadwork is *not* an ancient art from "before the time of the white man." Nor are the more intricate of the bone carvings. These were made possible through European trade. Beads and better tools led to a cultural and artistic Renaissance among many of the First Nations.

It was the habitant that destroyed Native societies, not the voyageur. The voyageurs were merely the unwitting advance guard of European encroachment, and in this they laid the groundwork for their own demise as well. In the voyageur's path followed surveyors, railways, farms, villages, cities—the very things that the fur trade, by its very nature, had been hostile towards. The Indians they had once lived amid, fought with, traded among and loved hard, were now cordoned off to the geographic and historical periphery of the nation.

Like the North West Company that it eventually absorbed, the Company of Adventurers is long gone. In 1970 the headquarters were finally moved from London, England, to Winnipeg, exactly three hundred years after its original charter. The Charter itself, one of the most important historical documents in Canadian history, is kept in an office building in downtown Toronto. On Bay Street, no less.

The Hudson's Bay Company no longer deals in furs. It has become a retail chain, with a distinctive dichotomy of glossy downtown department stores and small outposts among the far-flung communities of the North, supplying the wants of latter-day habitants. And the voyageur has disappeared.

You hesitate. The trees are entangled with menace.
The voyage is perilous into the dark interior.
But then your hands go to the thwarts.
You smile. And so
I watch you vanish in a wood of heroes.
Wild Hamlet with the features of Horatio.

This is the final stanza of a poem by Douglas LePan in *The Wounded Prince.* Beyond the simple nostalgia, we catch a glimpse of something else. A shadow across the mirror. The voyageurs, the *coureurs de bois,* the men of the north; they are the expression of a central Canadian archetype: the soul gone wild, the garden overrun, the heart that has made its peace with the primal unknown.

The voyageur stands opposed in intent and imagery to that of the habitant. The habitant doesn't enter into the landscape, he reorganizes it. He pushes the wilderness back to the edge of the yard and plants crops in rows and grids. That many habitants were also voyageurs is not important. The line is drawn firmly in our imagination: the settler and the traveller, the farmer and the nomad. He who stays and he who goes. One left his legacy in the land he cleared and the nation he built. The other moved like smoke through the forest, leaving little, taking less.

Canada is a land pinned between the memories of habitant and voyageur. We have grown crops and built cities, bypassed rapids, unrolled asphalt and smothered our fears under comforters and quilts. We are habitants, and the spirit of the voyageur lingers now only in the home movies of our nation, like the tiger dreams of a house cat.

Like a song from the far woods.

LOYALISTS
AND OTHER LOSERS

· · · · · · · ·

*T*HE AMERICAN revolution was—above
all—a civil war, one that tore families
apart and polarized the British colonies in North America.
The revolution may have been sanctified by the highest
ideals, but it was born of mob rule and violence. (High ideals and mob rule being a distinctly American blend.)

Although carried forth with great zeal by the average
unwashed rabble, the American Revolution was actually
a revolt of the *nouveau riche,* spearheaded by men like
George Washington, a wealthy plantation owner accus-
tomed to an opulent lifestyle supported by a large con-
tingent of black slaves. The crusader for liberty owned
hundreds of them.

As historian Christopher Moore notes in *The Loyalists*:

> That many of the leaders of the Patriot cause, who so vigorously proclaimed liberty, the rights of man, and representative government, were themselves slave-owners and defenders of a society built upon slave-holding had not gone unnoticed in Britain, where slavery had been prohibited some years earlier.

"Why," noted Samuel Johnson, "is it we hear the loudest yelps for liberty among the drivers of negroes?" One ex-slave who escaped to the Canadian colonies wrote, with deep irony, that it was only when he escaped America that he finally "began to feel the happiness of liberty."

The Patriots trampled on the very human rights they purported to be defending: they took hostages, they seized and opened mail, they staged violent boycotts, they orchestrated kangaroo courts, and they held what can only be dubbed "consciousness-raising" sessions, where people suspected of being loyal to Britain were badgered into swearing allegiance to the revolution. The Patriots also confiscated and auctioned off the land and property of suspected "traitors."

The persecution of Loyalists began in 1774, long before the first shots were fired. Those suspected of not supporting the revolution were beaten, imprisoned, tarred and feathered, and even murdered. (The term—and concept—of "lynch law" first described the treatment of suspected Loyalists.) The Loyalists retaliated in kind, and the two sides became increasingly violent.

I don't care whether it is the French Reign of Terror, the Soviet Vanguard, the Chinese Red Guards or today's

Politically Correct Movement; in practice all revolutions are based on extremism and intolerance. Without these, there could be no revolution. Open dialogue and compromise must be ruled out from the start if any revolution is ever to succeed.

Who were the Loyalists? Myths to the contrary, they were not simply dispossessed aristocrats. Most were farmers, but a good many were craftsmen, merchants, fishermen, professionals, labourers, ministers and officials. Some were newly landed immigrants, others had roots that went all the way back to the *Mayflower*. Nor was it simply a matter of Liberty vs. Loyalty. As often as not, it was The Majority vs. The Minority. Most Loyalists came from besieged ethnic minority groups: German and Dutch enclaves, Quaker and Mennonite pacifists, northern Anglicans, southern Presbyterians, Maryland Catholics, French Huguenots, members of First Nations and slaves. In other words, huddled masses yearning to breathe free. They were far more afraid of the liberty-loving majority than they were angry with a distant, neglectful British administration.

The aim of the Loyalists, writes historian W.G. Shelton in the *Dalhousie Review*,

> was not to reimpose harsh foreign rule, . . . but to liberate their homeland from the usurped authority of a ruthless faction claiming without justification to be acting for all Americans, and to restore the civil liberties guaranteed by the British constitution. They were fighting, in other words, for their own conception of freedom.

The majority of Loyalists were in fact sympathetic to colonial grievances; they simply disagreed with the methods being used. They were not united so much in what they believed as in what they abhorred: mob violence. Instead of calling them Loyalists, it would be more accurate to refer to them as anti-Revolutionaries.

As you can see, the Canadian Way was already taking shape long before Canada itself was invented: evolution rather than revolution; slow gradual change rather than sudden, traumatic upheaval; incrementalism as opposed to sweeping agendas. (This is one reason that both Meech Lake and the Charlottetown Accord failed, by the way. Mulroney's American approach of presenting one big package, love it or leave it, flew in the face of the Canadian preference for methodical, step-by-step changes.)

Today, Canada is an independent, stable democracy. With only the vestigial remnants of the Royal Family clouding our vision, we have attained a degree of civility and success that most revolutionaries can only dream about. And we did it without ideology and with a minimum of bloodshed.

Someone once described Canadians as "Americans with manners," but I would put it a different way. Historically and culturally, Americans are just Canadians in a hurry.

THE BREAK BETWEEN Britain and the Thirteen Colonies began, ironically, with one of Britain's greatest triumphs: the Conquest of New France. When the threat of French encroachment was finally removed, the Americans found less and less benefit in being part of an empire. Angered by British taxes and the limits imposed on westward expansion (Britain had reserved the west as First Nations territory), Patriots began massing arms and resisting British rule. And Loyalists began resisting the resistance.

As fighting intensified, the British issued a proclamation offering freedom to any slaves who would join them. It was a contradictory stance, because many of the Loyalists themselves were also slave-holders. (The same proclamation that guaranteed freedom for the runaway slaves of rebel overlords also guaranteed Loyalists the possession of their own slaves.) Still, the effect of the proclamation was immediate. It sparked the first mass escape in the history of American slavery. Thousands of ex-slaves, dressed in British uniforms, now marched against their former owners. This drove the Patriots into an even greater fury. At the same time, the British made tactical alliances with breakaway nations of the Iroquois Confederacy and established a "benevolent neutrality" with the recently conquered French that would prove crucial when Washington's army invaded Québec.

In March 1776, the American rebels drove the British out of Boston. A few months later, on July 4, the Declaration of Independence was adopted by the American Continental Congress. But the civil war was not yet over. British troops regrouped and returned in force for a counteroffensive, taking first New York and then much of the south. The reconquest of America foundered at Yorktown, when an overly ambitious British general named Charles Cornwallis marched into a trap. The war might have raged on—and the Patriots might have been subdued—but by then France, Spain and Holland had all joined forces against Britain. To cut their losses and protect their possessions elsewhere, Britain conceded defeat.

The south was abandoned as the British fell back to the last Loyalist stronghold, New York City.

With the American victory of 1783, the persecution of the Loyalists reached new extremes. The only thing more violent and vindictive than a thwarted revolutionary is a *successful* revolutionary. As well as the usual beatings, tarrings, imprisonments, poisoning of livestock, extortion, lynch mob hangings, stonings, assassinations and the confiscation of private property, several states also imposed double or even triple taxation on Loyalists—this from a revolution that began with the cry of "no taxation without representation." As popular historian Stuart Trueman writes in *An Intimate History of New Brunswick,* "Loyalists soon became non-persons in many states, unable legally to sell or buy land, work, speak or write their opinions, collect debts by legal means, or seek the law's protection if physically attacked." It was a grand victory for liberty.

In New York City, under the direction of Governor Guy Carleton, one of the largest mass migrations in modern history was launched. In many ways, the Loyalists were the original boat people. A flotilla of ships crowded in along the docks, and close to 100,000 people fled the advancing forces of the American Revolution. Of these, 50,000 went north to Nova Scotia, Québec and the inland wilderness above the Great Lakes. When a triumphant George Washington led his army into New York, he took possession of an abandoned city. The exodus of Loyal Americans had begun.

Moore writes, "All the experience of the loyalists' war—persecution, flight, loss, and service in loyal military regiments—reinforced and made permanent the sense of exile . . . [T]hough they certainly had not become British, [they] had ceased to see themselves as Americans." English Canada would be born of this identity crisis.

SO GREAT WAS the influx of Loyalists that three new colonies were created to deal with them: New Brunswick, Cape Breton (which was later returned to Nova Scotia) and Upper Canada (which later became the heartland of Ontario). Nova Scotia, an underdeveloped colony with a population of less than 19,000, was flooded with 35,000 Loyalists.

They landed unprepared, a bedraggled, defeated people. "Nothing but wilderness before our eyes," wrote a Loyalist refugee on the banks of the St. John River. "The women and children did not refrain from tears."

One woman recalled watching the sails disappear into the distance. "[S]uch a feeling of loneliness came over me that, although I had not shed a tear through all the war, I sat down on the damp moss with my baby in my lap and cried."

It was a long, hard struggle. The Loyalist families needed to be fed, clothed and housed. Many died from exposure and malnutrition, and more than one distraught head of a household committed suicide. Land surveys had to be completed, shelters built, rations allotted, mills constructed, land cleared, crops planted, tools and supplies distributed, civil administration established, streets laid out and plots of land assigned.

"Although their destination resembled a wilderness," writes Moore, "it would be an unusually organized one . . ." *An organized wilderness.* That, then, is the Great Canadian Allegory.

Somehow, through the chaos and confusion, a new society began to take shape, but one lacking the very elements that had given the American colonies their edge. The American Revolution turned North America, unintentionally, into a grand social experiment: two societies divided along lines of *temperament*. That line has defined North America ever since.

The Loyalists built entire cities, complete with harbours and mills and schools and garrisons. They were the second great wave of settlers after the habitants, the second great wave of people who came not to trade or fish but to build. From that first great Loyalist city of Saint John, New Brunswick, to the failed dreams of Shelburne, Nova Scotia, from the stronghold of Loyalist traditions of Kingston, Ontario, to the Eastern Townships of Québec, they transformed what had previously been a hinterland. True, they didn't mix well with the more than 150,000 French Canadians and returning Acadians, who had been settled in the area for 180 years prior to the Loyalists' arrival, but that too is a part of who we are: *canadiens* and Loyalists, British institutions and French forebears. Canada, as we know it, was taking shape: French roots, Loyalist perseverance and Native enclaves. Three people united in their separate tales of defeat.

The Black Loyalists and the Native allies suffered the worst. As Loyalist refugees crowded into New York, George Washington had sent an ultimatum demanding the return of slaves along with other "property." It caused a chest-tightening panic and fear of reprisal among the thousands of ex-slaves, but Governor Carleton refused Washington's demands and insisted that they were now free men and women. The thousands of ex-slaves who came to Nova Scotia had a much harder time of it than the other Loyalists. Blacks were barely tolerated. Race riots, inequality and induced poverty all took their toll. Although a small population of Black Loyalists remains in Nova Scotia to this day, almost half left in 1792, just nine years after their arrival, on board ships bound for the free African colony of Sierra Leone—where even greater hardships and misery awaited.

The Iroquois had fought alongside Loyalist troops and British regulars, but in the aftermath of war they were sold out by Britain, which ceded the vast western interior south of the Great Lakes to the Americans. Following their charismatic leader Thayendanegea (better known as Joseph Brant) into exile, the Iroquois allies settled on the northern side of the Great Lakes, far from their homeland. Of all the people displaced by the war, they were the true exiles, for they had not come from somewhere else. The Loyalists lost their land, their savings, their positions and livelihood. The Iroquois lost their ancestral home. Even today a division exists between the New York Iroquois who stayed neutral and those who fought for Britain and now live in Ontario and Québec.

In time, both the Loyalists and the *canadiens* would in turn be swamped by successive waves of immigrants, exiles and refugees. But they were the ones who broke trail, and it is in their path that we follow. It is easy, and even tempting, to dismiss Canada as a land founded by losers. There is a great deal of truth in this: the First Nations fought and manoeuvred, but were ultimately overwhelmed; the *canadiens* were conquered by the British; the Acadians were expelled and almost destroyed as a nation;

the Loyalists were chased out by the Americans; the Irish came to escape famine; the Scots to escape the Highland Clearances, and so on. But there is more to this than mere defeat. If the Loyalist exile was the end of one saga, it was also the beginning of another. The Loyalists' discovery of Canada was that it was not simply a wilderness: it was also a Land of Second Chances. Even in defeat, Canada was founded as much on stubborn optimism as on exile.

The Loyalist migration was Canada's own declaration of independence. In the words of historian J.M.S. Careless, it was "a declaration of independence against the United States." As the heirs of the Loyalists, we are a society founded not on ideology, noble or otherwise, but on principles of fair play and on the notion that whatever the issue and whatever the problem, taking up arms should be the *last* resort, not the first. These two world views—one ideological and the other pragmatic, one American and the other Canadian—exist today on opposing sides of a border that is as subtle and profound as these distinctions.

Whether it be Native, French or Loyalist, Canada is a nation built on survival. And survival in the face of overwhelming odds is more than mere subsistence, it is an act of defiance. It needs no apology. It says to the world, "Fuck you! We made it anyway." A cause for celebration, a triumph in its own right, survival is a form of victory.

We lost a battle. We won the war.

THE COLD WAR
ON ICE

. . . .

*R*EMEMBER THE Cold War? The dark fears. The spectre of nuclear destruction. The world's scariest staring match. It was a nerve-racking time, and it had a deep effect on the human psyche. The Americans saw it as a shoot-out at the O.K. Corral, two gunslingers facing off across a dusty street at high noon. The Soviets saw it as a messianic war for world domination. And Canadians? What dark demons did the Cold War conjure up for us? How did our subconscious absorb these tensions?

The following is a transcript of a psychological test given to an anonymous Canadian—let's call him J. Canuck—at the very height of the Cold War:

Analyst: I would like you to relax and say the first thing that comes into your mind. Are you aware of the term Intercontinental Ballistic Missile?

J. Canuck: Yes, I am.

Analyst: And what do you think of when you hear the word ICBM?

J. Canuck: Ice hockey.

Analyst: Hmmmm. How about "limited nuclear strike"?

J. Canuck: Roughing.

Analyst: The Cuban Missile Crisis?

J. Canuck: Too many men on the ice.

Analyst: Thermonuclear Armageddon?

J. Canuck: Sudden death overtime.

Analyst: I see. Now then, tell me about your mother—

J. Canuck: Gordie Howe.

Ice hockey and ICBMs. Missiles and rubber pucks. In Canada, hockey is war, and war—or at least the threat of war—was ever-present. It all came down to geography. During the Cold War, Canada found herself wedged in between the competing ideologies of Lenin and Locke, Stalin and Smith, borscht and the Big Mac. In the words of one Soviet ambassador, "Canada was the ham in the Soviet-American sandwich."

Comedian Dave Broadfoot once argued that Canada was a very important country because, without Canada, the Japanese could sail right across and invade Denmark— and Broadfoot wasn't that far off the mark. Without Canada, you see, the Russians could have flown right over and dropped bombs directly on New York, San Francisco, Cape Kennedy, Washington, D.C., and—with a little luck—

Buffalo as well. Fortunately, these long-range nuclear bombers of the Soviet Air Force, stuffed with nuclear warheads and commie propaganda, could be intercepted over the majestic barren lands of Canada's Far North, which, with the exception of a few dissenting Inuit, seemed like a good idea to everyone involved.

Canadian leaders, caught in the middle of this apocalyptic game, decided that the time had come for Canada to assert itself as—what else—a Middle Power. It was like declaring to the world that you are a C student. "We are a Middle Power!" we said, and the two Superpowers responded like a husband behind a morning newspaper, "That's nice dear." It was not unlike giving an office worker a fancy title, but then continuing to have him make coffee. "We are a Middle Power!" we said, to which they replied, "Fine, great. And while you're up, you wanna pour me and Boris a cup a java?" The staring match went on.

Canada had hoped that being in the middle of this mess would give her some kind of leverage, but it never worked out that way. The Russians and the Americans continued to growl and glare at each other from across the room, gnashing their sabres and rattling their teeth (or was it the other way around?). Canada, meanwhile, scurried about pouring coffee and making small talk. Yet, for all the gnawing fears and heart palpitations the Cold War engendered, Canada just may be the only nation on earth that secretly *misses* those days. Canada, after all, was where the Cold War began. It was September 5, 1945. Igor Gouzenko, a soft-spoken cipher clerk at the Soviet embassy in Ottawa placed confidential papers into his attaché case and walked away—from his job, his country, his life.

He then quietly defected. Or rather, *tried* to defect. Prime Minister Mackenzie King, the Spineless Wonder, was distraught and wanted to hand Gouzenko right back to his Soviet masters. ("Welcome back, Igor. Heh, heh.") It was only after the Soviets bungled an abduction/assassination attempt that asylum was—reluctantly—offered.

The papers that Igor smuggled out of the Soviet embassy revealed the alarming extent of Soviet espionage in the West, including two spies operating in Canada under the code names (and this is true) "Back" and "Bacon." In their pursuit of atomic weaponry, Soviet moles had tunnelled deep into the U.S. via a convenient side door called Canada. The safety of the Free World had been compromised and the fate of Western civilization hung in the balance, all due to Canada's lackadaisical security standards. ("Sorry, eh?")

Using the information Igor supplied, the RCMP rounded up eighteen suspects and—here is where it gets *really* gruesome—subjected them to a rigorous inquiry. That's right, a Royal Commission. If James Bond had been a Canadian, it would have been 007—*licence to thoroughly investigate!* Some countries have witch hunts, we have endless meetings and government inquiries. I leave it to you to decide which is the more cruel punishment. Several Soviet spies were later convicted and sent to prison, but the damage had been done.

Igor himself was clouded in secrecy. His face was carefully concealed, and he became known as "The Man in the Mask." (It was actually more of a pillowcase than a mask *per se*, but "The Man with the Pillowcase over His Head" didn't have quite the same ring to it.) Igor went into hiding, wrote his memoirs and even a novel, *The Fall of a Titan,* which earned him a Governor General's Award. He remained in hiding until his death in 1982, eight years before the fall of the Berlin Wall and the end of the Cold War that he had helped start.

But what does any of this have to do with hockey, I hear you figuratively ask. Was Igor's new identity that of a professional hockey player, perhaps? The Man in the Hockey Mask, the ultimate secret identity? Well, not quite.

The Gouzenko Affair threw Canada and the rest of the world into the thick of a dangerous undeclared war, a war fought in Cuba. Afghanistan. Angola. Vietnam. Cambodia. Czechoslovakia. Berlin. Warsaw. And Winnipeg, Manitoba.

That's right, in Winnipeg. On ice. And in Montréal. And Vancouver. And Toronto. And finally, in Moscow itself. A five-city, eight-game, limited nuclear engagement. The year was 1972, and the game was hockey.

Canada has never been a world power, but this is only true as far as Everything Except Hockey (EEH) is concerned. EEH includes politics, economics, fashion, technology, military arsenal, the number of A-bombs dropped, the number of H-bombs built, the number of Third World governments toppled, the number of burgers consumed, the number of East European nations ingested—in short, all those trivial non-hockey things that daily crowd our attention and distract us from the *real* matter at hand: who plays the best game of shinny?

Sure, Canada has never been able to muster enough of an arsenal to carpet-bomb a small throw rug, let alone a southeast Asian country, and true, Canada's military ranks just above that of Tonga's—and all that *their* military consists of is a tape-recorded message yelling "I surrender!" in thirty-two languages. We may not have a Big Stick, or even a Small Twig, but by God, when it comes down to who carries the biggest *Hockey* Stick, the rest of the world had just better watch out.

In hockey there is one, and only one, Superpower. Or at least, that is what Canadians had been indoctrinated to believe. In fact, those sneaky Soviets, in addition to developing intercontinental ballistic missiles, vodka and baseball, had also been working in secret to perfect The Ultimate Hockey Player. They did this behind our backs by taking average players and injecting them with all kinds of illicit substances such as speed, finesse and fair play.

Such underhanded tactics had allowed the Soviets to dominate amateur hockey and the Olympics for years, but Canadians mocked Soviet claims to the hockey crown nonetheless. After all, the Soviets had never been tested against Canada's finest. Let them meet an all-star cast of our best *professional* players, and then we'll see who is really the best. And so the gauntlet, or in this case, the hockey glove, was tossed at their feet. Unfortunately for Canadian pride, the Russians picked it up.

The Cold War was about to get a lot colder, as the geopolitical competition between conflicting economic systems faced off, quite literally, in a hockey arena. (This direct connection between ice hockey and Canadian/ Soviet military aggression has, I feel, been scandalously underplayed by those who would foist themselves on us as our national historians. Remember, hockey is not a metaphor for war; war is a metaphor for hockey.)

After extensive negotiations on the part of Alan Eagleson, head of the players' union and chief organizer of the series, a two-nation, eight-game tournament was arranged between their best and our best. Well, not quite. It was more their best and *the* NHL's best. The fledgling World Hockey Association was cut out of the competition, leaving hockey great Bobby Hull ineligible. It was dirty pool, and Bobby never forgave them.

Canada's first confrontation with the might of the Soviet Empire took place on the second day of September 1972, in that bastion of free speech, Montreal (sorry, *Montréal*). With the likes of Phil Esposito, Frank Mahovlich and Bobby Clarke up front, Igor Gouzenko in goal, and Robin Goodfellow appearing as Puck, it looked like Team Canada couldn't lose. But they could lose. And they did.

The Canadians were confident to the point of being insufferable. The scouting reports had all but laughed at the Russian players. The young Russian goaltender, it was said, couldn't stop a beach ball. His name? Tretiak something or other. Alan Eagleson, never one to put undue pressure on his boys, said that anything short of a complete sweep of the series by Team Canada would be considered a national disgrace.

Canadian though I am, I have to say that we really had it coming. I mean, we *deserved* what happened. We really did. The game started according to script; Phil Esposito scored just 30 seconds into the game and everyone settled back to watch the humiliation begin. Well, it *was* humiliating, but not for the Soviets. They, apparently, hadn't read the same script as we had, and they proceeded to beat Team Canada 7 to 3. It was a humbling experience. As sportswriter

James Marsh notes, "the Soviets displayed speed, skill, and a haughty disregard for Canadian confidence."

Team Canada came back and won the next game in Toronto, but that was to be their only victory on Canadian ice. In Winnipeg they barely managed a tie, and they were so badly outplayed in Vancouver that their own fans turned on them. The Vancouver crowd booed Team Canada to a 5–3 loss. "We're doing our best," said a dejected Esposito, "I can't believe people are booing us."

The series now moved to Moscow. Canada needed to win three out of the next four games to take the series and salvage their pride. But the Soviet juggernaut continued to roll, beating Team Canada 5–4 and putting the Canadians—who had so far won only a single game—in a hopeless situation. They would have to win all of the final three games. It was war. The newspapers—*and the players*—had turned it into a bizarre democracy vs. communism battle.

You may think I exaggerate, but no, from all sides, especially that of the players, the series had been turned into Something Significant (as opposed to, say, a hockey game). Phil Esposito became convinced that the Soviets would try anything to win, even—he said ominously—"kill." "It was our society against theirs," Esposito intoned, "and as far as we were concerned it was a damn war."

Then came the beer incident. It was an outrage. The large supply of Canadian beer that the players brought with them somehow disappeared when it went through Soviet customs. You can kick a Canadian when he is down, you can piss on his tuque and shoot his favourite malamute, but you had damn well better stay away from his beer. The

Soviets had crossed the line. "Remember the missing beer!" became a battle cry, as stirring to the Canuck hockey players as "Remember the Alamo!" was to a Texas Ranger.

The Free World vs. the Commie Hordes. Vodka vs. beer. "It was a series of democracy versus communism, no question," said Alan Eagleson, who later helped the cause of international good will by giving the finger to the Soviet fans. "I just told the world we were number one," chortled Eagleson, "but I guess I used the wrong finger." (Is it any wonder they started calling us "Team Ugly"?)

In fact, it wasn't the Russians who were willing to do anything to win, it was the Canadians. My favourite heart-warming moment of Canadian determination occurred when Team Canada's assistant coach, John Ferguson, pointedly told Bobby Clarke that the Russian's dominant forward, Valeri Kharlamov, had a sore ankle. Clarke went out and laid a two-handed slash across Kharlamov with his stick, bruising the Russian's ankle so badly he was out of the lineup for the next game. That Bobby, what a rascal. And you know, it was just that kind of work ethic that earned the Canadian team its reputation as a bunch of "international hooligans." That's right, in '72 *we* were the assholes. We were the bullies. We were the loud-mouthed, winning-is-everything cretins. It was great.

The lively crowd of Canadian fans who made the trip to Moscow had a catchy chant as well: *"Da, da, Canada! Nyet, Nyet, Soviet!"*

Game Six. Canada fought back to a narrow victory, 3–2, with the winning goal coming from a talented young player named Paul Henderson. Game Seven. Another one-goal victory for Canada, 4–3, as Paul Henderson *again* provided the game-winner, going through two Soviet defensemen to do it, with only two minutes left on the clock.

It now all came down to a single game. The standings: three wins for the Soviets, three for the Canadians, and a single tie. On September 28, 1972, Canada came to a standstill. It is estimated that 15 million people—two thirds of the population at that time—were listening to the game on radio or else watching it on television. Classes were cancelled. Downtowns were deserted. For one brief glorious evening, the nation stood united before a common foe: French, English, West, East, all those differences now dissolved into a pathological hatred of the Soviet Union. It was inspiring.

I was seven years old, and for the first time I became aware of belonging to this group, this *thing* called Canada. We gathered around the radio and listened, and we were all a part of it, this event, this crusade. We held our breath and waited.

And so it was that the largest viewing audience in Canadian history tuned in to watch Team Canada get pelted by pucks for two periods. It was all going horribly, horribly wrong. The series was slipping away. Canada was going down, down, down. With one period left, the Soviets had a solid two-goal lead. There were only twenty minutes left to play and Team Canada had to score three unanswered goals. It would take a miracle to pull this off—and not some minor water-to-wine, heal-the-lepers type of miracle. No, it required a *real* miracle, a *hockey* miracle.

Phil Esposito, having managed to elude Soviet assassins, scored, but the clock was ticking down. Ten minutes, nine minutes, eight minutes. Then, at the seven-minute mark, Yvon Cournoyer picked up an Esposito rebound and tied the score. The game reached a fever pitch. Five minutes remained. Four. Three. Two. One, and now we were counting down in *seconds* to the end of the series. And then, and then, it happened. The Goal.

With thirty-four seconds remaining—*thirty-four seconds, mind you*—Paul Henderson picks up his own rebound and flips it into the net. Team Canada goes wild, and back home, a roar rolls across the country from sea to sea and back again. It is New Year's and Christmas and the First of July all rolled up in one big neonationalistic package. Pagan shrines dedicated to Paul Henderson appear within hours and small children and animals are offered up in sacrifice. A petition circulates demanding Sainthood, Knighthood— even Commercial Endorsements—for the Thirty-Four-Second Kid.

The Soviets came roaring back in those last thirty-four seconds. They didn't roll over and die, and they even came within a heartbeat of tying it in the final seconds of play. But it didn't matter. Canada won the series, with four wins, three losses, and a single tie. The nation was ecstatic. Paul Henderson, who had scored the winning goal on all three of Team Canada's final victories, says that even now, more than twenty-five years later, a day hardly goes by that someone doesn't ask him about it. He later became a born-again Christian.

We ran outside and screamed, primal tribal screams to the sky. A friend of mine remembers it well: "It was the only time I ever saw my father cry." My own memories are an Armistice-Day mix of joy and relief that swirled around me like a ticker-tape parade. That was the day I became a Canadian. Forget Confederation, Vimy Ridge and

Expo '67—the real pinnacle of Canadian civilization occurred on September 28, 1972, when Saint Paul scored that winning goal.

But beneath the celebrations, the bravado and the swagger-happy pride, Canadians realized that a new age had dawned. Canada's days as the sole Superpower of The Game had come to an end. In *Home Sweet Home,* Mordecai Richler recalls: "After the series, nothing was ever the same again in Canada. Beer didn't taste as good. The Rockies seemed smaller, the northern lights dimmer."

The Soviets had changed hockey in Canada forever. Moving passes and floating wings replaced the old crunch-and-grind of the Canadian game. The Broadstreet Bullies of Philadelphia eventually had to give way to the kind of 300-mile-an-hour chess perfected by the Edmonton Oilers in the mid-eighties. Hockey became a more fluid, free-flowing game, and for that the Canadians owe the Russians no small debt of gratitude. And herein lies the very key to understanding Canadian foreign policy during the Cold War. All through those dark and terrible days, as the Americans pounded the tables and decried the Evil Empire, Canada nurtured a secret affection, even respect, for the Soviet Union. Simply put, Canadians, in their heart of hearts, could never *really* bring themselves to hate a nation that played hockey so well.

In fact, the Soviet prowess on the ice may very well have *helped* the communist cause in Canada. I can well imagine yer average Canadian hockey fan, beer in hand and tuque on head, watching the Soviet team and saying to himself, "Y'know, maybe there is something to this dialectical materialism after all."

Alas, the Cold War is over, the Soviet Union has dissolved into a collection of fiefdoms with names like Khaliazherbajianihstan, and the hockey wars are gone forever.

The last campaign was in 1987. Following the '72 series, the Canada Cup was created. Every few years Canada would invite the elite HPN (Hockey Playing Nations) of the world, from Sweden to Norway all the way to Finland, to send their best to Canada—where they would get mugged by either the Canadians or the Russians. The Canada Cup passed back and forth between Canada and the Soviet Union, across the carcasses and rubble of Swedes and Finns. In 1976, Canada won. In 1981, the Soviet Union won. In 1984, Canada.

By the time the 1987 series came around, the level of hockey was far, far superior to that of the 1972 series. (Read that sentence in any bar in Canada and you are guaranteed to have a raging sports debate on your hands, but it is true.) Gone were the goon-squad tactics and the bench-clearing brawls—those were left for the junior leagues. It was hockey as it was meant to be played: fast, hard-hitting and with a touch of razzmatazz.

In 1987, having swept away the other HPNs like so much debris in front of a Zamboni, Canada and the Soviet Union faced off for a three-game final. No one knew then that it would be the last series of an era.

Game One was an exceptional—almost transcendental—hockey game, up and down the ice without pause or quarter given. The game, tied at 5–5 after three periods of regulation play, went into sudden death overtime; the first goal scored, be it after ten seconds or three hours, would win the game. Just six minutes into overtime, Alexander

Semak of the Soviet Red Army snapped a shot high and inside. The game was over.

Game Two was played at the Copps Coliseum in Hamilton, and it has gone down in history as the single greatest hockey game ever played. It was magnificent. One extended end-to-end rush all night, with both teams playing at their peak. The Game was elevated to new heights, and after three periods of in-your-face parry and thrust, the score was again tied at 5–5. And again they went into sudden death overtime. It was electrifying, relentless. If the Soviets scored the next goal, they would win the Canada Cup; if Canada scored, the series would be tied. Everything rode on the next goal. This was the stuff of hockey dreams and sports thesauruses. (You know the ones, they contain words that no one except sportswriters use. As in "assiduous assists," "scintillating saves," "bounteous bodychecks," "tendentious teamwork" and "a veritable gallimaufry of goals." Roget has nothing on sportswriters.)

Overtime. A darkling ice where desperate armies clash by night. The players gave everything they had, but after a full twenty-minute extra period of play, neither team had scored. It now went into *double* sudden death overtime. Exhausted, the players took a ten-minute break and then began all over again. Finally, at 12:45 in the morning (!), in a mad scramble, Mario Lemieux flicked the puck past the Soviet goalie and the Greatest Game Ever Played came to an exhausting end. Pressmen rushed out of the Coliseum to make their deadlines, car horns blared, crowds spilled into the streets, and people kissed perfect strangers (or at least I did).

After the elation over winning Game Two, Team Canada came up flat in the early stages of Game Three. The

Soviets punched holes through the Canadian defence and scored *three* unanswered goals before the Canadian players noticed that a hockey game was going on around them. Slowly, they fought their way back from a 3–0 deficit. They caught up with the Soviets—and even pulled ahead. They were leading with a score of 5–4 and only eight minutes remaining when, in a shameful display of bad manners, Alexander Semak, the same player who had given the Soviets their first overtime victory, scored to even up the game. The Semak goal took the wind out of Team Canada. The clock was running down, and a third sudden death overtime seemed to be in the making.

But then, *with less than a minute and a half remaining,* as the two teams jammed away at the puck, out of the melee Wayne Gretzky broke away. The crowds jumped to their feet. Gretzky crossed into Soviet territory, followed in by Mario Lemieux and Larry Murphy. In front of them was a single Russian defenseman. The Soviets had been caught pressing too deeply into Canadian territory, and now, suddenly, they were on the wrong side of a three-on-one breakaway. And then, and then, it happened. The Pass. Gretzky to Lemieux. The puck floats across the ice and onto the stick of Super Mario, who delivers a pre-emptory nuclear strike all his own, snapping it high and to the glove-side corner. It was a wrist-shot heard round the nation, emblazoned on newspaper front pages in a type size usually reserved for D-Day landings.

With a score of 6–5 (all three games ended with that same score, 6–5), Canada had won what turned out to be the final battle of the Cold War. Hollywood scriptwriters couldn't have come up with a better ending. The Soviet coach was dismayed. He later listed several key attributes—

discipline, speed, stick-handling—and said that the Soviet team was superior to the Canadians in every regard except one: *heart*. The Canadians wanted it more, and in the end that made all the difference. It was the highest compliment ever paid to Canadians. We had more heart.

It seems so long ago now. Today, Russian players are signing NHL contracts and crashing sports cars and learning useful phrases such as "more money" and "trade me to L.A." Lenin is just a mouldy old mummy piece, the Titans truly have fallen, and Armageddon now seems like a bad dream. Those two moments—those two *goals*—the first in 1972 and the last in 1987, were the opening and closing shots fired in the Really Cold War, the bedtime stories of a nation. "Daddy, tell me again about how Paul Henderson scored with thirty-four seconds remaining." "Well, it begins a long, long time ago. An Evil Empire was threatening the world and only a brave and plucky band of Canadians could stop them..."

In 1997, on the twenty-fifth anniversary of Paul Henderson's goal, the Canadian mint issued a commemorative gold coin, the post office produced a commemorative stamp, and Douglas & McIntyre published a book entitled, simply, *Cold War*. After a quarter of a century, the '72 series is still remembered with awe and reverence. After a quarter of a century, it can still sell stamps, books, gold and national pride. It was our one brief shining moment. It was just a hockey game, true, but we'll never get over it.

Paul Henderson said that when he scored that winning goal, he finally knew what democracy was all about. Fifteen years later, Wayne Gretzky was more objective about the whole thing. In his autobiography, *Gretzky,* he reflects about the Really Cold War—and its passing:

[The 1987] series was the end of the Soviet-Canadian hockey wars. Two years later, the Soviets allowed their stars to join the NHL. The mystique of defeating the Soviets is now gone. Oh, we'll play them again, but look around. The Berlin wall is down, the domination of the Communist Party is history, the Soviets are moving toward freedom of speech and freedom of the press. It's a far better world than it was just a year ago. And because of it, the Canada Cup will never be the same.

I can live with that.

And who knows, but maybe somewhere a Soviet hockey fan once sat, vodka in hand, big furry hat on head, saying to himself as he watched his country play the Canadians, "Y'know, maybe there's something to this democracy thing after all."

FROM SUEZ TO

SOMALIA

· · · · · ·

*P*EACEKEEPING IS the ultimate Canadian endeavour. Not just because it is noble and selfless and nice, but because it is such a *non*solution. Rather than confront a problem head on, you diffuse it by creating separate solitudes, by living parallel lives, by maintaining duality and by limiting contact. Sound familiar? It should. It is the very blueprint of our nation. And peacekeeping is simply Canada projected outwards onto the world. In spite of this—perhaps even because of this—peacekeeping is heroic. It is such a lost cause, you have to admire the men and women who are giving it everything they have—up to and including their lives.

Upon the Afghan plains, amid the rubble of Beirut, at sunrise on the Golan Heights and at dusk in the jungles of Cambodia. Across the sun-baked deserts of Africa, past pock-marked churches in El Salvador, through the chaos of Yugoslavia, we find them: international peacekeepers acting as human buffers between warring factions. It is the most thankless job on earth. It is also one of the most rewarding.

Peacekeeping—like Greenpeace—is a Canadian invention that now belongs to the people of the world, whether they like it or not. Canada developed the notion of peacekeeping, and Canada remains its biggest supporter. We are the only country on earth to have contributed peacekeepers to every single UN mission. Including Somalia.

Peacekeeping began in 1956, after a bizarre domino effect of conflicts took us to the brink of World War III. Egyptian President Gamal Abdel Nasser, frustrated at a lack of Western financial support for a costly dam project, seized the Suez Canal and nationalized the shipping lane that cut through Egyptian territory. His actions angered Britain and France enough to warrant a retaliation. Striking a secret pact with Israel, these two aging imperial powers came up with a scheme to topple Nasser and reclaim the Suez as an international waterway. At daybreak on October 29, Israeli armed forces invaded Egypt, crossing the Sinai desert in a single day, splitting Egyptian defences and storming to within striking distance of the Suez itself. Britain and France then issued an ultimatum, ordering both Israel and Egypt to leave the canal zone or face an all-out assault. Israel fell back, as secretly agreed, leaving Nasser's forces to take the brunt of Anglo-French fire. On Halloween—a day when the dead and the near-dead walk again—the bombing of the Suez Canal began.

It was the last hurrah of European imperialism and gun-boat diplomacy.

The Americans, enraged not so much by the flouting of international law as by the lack of advance notice, fumed loudly and publicly against the Anglo-French aggression. The Soviets, equally enraged, threatened to bomb Paris and London. Nasser had achieved the unachievable; he had both the Soviet Union and the United States on his side. The Soviets, in turn, showed their support for Egypt by rolling tanks into Hungary. It was all very confusing.

The Soviet power grab in Hungary was well-timed. How could NATO condemn Soviet aggression in eastern Europe when two of their own were bombing a Third World country? Europe and the Middle East were about to ignite, and as the rhetoric and missiles flew, into the melee wandered a history professor named Lester who wore a bow tie and spoke with a slight lisp. He was the right man at the right time in the right place. Lester would save the world!

As the United Nations scrambled to contain Armageddon, the Secretary General, Dag Hammarskjöld, turned to the chairman of the UN Security Council, Lester B. Pearson (nicknamed "Mike" by an air force commander who thought "Lester" didn't sound tough enough). Lester and Dag were close friends as well as colleagues, and together they set out to unscramble the omelette.

There was no small amount of irony in asking a Canadian to deal with the transgressions of Britain and France, the two imperial powers that had founded the colonies which had become Canada. Pearson was uncowed, however. He noted that this was not a time for Canada to "be a colonial chore boy running around shouting 'ready, aye, ready!'"

The strategy Pearson proposed was stark and straight-forward: a neutral force of armed soldiers sent in to take up a position between the two sides, a physical presence that would separate the combatants and enforce a cease-fire until a compromise was worked out. As peacekeepers, they would be, in Pearson's words, "a moral force against aggression." When it was first proposed, no one took the notion seriously, but Pearson pushed ahead, determined to use the United Nations as a forum for something more substantial than mere gestures and propaganda. The idea soon gained momentum and on November 5, just five days after the Anglo-French bombardment began, a resolution calling for the first United Nations Emergency Force (UNEF) was passed without opposition. And the very next day, in a gesture of good will and tact, Britain and France launched an invasion.

As paratroopers landed in the canal zone, Pearson's initiative foundered. But Canada's ambassador to Egypt, the talented Herbert Norman, saved the day by convincing Nasser to publicly embrace the Pearson initiative. Britain and France, humbled by a colonial countermove, now found themselves pariahs on the world stage. Grudgingly, they gave in. (Norman's life, however, ended in tragedy just six months later, when—hounded by American accusations of communist leanings—he leapt to his death from atop a Cairo building. Murdered by slander, Herbert Norman remains one of the many uncounted casualties of the Cold War.)

Nasser had accepted the notion of peacekeepers, but he balked at allowing Canadian soldiers to be involved, something that Pearson had assumed as a matter of course. How, Nasser wanted to know, could Canada claim to be a disinterested participant when its flag still contained a Union Jack? Or when a third of its population was French? Or when its uniforms were identical to those of the British? Or when the name of its best regiment—and the one it wished to dispatch to Egypt—was the Queen's Own Rifles? The name, the flag, the uniform—they would inflame Egyptian sentiments, and Nasser was adamant: no colonials, no Canadians. In response, the UN hurriedly shipped in thousands of surplus army helmets and spray-painted them sky-blue as a sign of nonalignment. But blue helmets or no blue helmets, Nasser refused to relent: no pseudo-British Canadian troops marching under the name of an Imperial Queen. In 1956, Canadian identity and independence—tempered in two world wars and given substance in the Statute of Westminster—were still not perceived beyond her own borders.

Pearson had learned an important lesson: national symbols are the clearest message of national character. In spite of Nasser's objections—or perhaps because of them—a Canadian general was put in charge of the UN's Emergency Force and one of his first moves as commander in chief was to bring in Canadians to handle administration and ground support, effectively circumventing Nasser's protests.

By the end of December a treaty had been signed, a face-saving withdrawal agreed upon, and a world war averted. In 1957, Lester Pearson was awarded the Nobel Peace Prize, the first and only Canadian so honoured. "Lester Pearson saved the world," said the Nobel Prize Committee. To which Pearson replied, "Gee, thanks."

At home, Pearson was vilified and attacked. The public was against him, both in French Canada and in English

Canada—united in a common colonial hysteria. Canada had betrayed her Mother Countries, cried the opposition. Pearson, it was hinted, might even be a commie himself. But as esteem for Pearson grew outside of Canada, opinion—predictably—began to change. (As Canadians, we opposed the Pearson peace initiative of 1956 and *supported* the War Measures Act of 1970; remember that the next time you hear someone going on about how innately nice we are.)

Success breeds support, and Canada now takes great pride in its role as peacekeeper. And so it should. Over the years, the blue helmets of the UN have become a symbol of hope, a promise that someday we may yet outgrow war—or at least stem the tide. And maybe, against all odds, maybe we will survive. It is a very Canadian outlook, one that manages to be both pragmatic and naive at the same time.

Since 1956, the UN has sent more than twenty-five missions across the world, from war-weary Lebanon to the killing fields of Cambodia, from the Gordian knot of the Balkans to the jungles of Laos. More than sixty different nations have contributed members, but the core support comes from Canada, Sweden, Finland, Austria and—to a lesser degree—Ireland, New Zealand, Pakistan, Ghana and Fiji. There have been successes, such as in Namibia, when UN peacekeepers stabilized the nation and helped in its transition to democracy following independence from South Africa. There have been failures, such as when the Israelis—ignoring international law—drove their tanks right through UN positions to invade Lebanon. And there have been stalemates, most notably on the Mediterranean island of Cyprus, claimed by both the Turks and the

Greeks, where 158 peacekeepers have been killed over the last thirty-four years without any resolution in sight, making it the world's longest and most absurd conflict. (As humour writer George Mikes noted, Cyprus, having given up on ever being a world power, has settled instead on being a world nuisance.)

As the world's most experienced and respected peacekeepers, Canada enjoyed an enviable reputation. Then came Somalia. It was anarchy. Freebooting warlords ran wild, robbing relief convoys and medical centres with impunity. American personnel were killed and dragged through the streets. Looters and snipers scoured the ruins, and into the maelstrom came the Airborne Regiment, Canada's answer to the Green Berets.

What many people don't realize is that the Airborne was *not* sent to Somalia as peacekeepers. They did not don blue helmets and UN insignias; they went in as fighting soldiers on a military mission: to stabilize and resupply an especially volatile region of the country. It was a dangerous mission, but the Airborne were an especially ruthless group. As looters plagued their camp, word came down from the commanding officers to shoot trespassers who tried to flee and to "rough up" those captured to discourage further theft. On the night of March 16, 1993, the men of the Airborne went a bit too far. A sixteen-year-old boy named Shidane Abukar Arone was caught, beaten, burnt, choked, tortured and eventually killed. Over a dozen people knew what was going on and either stopped by to watch or ignored the screams echoing through the camp. The boy died pleading with his tormentors for mercy, repeating again and again the only word of theirs he knew: "Canada, Canada, Canada."

The ensuing scandal would taint the Canadian military and disgrace the flag under which these men, these few bold men, were operating. As the sadistic hazings, the racist taunts, the neo-Nazi imagery, the incriminating videos, the white supremacist cells, and the accusations of coercing sex and abusing refugees in Bosnia came to light, the military found its reputation in tatters.

The murder of Arone, as well as the deaths of three other Somalis in Canadian hands, was one of the nastiest scandals in our nation's history—and what did we get? An inquiry. A very long, plodding inquiry. The investigation would drag on for years before eventually being put to sleep in an act of politically motivated euthanasia. If lynch mobs are a sin, so too is the other extreme: lethargic inaction. Royal Commissions and dithering federal inquiries are as Canadian as maple syrup. It is a strategy of half-measures and muted responses; we talk a crisis to boredom and eventually to death.

The Somalia Inquiry was a fiasco, the truth was debauched and we had to witness the squirrelly antics of General Beady-Eye Boyle showing all the fortitude of a wet noodle. They should have had Boyle's balls—but no, the Airborne was disbanded, a few perfunctory sentences were handed out, and the issue sank into a sea of paper. Ben Johnson suffered more as a steroid-user than did most of the Somali-beating, violence-encouraging officers and soldiers in the Airborne. The solution? I say we call a Royal Commission *on* the Royal Commission, an investigation into the investigation. And so on into infinite regress.

We need to re-evaluate our stopgap approach to peacekeeping. The Airborne wasn't on official peacekeeping duty, true, but they had been before—and had they not been disbanded, they would have served as peacekeepers again. (Sending in the Airborne to maintain peace is like asking the Hell's Angels to work security at a Rolling Stones concert. Not a good idea.)

Part of the problem is that we have been using regular recruits as peacekeepers. It is an odd paradox, as reporter Rae Corelli notes in *Maclean's*: "They are soldiers, men and women, prepared for war and trained to kill, but their enviable reputation rests on 45 years of peacekeeping, not fighting." What we need is a truly elite corps of peacekeepers—a *moral* elite, not a combat elite—one specially created and specially trained for peacekeeping.

In the splintering post–Cold War world, the key to stability—and perhaps the next step towards transcending the nation-state itself—is the creation of an international standing force trained specifically for UNEF work, on call and ready for deployment, with the moral authority of the United Nations Charter of Human Rights behind it. Unfortunately, the call for a UN standing army has been resisted by all sides, especially by the American government, which has no intention of relinquishing its self-anointed role as the world's policeman and which refuses to consider allowing Americans to serve under the command of anyone other than Americans. Nationalism dies hard.

And whatever became of Lester B. Pearson, the Hero of Suez, the Man Who Saved the World? Well, he went on to become the Prime Minister of Canada (a step down, granted), and his main achievement in office was symbolic, but significant. He gave us a flag of our own, free of any colonial overtones or Old World fixation: a red maple leaf on a white standard, one of the most striking flags in the world. Its origins can be traced back to the stinging insults that an Egyptian president made to a Canadian diplomat, and even after being dragged through the mud by the thugs of the Airborne, it is still magnificent. Ranked thirty-first in population, Canada is the fourth largest contributor to the United Nations and still the most reliable peacekeeper on record—and all the Airborne war crimes and Royal Commission sleights of hand will not change that.

Oh, yes. I almost forgot. Five Canadian soldiers were awarded Medals of Bravery for acts of valour while in Somalia. One of the soldiers—Corporal Joseph Charette of Gatineau, Québec—single-handedly contained *and disarmed* a violent mob that was threatening a relief hospital. But of course, in the aftermath of the Somalia Affair, the heroism of Corporal Charette has been forgotten—and that in itself is a tragedy.

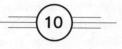

THE DAY CANADA
BECAME NICE

· · · · · · · ·

*O*CTOBER 1995. A woman is found
wandering beside a highway north
of Los Angeles. She doesn't remember who she is or where
she came from. The U.S. police have only a single clue: the
woman is polite, *very* polite. So polite, in fact, that they figure she must be a Canadian. They send a bulletin to news
agencies and police desks across Canada, and sure enough,
the woman *is* a Canadian. Her identity is established as
Ms. Susan Simpson, who mysteriously disappeared from
her Edmonton home several weeks earlier.

The two important things to note are (A) even in a state
of total amnesia, she still retained her basic Canadian
niceness, and (B) this alone was enough to distinguish her
from an American. Frightening, isn't it? If it ever comes to
war, all that will stand between us and death is the use of

a well-placed "thank you." You can whack a Canadian on the head, you can scramble his brain and erase his memory, but he—or she—will still be nice.

So when did this happen? At what point did we, as Canadians, officially become *nice*? When did we cease to be a nation of voyageurs and become, instead, a nation of habitants, a nation of Associate Professors, a nation of nice people?

It was a slow process. We rejected revolution, we tamed our frontiers by sending in law and order first (the Canadian Mild West, as it is known), and we founded our nation not on political ideals or on ethnicity but on very practical, pragmatic reasons: peace, order and good government. And yet, as history has repeatedly shown, we were not always such a swell bunch. I repeat: the only reason our history seems so sweet and gentle is because we compare ourselves—incessantly—to Americans. Jeez, who *doesn't* appear kind and gentle when compared to them?

And even then, we are often worse. A recent study by the European Banking Federation named Canadian banks as by far "the most robbed banks in the world," with 1 in 6 being hit in any given year compared to 1 in 12 in Italy—the home of organized crime—and 1 in 924 in Japan.

In *Canadian Forum,* columnist Morris Wolfe writes, "Canadians, it seems, have the shortest memories of any people on earth when it comes to remembering the awful things we've done to each other."

It's true. A survey of Canadian history from the fun-loving days of the slave trade (usually unacknowledged) to the annihilation of the Beothuk Indians (shame about that) to apartheid (our reserves and residential schools), internment camps (the tale of Japanese-Canadians), eugenics (Canada's not-so-distant racist past), as well as our contribution to the Holocaust of World War II (none is too many), our run-amok Mounties and the suspension of human rights during the October Crisis, indicates a less than holistic approach to nation-making.

I suppose, like any birth, the creation of Canada was bound to be messy and more than a little bloody. Rebellions, oppression, scandals, uprisings, war. But at some point we crossed the line, at some point we became a Bland and Happy Land, the Valium of Nations. When did this happen? When did we become so damn nice? And what's with all the rhetorical questions?

Well, you will be relieved to know I have come up with an answer. After years of exhaustive research, often late into the night, I have pinpointed The Exact Moment Canadians Became Nice. It occurred at 8:05 A.M., November 16, 1976. This was the morning *after* the day the Parti Québécois was first elected, when René Lévesque was *not* assassinated. When René Lévesque woke up and was still alive, at that moment Canada became irretrievably "nice." After that, there was no turning back. True, we had been nice before that, and there have been pockets of nastiness since (Somalia being a prime example), but on November 16, 1976, we passed the point of no return.

Consider this: in 1970, the government of Canada invoked the War Measures Act, suspended civil liberties, put Canada under martial law and arrested hundreds of separatists without bail or due process. Ten years later, in 1980, the same government allowed the province of Québec to vote on negotiations aimed at breaking the nation apart. In just ten short years, something had shifted. In 1970 we still had an edge. In 1980 we had become a nation of eunuchs. The watershed was in 1976, at the peak of Disco Nationalism, when Canadians proved that there really was such a thing as being *too* nice.

With the election of the PQ, Canadians decided—by default—that a party sworn to destroying the nation would be allowed to hold public office. It was here that the much-heralded tolerance of Canadians reached a new height, and one that would lead inexorably to the absurdity of the Bloc-Heads Québécois (a *federal* separatist party—surely a contradiction in terms, no?) and the possible end of Canada.

The ramifications of this are alarming. Think about it: we have been nice for little more than twenty years. Not coincidentally, the last twenty years have also pushed Canada to the brink of collapse and dissolution. Maybe it's time we went back to being just a little bit nasty. I don't mean we should start blowing up bridges or taking hostages, but we could at least show a little backbone. After all, we are the proud descendants of rogues, refugees, misfits and lost causes. Rather than deny this, we should glory in it. *Je suis un homme du nord!*

During the divisive Free Trade debates of the 1980s, I remember how upset columnist Rick Salutin became at the muscular rhetoric used by the government as they rammed through the necessary legislation. Donald Macdonald, the chairman of the Royal Commission that recommended Free Trade, argued that Canada needn't fear economic union with the largest consumer society on earth: "I don't see Canada as a sort of sheltered workshop for the inefficient, the incompetent or the less than capable."

To which Salutin, comparing Macdonald to a chest-beating Tarzan, replied: "This imagery is Ramboesque and Nietzschean, full of taunts of cowardice and fear, the language of tough, lean, and mean, of winners and losers."

In other words, it just wasn't very *nice*.

What Salutin was probably not aware of is that Rambo—that icon of Ronald Reagan's America—was created by a Canadian: author David Morrell of Kitchener, Ontario. (The hero's name is a sardonic twist on the French poet Rimbaud.) The first Rambo movie was directed by a Canadian and filmed in British Columbia, making it Canadian in content if not in theme.

And a nation that has produced Rambo, voyageurs and ice hockey can't be all bad. Or rather, can't be all *nice*.

Part Three

THE TROUBLE
WITH CANADIANS

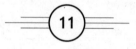

AMERICA IS SEXY

. . . .

I CAN SEE AMERICA from my bedroom window.

It lies across the St. Croix River, steeped in shadows, a wooded bank with a few forlorn points of light. It is a dark land, America. Our Doppelgänger; Canada reflected through the fun-house mirror, warped and wild, colossal.

Nothing from my window suggests this.

I was born in the northern Alberta town of Fort Vermilion (or, as my brothers and I insisted on calling it, "Fort Vermin"). We were closer to the Arctic Circle than the American border. The rest of Canada lay south, past the curve of the horizon. Fort Vermilion, far beyond the nettoss of television signals, existed in a vacuum. Toronto and Chicago were equally unreal and foreign. It was not until the Anik satellites of the 1970s were skyrocketed heavenward that we were finally able to pick up the dim glimmerings of even the CBC. I remember watching *Hymn Sing* with unblinking awe.

Living in the north was like living in a colony, a northern colony of a distant, unresponsive land called Canada. Only later did I learn that mine was not a typical Canadian childhood. In the south, living within the media fallout of American pop culture, other Canadians—real Canadians—were growing up under a radioactive cloud of Americana. Real Canadians lived on the fringes of the American Empire; we in the north lived on the fringe of Nothingness.

I haven't been home for many years, but I understand that things have changed. Satellite dishes are now pointed low along the horizon, almost vertical as they strain to catch signals from the south. There is no longer the ten-year time lag between current pop culture and northern tastes, and a few tourists have even begun to stumble in, looking around with outsiders' eyes.

I didn't leave the North, I escaped. And eventually, I ended up here in St. Andrews, New Brunswick, with just a river separating me from that Great Carnival, America.

The St. Croix is a deceptively narrow river, yet down its spine runs both an international boundary and a time zone. On one side, the province of New Brunswick. On the other side, the state of Maine. The provincial vs. the stately. This is where the American Dream ends and the Canadian Dream begins.

Further upriver on the Canadian side is the town of St. Stephen, home of the world's first chocolate bar and sister city to Calais, Maine. Calais and St. Stephen are mirror reflections, with only a short bridge between the two.

Like St. Stephen, Calais is a goodhearted but tawdry little place. It lies huddled along the border, selling trinkets and cheap gas, living and dying on the Canadian exchange rate. After Calais there is two hours of forest along the Airline Road, two hours of ruts and claustrophobic woods, before you get to the next outpost of civilization—if Bangor can be considered civilization.

You can use Canadian money anywhere in Calais and in most places in Bangor. Canadian flags fly over Wal-Mart and McDonald's, the International Hotel offers special discounts to Canadians, and Bangor holds an annual Canadian Appreciation Days, with a flurry of maple leaves and signs declaring *Welcome Canadians! To Your Home Away from Home!* Loonies and twonies and Queen Elizabeth's formaldehyde hair are everywhere in evidence, and—unfettered by our own fetish with language—the American Border Patrol has even put up a bilingual welcome sign: *Bienvenue aux États-Unis. Toutes les voitures doivent arrêter pour l'inspection.*

The Americans, to their credit, are not dismayed by any of this. There is no talk of cultural encroachment or Canadian colonialism, no intellectual nationalists debating the issue, no outraged letters to the editor. Why? Because Americans have the ability to separate commerce from culture. Canadians do not.

On the Canadian side of the Great Divide, meanwhile, the town of St. Stephen has no fewer than four flags over its wharf-side park: the Canadian flag, the American flag, the New Brunswick provincial flag and—for good measure—

the Union Jack. Calais and St. Stephen are so close you could throw a stone from one to the other. Marriages and friendships straddle the line and fire-trucks answer calls on either side. During the war of 1812, nervous British officials sent a shipment of gunpowder to St. Stephen for defence against American marauders. It wasn't necessary. The two towns simply agreed not to fight, and the good people of St. Stephen later *gave* their gunpowder to the Americans in Calais to help them celebrate their July 4 holiday. All this while a war was raging. (Even today, a horn of gunpowder is sometimes ceremoniously exchanged between the two communities.)

St. Stephen and Calais have enjoyed more than two hundred years of civility. You would be hard pressed to find any two towns—let alone two on different sides of an international border—that get along as well as do Calais and St. Stephen. Yet, when you cross that bridge from St. Stephen to Calais, everything changes. The accents change, the spellings change, even the units of measurement change. Handguns for sale at the local department store, mace for sale at supermarket checkouts, smutty magazines displayed without those paternalistic and highly annoying little black tags required on the Canadian side of the river: everything reminds you that you have entered another country. You cross time zones as well when you cross that bridge; the two sides exist in different hours of the day and different frames of reference.

That odd American blend of puritanism and anarchy, the Yankee pride, the abrasive patriotism—it lingers like vapour halfway across the bridge. From St. Stephen, you can walk to America. And the closer you get, the more things change, and the more aware of nationality you become. It is like examining a pointillist painting under a magnifying glass; when you are right up against the edge that divides Us from Them, the differences are minute—and myriad.

Border towns are always slightly surreal, and in a sense Canada is one extended border town.

"Canada is a land of multiple borderlines, psychic, social and geographic. Canadians live at the interface where opposites clash." So wrote Marshall McLuhan (quoted in *Mondo Canuck*) in one of his more lucid moments, incomprehensible aphorisms being something of a Marshall McLuhan speciality.

If Canada is a land of borderlines, none is as deeply etched or as ephemeral, as carved in granite or as light as air, as that which runs between Canada and the United States. Pessimists like to point out that 80 per cent of Canadians live within 160 kilometres of the United States, the suggestion being that we long to live as near to America as humanly possible. But this assumes intent where none existed: it projects modern insecurities on powerful past forces. We live as far south as possible because it makes sense. It is as primal an urge as the need to huddle near a campfire. The border between Canada and the U.S. was forged in geography, trade routes, blood, war, threats and ultimatums. It was not a psychological yearning that kept us clinging to the border, it was the combined threat of frostbite and Manifest Destiny.

In the east, the St. Lawrence River and the protective cuddle of the Great Lakes dictated where we would settle. Further west, however, it becomes less logical: the 49th parallel cuts as cleanly as a scalpel blade across the prairies and over the mountains, jogging south only to include the tip of Vancouver Island in Canadian territory.

Borders—even arbitrary borders—matter. They may be simple lines drawn in the dust, but once drawn, they begin to shape us. They both limit and define us. They give us an outline to grow into. In western Canada, differences in agriculture, irrigation and settlement have made the 49th parallel—once an arbitrary line on a map—a geographic reality that is visible from outer space.

All along the Canada/U.S. border, the relationship between the two countries is reversed. For us, the border is our southern sunbelt, the most populated stretch of land in Canada. But for the Americans, the border is the northern attic, a frontier hinterland, sparsely populated and generally quiet. There are exceptions, of course, Detroit/Windsor being the most glaring, but generally along the border, the Americans are the hicks and the Canadians are the urbanites with the big cities and spacious shopping malls.

Living so close to the States makes us compulsively aware of both small differences (the body language, surnames, pronunciation and even hairstyles) and large (our deference to authority, our fascination with language laws, our secret smugness, our insecurities, and—most striking of all—our lack of ideology). Though we generally speak a common language, our words have different meanings. In Canada, *freedom* refers largely to negative freedoms: freedom from crime, freedom from fear, freedom from risk. In America, *freedom* is understood in its baldest, simplest form: the freedom to do anything you damn well please.

The American version of freedom includes the freedom to soar with the eagles—and to shit on those below you. In Canada, freedom-as-security has a kind of self-censoring, levelling effect. It enshrines mediocrity.

Mediocrity vs. anarchy. Tough choice.

LIVING IN ST. ANDREWS after five years in Asia was like taking a crash course in being Canadian. St. Andrews is a Loyalist town, proud to the point of obstinacy, yet catering to American tourists. In St. Andrews, America is inescapable. It is everywhere. I can almost reach out and stroke its sleeping northern flank.

For the first time in my life, I had cable television. The World According to the U.S.A. spilled in through my TV set, and I slipped into a sort of protracted orgasm, my thumb hitting the channel changer again and again like a laboratory rat hooked on pheromones.

This absolute saturation of American images is one of the compelling facts of being Canadian, and it is something that causes intellectual nationalists no end of garment-rending, angst-ridden dismay. Fuck 'em. I was too busy watching *Jenny Jones* and *Judge Judy* and *Baywatch* and *Geraldo* and *The Price Is Right* and O.J. retrospectives and the *A&E Biography* of Jeffrey Dahmer.

The basic theme of American television, as near as I can deduce, is wholesome family values and gruesome celebrity murders. Or maybe wholesome celebrity murders and gruesome family values. It's hard to tell sometimes.

Still, as I sat there in my underwear, with the frenzied caffeine montage that is America flipping past, I felt a warm, almost tearful, sense of belonging wash over me. So this is what my fellow Canadians had grown up on. And when, at the age of thirty-one, I finally watched an episode of *The Brady Bunch*, I almost cried. I felt so very, very *Canadian*. Here, at last, was the missing part of my Canadian identity: American pop culture.

Depending on your bias, living in Canada is either like living beside a parade route—or downstream from a sewage treatment plant. American pop culture permeates our existence as Canadians, and from this our intellectual nationalists have concluded that Canadian culture is doomed.

Here is author and diplomat John W. Holmes (as quoted in *Canada Inside Out*), long before the ascendancy of cable television:

> If Canada ceases to exist it is more likely to be death by hypnosis than by foreign investment. The vitality of American media, from NBC to Penthouse, is such that Canadians are losing consciousness of themselves... We are in danger of becoming a zombie nation, our physical structure intact but our souls and minds gone abroad. Having gloriously resisted with our loyal muskets the Yankee invader on the slopes of Québec and Queenston, Canada may well be conquered by American television. That's a hell of a way to die.

This is typical of the hyperbole used by nationalists, the kind to which I refuse to stoop. I assure you, they are a million, billion miles off the mark. Canadians do *not* lose consciousness of themselves through exposure to American pop culture. Quite the opposite. They gain a heightened awareness of being outside it all, of being not-American. Of being Canadian. It is not a form of indoctrination, it is a form of inoculation.

The Belgians are inundated with French television, French music, French films—but they are still proudly Belgian. It hasn't turned them into Frenchmen.

Our wet-blanket nationalists are confusing exposure with surrender. If anything, this prolonged contact with American media has left us less enamoured with America, not more. Up close and in your face, breathing its heady halitosis and invading your personal space, America is hardly awe-inspiring. It is more like a traffic accident on a grand scale, and Canadians slow down to gawk. We are reminded how different we truly are from Them. The issues that ignite Them—race, money, street crime, Latin gangs, handguns, international entanglements, ground wars in Asia, the pros and cons of breast implants—these fixations are, to Canadians, deeply, undeniably *foreign*. American programs broadcast in Canada should carry a label: Warning—prolonged viewing may cause nausea and/ or delusions of moral superiority.

We are not so much spectators as voyeurs, peeping Toms peering in through our neighbour's window, clucking under our breath even as we get all hot and bothered. To Canadians, America is not a real nation: it exists on the other side of the looking glass, one part Rorschach test and two parts soap opera. It is *Lifestyles of the Rich and Aggressive*. It is Disneyland on speed. It is everything and anything, but it is not this: it is not Canada.

Can anyone doubt that the host of *Jeopardy!* is Canadian? Or that the prize money is American? Could any other nation except the U.S.A. produce something as compellingly tacky as *American Gladiators* (a spectacle that blends the worst elements of pro wrestling, game shows and amateur athletics)? Watch the *Jenny Jones* show and ask yourself if you feel any cultural or national affinity with these people—these dregs of self-indulgence, these utterly shameless people. And then ask yourself why you are watching. It really is the moral equivalent of a peepshow. If Americans are exhibitionists, Canadians are voyeurs. Our fetishes mesh nicely.

It is also why Canadians excel at subversive skit comedy. Satire requires both the intimacy and objectivity of the Overwhelmed Observer, immersed in the medium but still existing on the fringes, looking in. (In a way, this reflects my own relationship with mainstream Canadian culture; although immersed in it, I still feel like an outsider.)

Such were the epochal lessons I learned while vegetating in front of my television. And I might still be there, sitting in my underwear, slack-jawed, with my thumb spasmodically changing the channel every 2.6 seconds like a hapless tourist at a Vegas casino. "Hit me. Hit me. Hit me. Hit me." But fortunately, rugged northern Albertan that I am, I have been endowed with a certain degree of will power and self-control.

That, and the fact that the cable company discovered the illegally spliced wire running into my apartment and cut the signal.

I was once again reduced to watching PBS from Maine (featuring the *Red Green Show*) and fuzzy images of anchorman Steve Murphy and the ITV Live at 5 Action News Excitement Team. *"Salmon Fishing on the Miramichi! A Live at 5 Exclusive, Coming up Next."*

I went through withdrawal. But I'm okay now.

THE THREE GREAT THEMES of Canadian history are as follows:

1. keeping the Americans out
2. keeping the French in, and
3. trying to get the Natives to somehow disappear.

These three themes represent the political/social mission of Canadians. Americans: *out*. French: *in*. Natives: *invisible*. If Canada were a hockey team, this would be our chant.

These three forces push us and pull us, they haunt us with doubts, they enrage us, they engage us, they *are* us. They are so fundamental as to be embedded right in our DNA.

There are other minor themes as well: Sucking Up to the Royal Family; Waxing Poetic About Nature While Huddling Inside Shopping Malls; Electing Boneheads; Trusting Authority; Avoiding Extremes; and Resenting Success. All of which are played out against the larger Myth of Niceness.

Of our three great themes, I began with the Americans. Why? Because without the Americans there would be no Canada, at least not in the political sense. I imagine the people living on the northern half of this continent would be an odd, introspective, stir-crazy bunch no matter what course history had taken, but the fact remains that *two* nations were created by the American Revolution. It was the Revolution that drove the final stake between Us and Them.

Bloodied but still standing, the U.S. of A.—last of the Superpowers—is at once obnoxious and enticing. Love them or hate them, and Canadians manage to do both, Americans are impossible to ignore.

My brother Ian is a playwright. He is talented and intensely patriotic. "We live in an occupied country," he says bitterly whilst eating a French cruller in Tim Hortons at three o'clock in the morning. If there were a Liberation Underground, Ian would have joined. He once beat the living hell out of a *USA Today* news box, which he saw as a symbol of the stifling pillow of American culture pressed up against our face. "We live in an occupied country," he says, and he may be right. And he may be wrong.

"But you would be better off beating up the Canadians who read *USA Today*," I said. They didn't appear at random, these advance-guard news boxes, they were summoned. Summoned by a yearning. My brother Ian is a proud Canadian. He is a die-hard fan of the Edmonton Oilers, Gordon Pinsent and Gabriel Dumont. He is also a fan of Clint Eastwood and Arnold Schwarzenegger, who are the very epitome of American values, and he never misses the Academy Awards. "Long after the U.S. dies," says Ian, "and long after capitalism goes tits up, Hollywood will still rule the planet."

This American presence is so pervasive we often have trouble recognizing it. It surrounds us like air, as unavoidable as gravity, as unfathomable as identity. Unfortunately, when the average Canadian does react to it, it is often in a nasally voiced, whiny way.

In *Last Train to Toronto,* American author Terry Pindell chronicles his journey across Canada in the twilight of the Age of Rail, culminating in the melancholy January 14, 1990, run from Vancouver to Toronto, the last passenger train along the old CPR line, the one that first bound Canada together as a nation.

Throughout his travels, Terry runs up against nasty anti-American comments and paranoia. He takes it all in stride. "Every province has grievances against some other, and all distrust the dominant Ontarians," he notes. "There is only one neighbor that unites Canadians in a national prejudice—Americans. We are mean, rapacious despoilers of the continent—somewhat akin to Ontarians."

When a group of tourists are identified as Americans— in a searing *Invasion of the Body Snatchers* scream, I imagine—Terry writes, "Having been immersed in the Canadian milieu for some time now, I am struck by how [the American] presence changes the atmosphere of the train."

At one point a man holds up a Canadian five-dollar bill and insists that the tiny, illegible flag depicted over the Peace Tower is in fact the Stars and Stripes. An American flag on Canadian money, a conspiracy!

The supreme, delicious irony of it all is that the very people who rant and rave to Terry about Americans never realize that Terry himself is in fact an American. They cannot tell the difference. But I can. The Canadians are the ones carping on and on about Americans. And what they are saying is so familiar and so very petty, it is embarrassing to read. (It is to Terry's credit that he didn't throw half a dozen or so Canadians from the back of the caboose.)

Which brings me to the infamous Skis on the Car Roof Mentality. Memo to any Canadian nationalist muttonheads out there: No American has ever—*ever*—shown up at the Canadian border in the middle of July with skis strapped to the roof of his car, asking "Where's the snow?"

I must have heard this stupid story a hundred times. If I hear it one more time, I'm going to scream. Or puke. Or both. Either way, it won't be a pretty sight. So the next time some whiny Canuck bastard starts in with the old "skis on the car roof" story, I reserve two boots to the head.

And while we are at it, Americans do not think we all live in igloos. No one thinks we live in igloos. These folk legends reveal more about Canadian insecurities than they do about American attitudes.

Our feelings towards America are complex, but they can be summed up in the following five (5) axiomatic propositions of Canadian Nationalism *vis-à-vis* the Americans:

1. Boy, we hate Americans.
2. We really do.
3. Really.
4. I'm not kidding. We really hate them.
5. So how come they never pay us any attention?

It is a classic love/hate obsession, and it defines us in ways we can never transcend. We measure ourselves against Americans. We crave their attention and their approval, we revel in their ignorance of us, and we take masochistic glee in slights, perceived or real. It is a form of neurosis, one step away from a compulsive high school crush. We pout, flirt, throw pencils, pass notes and talk maliciously about the object of our fears and desires. And they ignore us.

There are two examples, two thin books, each written by an icon of Canadian culture, that best illustrate this: the first is *My Discovery of America* by Farley Mowat, and the second is *Why We Act Like Canadians* by Pierre Berton.

Farley's book is a blow-by-blow account of his "war" with the U.S. Immigration and Naturalization Service (INS) back in 1985, when he was denied entry into the United States on vague charges of possible communist links. The book even begins with Farley's own version of the "skis on the car roof" tale, as he explains why a professor in California invited him to America in the first place:

[H]e thought I would be a good person to help dispel the myth of the Great White North. This is a delusion afflicting many Americans, one that makes them shiver apprehensively on those rare occasions when they acknowledge the existence of a frozen wasteland lying mainly to the north of the 49th parallel of latitude, inhabited by a meagre scattering of beer-drinking, parka-clad bacon-eating lumberjacks, polar bears, and scarlet-coated stalwarts of the Royal Canadian Mounted Police.

That second sentence is quite a marathon, but Farley eventually does come up for air, just short of saying "And they think we all live in igloos! Boy, I hate Americans. I really do."

What happened to Farley was a minor bureaucratic adventure, wherein stale McCarthy-era sentiments were used to justify barring writers whose ideas differed from the reigning Reaganites of the 1980s. The U.S. has been excluding suspected commies and anarchists for years, and the list includes such luminaries as Pierre Trudeau, George Woodcock, at least one Attorney General, and even a classical violinist—and we all know how dangerous they can be. The U.S. of A. tends towards paranoia. And no matter how much we like to assume otherwise, when Canadians cross into the U.S. *we* become foreigners.

The odd thing, and one that Farley notes with genuine surprise, is that throughout his "ordeal" his strongest support—and the sharpest criticism of the INS—came from south of the border. Newspapers across the U.S. ran editorials denouncing the decision to exclude Farley. They mocked the INS and sent letters of apology and support to

Canada. The issue even worked its way up to Capitol Hill and was championed by U.S. senators. Of the hundreds of letters Farley received from Americans, only three thought the INS was justified in their actions.

It also turns out that the information used to bar Farley probably came from Canadians: those scarlet-coated stalwarts, the RCMP. Later, Farley writes, "We Canadians are hardly more than house slaves to the American Empire."

And therein lies the crux of the Canadian neurosis. Not that we are actually "slaves"; to argue this is to demean the very real suzerainty of the economic slave-states of the Third World. No, we are not slaves. But we *feel* like slaves, or more accurately, like underappreciated housewives in prefeminist days.

Canada's intense preoccupation with America reminds me of nothing so much as those old black-and-white 1940s flicks where the heroine beats her fists on the man's chest, sobbing "I hate you, I hate you, I hate, I hate you," only to collapse into his embrace.

Let's face it, America is sexy. It is exciting, dangerous, crass, brash and violent.

The problem is not that America is screwing us daily—which they are—but that they never send flowers or call afterwards. They barely remember our name. "See you around, doll. Here," as they toss us a coin, "buy yourself something nice." It is intercourse without foreplay, when all we needed was a little respect. (Cue the sobbing, chest-beating litany of "I hate you's.")

Farley Mowat was thrown into a foot-stomping tirade because the Americans wouldn't let him in. There was a party planned, but he couldn't get past the front gate. In this, then, *My Discovery of America* is a key book for understanding something deep in the Canadian psyche, something I call "the Angst of the Spectator." As the United States careens by like a parade on crack cocaine, amid fireworks and gunplay and racially sparked riots, we watch from the sidelines, from the curb, thankful we are not caught up in it and yet—and yet, somehow wishing we were.

Existing as we do, somewhere between Voyeur and Spectator, we know in our hearts that we will never be invited to actually participate. We will never be the biggest or the strongest or the richest.

So why should we care? There are many quiet, backwater countries that have attained a degree of civility and social order that the Americans can only dream of. Sweden. Switzerland. Singapore. The problem is that Canada is still very much a *North American* nation, a New World country; we are a frontier-bred people and we will never be satisfied with mere comfort and security. We are nagged by dreams of greater things, a promise of something more. It is a state of mind we share with the United States, Mexico and the separatists of Québec. For all our angst, it is a resolutely optimistic and materialistic world view, one based on the idea that we can be anything, dream anything, achieve anything. And therein lies the problem. Deep inside, we are not satisfied with the safety of the suburbs. We have grasped the brass ring: security, peace, prosperity. But we were bred for bigger things, and this knowledge gnaws away at us like a rat on a bone. We have settled for less. We have made our peace with the world, but not with our dreams. Canadians, under the cottage calm and the down-filled comforter blankets, are restless.

If Farley Mowat really doesn't give a shit about the United States, then why does he expend so much emotion and energy when they won't let him in?

The other book, and one that ought to be standard reading for every Canadian citizen, is Pierre Berton's succinct inventory of our national traits entitled *Why We Act Like Canadians*. Whatever you may think of Pierre Berton the celebrity/institution, you have to admire Pierre Berton the author. As a popular historian, he has done more for Canadian self-awareness than any other writer.

He is also a nationalist of the Old School, and it was in this capacity that he set out in 1982 to explain what exactly makes us Canadians. With all due respect to Mr. Berton, this is one of the biggest nonmysteries ever. If he had only thought to give me a call, I could have cleared it up for him in a few minutes. What makes us Canadians? The answer is both paradoxical and self-evident: *Canada makes us Canadians. Canadians are what we all are. Simply put: I am. Canadian.* But that would have made for a very short and very esoteric book. And anyway, a beer company already had dibs on it. Instead, Pierre focussed on law and order, the French, the Loyalists and our lack of blacks. Other than that last somewhat disturbing assumption, Pierre's book is fairly straightforward.

What is unsettling is how it is presented. *Why We Act Like Canadians* is in the form of an open letter. And to whom is this letter addressed? Is it addressed to new Canadians seeking to learn more about the land they have chosen? Or landed immigrants who have just begun the journey to citizenship? Or to young Canadians? Or Native Canadians? No.

It is revealing that Pierre chooses to address not his fellow Canadians, but the people of the United States.[1]

"Dear Sam," he writes (Sam as in *Uncle Sam,* get it? Get it?) "Today is Constitution Day in Canada! That doesn't mean much to you, I know—I doubt if it will make your front pages—but it's a big thing for us."

Farley rants and raves over American ignorance of Canada, Pierre tries to enlighten them, but the message is still basically the same. We hate you, we hate you, we hate you. Why don't you pay us more attention?

I remember one book exclusively devoted to the Americans' lack of understanding of Canada. The author, Walter Stewart, travelled across the U.S., asking average Americans what they knew about Canada and then recording the often flip remarks with a martyr's fastidiousness. The book managed to be both masochistic and smug. Stewart also ransacked archival sources to quote celebrities such as Al Capone saying things like "Canada? I don't even know what street Canada is on." The basic theme was, *Americans sure are dumb, huh?*

I tried to imagine another nationality that would undertake such a project—New Zealanders travelling across Australia to record Australian lack of knowledge about New Zealand; or Scots travelling through England, seething whenever an Englishman asked "What's a haggis?"— and the only one that seemed possible was Japan.

The Japanese, like Canadians, love to be misunderstood and underappreciated. I could perfectly imagine Japanese commentators travelling across the United States,

1. Like they care.

recording with painstaking accuracy American ignorance of Japan. I can even imagine the book doing quite well.

At best, this inbred anti-Americanism of ours is a survival technique. At worst, it is petulant and petty. In many ways, our relationship to the United States is remarkably similar to Québec's relationship with English Canada. No matter how much Québec nationalists would like to deny it, English Canada *defines* Québec. Just as America defines Canada.

Nationalism, as a force, often relies on the fear of outsiders, and this reveals itself in paired antagonism: Greece and Turkey, Japan and Korea, France and England, Québec and the RC, the United States and the Soviet Union. For English Canadians, anti-Americanism renders the world into easy opposites. Unfortunately, it takes two to play, and the Americans don't realize they are being cast as the Bogeyman of Canadian nationalism. Even worse, it is getting harder and harder to hate them, especially now that they have that big marshmallow in the White House havering away about bridges to the twenty-first century.

There is, however, some good news in all of this. The United States acts like a forerunner for our own fears and apprehensions. In many ways, the Americans are not an invasion force, but are in fact our first line of defence, an Early Warning Line where the consequences of ideological decisions are played out in graphic detail: gun laws, private medicine, unchecked capitalism, the complete ghettoization of minority groups, and allowing too few people to get too rich too fast. We learn from their mistakes.

Unfortunately, as well as using the United States as a harbinger of things to avoid, we also use it as a measuring stick by which we judge Canada's place in the world. And this is where we run into trouble.

Whenever Canadians describe themselves as being kind, cautious, timid and nice, what they are really saying is that they are kind, cautious, timid and nice *when compared to Americans*. Christ, who wouldn't be? When you are comparing yourself to the wildest saloon in the West, of course you will end up appearing soft and angelic. This is the heart of the Canadian Myth of Nice. Just as we seem quieter when compared to the Americans, we also seem more modest, more polite and more self-deprecating. This is utter rot. We may not have an edge, and we may err constantly on the side of caution, but overall we are a loud, brash, gregarious people. Ask any northern European who has travelled in Canada.

I remember my Scottish cohort Marion saying with a mock Canadian accent, "Everything is bigger 'n' better in Canada!" She couldn't believe how relentlessly hand-shaking and back-slapping Canadians were. An English traveller said, "It was aggravating how the cashiers would smile at me as though we were dear friends and ask *How ya doing?* as though I were dying for their acknowledgement." There is nothing bookish or morose or European about us. We are North Americans, through and through. True, we are not as bad or as extreme as the citizens of the United States, but then, the only person as bad or as extreme as an American is another American.

My Japanese friends think Canadians are hopelessly slothful, slovenly, unreliable and fun. My Ecuadorian friends think Canadians are hopelessly uptight, punctual and obsessed with schedules. They can't both be right.

Or can they?

In *Hello World!*, Jacques Hébert's chronicle of Canada World Youth, a young volunteer recalls the shock of coming home after a stint in the Dominican Republic: "I realized Canadians live at a frantic pace and don't take the time to enjoy life's simple pleasures. Though Canadians are very sociable, their use of time is too rigidly structured and makes no allowance for the unexpected." However, when my friend Kerry returned to her hometown of Victoria after an extended stay in Japan, she found Canadians intimidating. "Everyone was wearing dirty clothes. The men were hairy and huge, and I felt threatened."

It all comes down to your standard of comparison. Canadians appear tidy, timid and soft-spoken only when standing next to Americans, in much the same way that I look slim when standing next to a sumo wrestler.

And while we are hammering away at popular delusions, let's take on another one: that Canada is facing cultural annexation by the United States, that we are in imminent danger of being absorbed, *Protozoa*-like, into the American soul. This is a vestigial fear, born of what was once a very real, very ominous possibility. The Americans have coveted our land for centuries. The annexation of Canada was official policy in the United States for over 150 years. They invaded us twice, encouraged sedition several times and were involved in endless border skirmishes. Canada regarded the United States as its biggest territorial threat right up until World War I. Until then, our major military plans involved defence against an American invasion. The United States themselves did not relinquish their pro-annexation sentiments towards Canada until 1923! So our suspicions that the Yanks are waiting to gobble us up are well-grounded in history.

But the old-style "annex and plunder" imperialism is dead, and it's time we got over it. Even if Québec goes, Canada will not be absorbed piecemeal into the United States. Why? Because Canadians do not want to become Americans. This is what created us in the first place, this desire *not* to be American, and it is a sentiment that is getting stronger, not weaker. In *Nationalism Without Walls,* columnist Richard Gwyn writes:

> Not a scrap of evidence exists that Canadians want to become Americans. In April 1995, a survey by Decima Research for the Canadian Council of Christians and Jews found that just 3 per cent polled favoured "union with the United States." This was down from a 5 per cent tally measured by an Angus Reid survey in 1991. It's entirely possible that fewer Canadians want to become Americans than do the citizens of almost any other country in the world.

Three per cent! That is less than the percentage of naturalized and second-generation Americans living in our fair land. Even our own domesticated Yanks are not big on the idea. Surely, three per cent does not represent any kind of Fifth Column threat, yet still the breakup and cannibalization of Canada is trotted out every time we face a domestic crisis. Let's lay this demon to rest. It isn't going to happen. The Americanization of Canada is a shadow-puppet spectre conjured up by intellectual nationalists and their ilk. Indeed, nationalists never shut up about the Americans in much the same way that fundamentalist preachers never shut up about Beelzebub and the Day of Judgement.

There is, of course, a flip-side to all of this: *pro*-Americanism. This is manifest in the ease with which Canadians have surrendered their autonomy, their economy and their confidence to the American juggernaut. Hate is only one half of any love-hate relationship, and Canadians have all too often crawled on their bellies for American approval. Again, this has got nothing to do with the Americans themselves. Just as Americans do not really deserve our hatred, neither do they deserve our love.

Yet there was Smilin' Brian up on stage, singing away to Cowboy Ron at the Shamrock Summit. It was March 1985 and Ronald Reagan was visiting Québec City, where—live on stage—our prime minister sang a warbled version of *When Irish Eyes Are Smiling* to the president. "The general impression you get," noted commentator Eric Kierans, dryly, "is that our prime minister invited his boss home for dinner." Heck, it was all Brian could do not to give Ronnie a big wet smooch right then and there on national television.

Canadians have long since disowned Mulroney, but in doing this we are shirking our responsibility. We voted that man into office twice—*twice mind you!*—so in a very real sense that was us up there on stage, crooning away like an infatuated schoolboy.

Brian Mulroney's serenade was a low point in Canadian pride. For those of you too young to remember, consider yourself lucky.

The key point is that Brian's performance, like the free trade that followed, was done with our approval—and usually on our initiative. Don't blame the Americans. They aren't the real threat—the real threat comes from our own insecurities and ambivalent feelings.

We worry far too much about America.

Why should we give a tinker's damn about how we stack up against the U.S.? Whether our gun laws are more civilized than theirs or whether our medicare is more humane doesn't really matter. We have nothing to gain by using the United States as our yardstick. We should be setting our standards by who we are and who we *could* be—not by what we aren't. And that is the heart of the matter: we must stop defining ourselves in terms of negation.

Let us put an end to the wailing, hair-pulling, woeful lamentations about our impending Americanization. That we share many similarities with those foreigners to the south is not a cause for despair. Given the similarities in geography, history and background, the surprising thing is that we are different at all. And we are. Whether we can agree on what makes us Canadian, whether we can articulate something so near the bone, is irrelevant. The deep silent chasm that separates us from the United States of America is one of the miracles of North American history—one of the *enduring* miracles. That Canada exists at all is remarkable, that we have made a damn good show of it is even more impressive. So let's stop treating the Americans like the Bogeyman. Let's stop blaming them. Let's stop admiring them. Let's stop hating them. Let's stop loving them.

We will always be something more—and less—than American. In the twilight of the twentieth century, we will have to redraw old maps and realign outdated thoughts. It is time we stopped looking, with a mix of fear and longing, across the river to that dark wooded shore.

OUR HOME

ON NATIVE LAND

. . . .

*W*HEN I RETURNED to Canada, I longed for landscape and space and familiar mythologies. I wanted to be comforted by *Canada*: the Peaceable Kingdom. *Canada*: the Great Lone Land. The True North. Land of the Silver Birch. Home of the Beaver. I wanted to see moose wandering at will. I wanted to see wigwams.

And so, I set off to look for Canada. Wisely, I let someone else do the driving.

I caught a ride from Vancouver with a friend. We threaded our way into the mountains of the interior, in a blaze of patriotism. The car radio didn't work (it only picked up CBC) so we sang ourselves hoarse with songs like *Canada Is,* with its shopping list of locales. "Canada is the Rocky Mountains, Canada is Prince Edward Island! And that's what Canada is!" Lists are like names, they identify through the very act of labelling. "From Vancouver Island to the Alberta highland, cross the prairies, the Lakes to Ontario's towers! From the sound of Mount Royal's chimes, out to the Maritimes. Something to sing about, *this land of ours!"*

The Rockies break suddenly, first into foothills, then into rolling farmland. And the farmlands go on forever. They are great backdrops for murky introspection, and as the euphoria faded, my thoughts turned in on themselves. The prairies were once eulogized as empty and primal, but today they are some of the most tamed stretches of land in Canada; not a square has been left untouched, not a horizon left untilled. We have imposed a strict geometry upon our landscape. Survey lines and access roads define and exclude. Grain elevators, the bucket-brigade that feeds us, are paced out in even strides. This is the loneliest suburb on earth, for we are a nation of city dwellers, and the plains are as docile as any lawn.

In Edmonton, I joined my brother Sean, who was driving to Montréal with his wife and daughter. The highway ran straight across Saskatchewan, through towns and cities pooled like lakes, through the methodical patchwork of our nation.

The most Canadian word I know is *subdivision.* It suggests both the lay of the land and the philosophy behind it; it is not enough to divide our property, we must *sub*-divide it as well. We have subdivided our world into suburbs and into submission. (Indian reserves are a natural extension of this world view. On reserves, people are sub-divided—not into submission, but worse—into shadows. And parentheses.)

One of the grievances that led to armed rebellion among the Métis in 1885 was the division of land. The Métis had already settled beside the rivers, along contours and curves, but the government insisted that their farms conform to the rectangular pattern that had been superimposed like a grid over the entire Northwest. A bloody uprising followed, and when the fighting stopped, over 125 Indians and Métis were prosecuted. Eight Crees were publicly hanged in the largest mass execution in our history. Such is the power of geometry.

Every line we have drawn since Confederation has involved right angles. Saskatchewan is nothing *but* right angles, superimposed on a globe like a square on a circle.

The highway runs from the plains into chaos. The Canadian Shield. Towns strung out like supply depots, a highway that hurries through the wilderness. Lakes too numerous to name. Names too numerous to remember. The Trans-Canada cuts across rock and river, through cities and towns separated by forests, across ravines and time zones. The broken yellow line rolls past like a repetitive morse code, in dots and dashes, sending a signal.

We have claimed half a continent as our own. Half a continent—but how? On what principle? By what right?

Highways do that. They ask questions.

Somewhere near Iron Bridge, Ontario, we ran into a wall of fog and the entire landscape vanished. It was unnerving how easily Canada disappeared. My brother slowed the car down to a crawl, the headlights groping ahead of us with only a few feet of vision. The Great Lakes were lost, the Canadian Shield was gone, the Silver Birch, the Mighty Moose. The Wigwam.

As we forced our way through the mist and damp, we talked in whispers about Japan. I told Sean about the *burakumin*. This is a euphemism for "human filth," meaning, roughly, "village dwellers." The Japanese never talk about them, and most people outside Japan don't know they exist. I didn't before I moved to Japan. They are the bottom caste, the descendants of butchers and leather workers, ostracized by a vegetarian society that had learned to eat meat but not to accept the people who provided it. The caste system of Japan still exists today. Family records go back for generations and are matters of public record. In Japan—a modern, democratic nation—parents forbid their children from marrying *burakumin* and companies refuse to employ them. They live on the margins, often in separate villages, the hidden outcasts of Japan, prisoners of history.

Sean nodded and, with a certain amount of pride, noted how much more enlightened Canada was in comparison. We don't have a caste system. We would never allow such covert discrimination, for we are much too tolerant for that.

This is a common enough sentiment—Canada as caste-free, progressive, nice—but it is also a false sentiment and a dangerous one. We do have a lower class that is segregated and marginalized. We too have our prisoners of history: the Natives, Inuit and Métis. Are they not segregated socially, legally, *racially*? Are they not our *burakumin,* our Third Solitude, the ones we never talk about? The brutal fact is we *do* have a caste system in Canada. We may ignore it—and we often do—but we can't deny it.

OUR HISTORY HAS been less than exemplary. This wasn't an empty continent we took for our own. From the start, the Europeans recognized that they were dealing with sovereign entities. In 1748, the Intendant of New France noted that "these Indians claim to be and in effect are independent of all nations, and their lands incontestably belong to them."

As the colonies became permanent and the New World became the adopted home of Europeans, the Indians became either ally or enemy. We waged wars, signed pacts, and slowly—ineluctably—we moved inland. The First Nations were up against a glacier. And they lost.

As more and more land was annexed, it became necessary, or at least expedient, to sign treaties with the various nations. The treaties were notoriously vague. Typically, they were ceremonies involving exchanges of gifts, vows of peaceful coexistence and gestures of mutual good will. To the Natives, they were friendship pacts. To the whites, they were legally binding documents, and as often as not, land deeds.

After Confederation, as the railroad pushed west, it became imperative to deal with the Native people living there, and several expansive treaties were signed, some stipulating reserve lands, others not. At this point, newcomers had killed off all of the buffalo and introduced epidemics that had destroyed well over half the Native population. The survivors began to starve. The Natives were not on equal footing during these negotiations. The surrender of land title was the only option left to them if they wanted to avoid extinction; the treaties were a pact with the devil, so to speak.

Often, the treaties were drawn up before the Indians even arrived for discussions. Tribes negotiated changes anyway, but few of them were ever written down, as the Native representatives assumed that verbal agreements would be honoured. In much of Canada—nearly half the total land area in fact—no treaties were ever signed, and the land was appropriated more by stealth and momentum than by any pretext of legality. In British Columbia, with only a few exceptions, and all of the Atlantic Provinces, and all of Québec, no agreements were reached.

At first, the Native groups were allowed to choose their own reserve lands, but that promise was quickly broken. Good farmland was excluded for the most part, and—devastating to tribal custom—large tracts were disallowed. Instead, Indian bands were splintered among small, unconnected plots of land. When they resisted, the government simply withheld food that was promised under the Famine Clause of the treaties. Thus it was that we coerced, shoved and blackmailed nomadic people into subdivisions and *sub*-subdivisions.

What's more, the reserves do not belong to the people living on them. All title and ownership remains in the hands of the federal government, making Natives both legally and psychologically charity-case tenants.

This system of divide and rule did not happen by accident; it was all carefully worked out as a matter of policy. The young Dominion of Canada did not consider Natives to be equal citizens, and as the Indian Act of 1876 made very clear, they were to be wards of the state. The paternalism was explicit and unapologetic. The government was to be the guardian of the Indians, who were deemed incapable of taking care of themselves. Indians could not vote, nor own property, nor take out loans, nor drink in public places. They were a caste created by fiat.

Paradoxically, the official goal of this enforced segregation was—and always has been—assimilation. Assimilation is a gentle-sounding word, but reflect a moment on what it means: simply, cultural extermination. Québec nationalists rail all the time about impending assimilation, but they have never had to face that demon in the eye. Native groups have. The process was less bloody than the American-Indian wars that were raging south of the border, but the goal was exactly the same: the permanent removal of Indians from the equation.

The result of this self-cancelling, dehumanizing process? In Canada, one of the wealthiest, most prosperous countries in the world, we have created an entire, racially segregated subclass, our very own Third World.

SEAN AND I argued the fog away, our voices getting louder and louder until we woke his wife and daughter who were asleep in the back. The landscape reappeared.

Sean conceded that Canada did have a racial subclass, but he refused to accept any sense of guilt over this. He saw it as a *fait accompli*. Why, he asked, should he be held responsible for something that had happened before he was born? Surely there is a statute of limitations on shame.

This quick absolution of guilt is perhaps the most common response in Canada to the issue of Native rights. It is also the most specious. Our caste system is still with us, here and now. It is ongoing, it is not ancient history. And we support it with our indifference.

Look at it this way: we are more than willing to take pride in our national achievements, but at the same time we are quick to dismiss our national failings. This contradiction is as obvious as it is unacknowledged. I, for one, am not *personally* responsible for the great wealth, peace and international image Canada has garnered over the years, but by God, I revel in it. If we accept Canada's good fortune—which did not suddenly appear, but is the product of our history—how then can we refuse to accept any culpability for our less glorious achievements?

The answer, of course, is that we cannot.

If we accept the good, we are compelled to accept the bad. It is that simple. Yet we rarely think these things out. We may, as some commentators tell us, be a self-deprecating nation. Perhaps. But we are not—by any standard—self-*critical*. We remain resolutely, blissfully, uninformed about ourselves.

Here is a sample of our reality. The following statistics are being updated and adjusted almost hourly, but rarely differ more than a percentage point one way or the other.

- The life expectancy of Canadian Natives is ten years lower than the national average. The infant mortality rate is twice as high.
- Over 60 per cent of all Natives are either unemployed or on welfare.
- Housing on reserves is far below the minimal accepted levels. A quarter of the homes on reserves still do not have running water. A third don't have indoor toilets.
- On reserves, about 75 per cent of all households are run by single parents. Off the reserves, the number soars to over 90 per cent.
- The Native illiteracy rate is double the national average.

Only 5 per cent of Natives graduate from high school, and 40 per cent don't make it to grade nine.

- The average Native male is three times more likely to end up in jail as graduating from high school.
- The average income of Natives remains between one half and two thirds that of the rest of the nation.
- Inquiries have shown again and again that the justice system is slanted against Natives. In the circumlocution of government lingo, Natives are "over-represented" in our jails. In Manitoba alone, over 50 per cent of the prison population is Native.
- 46 per cent of non-Native juvenile offenders are let off with a warning. For Native juveniles, the number is 15 per cent. Compare those two numbers: 46 to 15. That is our national score card. Natives get sent to jail sooner, and more often, than non-Natives.
- The most common cause of death among Natives is violence (accidents, assaults or suicides). The alarming suicide rate among Native Canadians is perhaps the most incisive judgement we have against our apartheid system. Young Natives are over five times more likely to kill themselves than are their peers in the general population.
- In Canada approximately 25 per cent of all family-related murders occur among Natives, a group that makes up less than 3 per cent of the total population.
- On the reserves and off, alcohol abuse is rampant. Estimates put the number of alcohol-related deaths and accidents at over 50 per cent.

These numbers are relentless, almost tiresome. Certainly, it is not all doom and gloom; many individuals lead healthy lives and many do well for themselves, but overall the situation is grim.

In the area of northern Alberta where I grew up, there were three reserves (Tall Cree, Little Red River, and Boyer River-Elleske). The Indian kids that used to beat me up after school certainly didn't seem like an oppressed minority. I am not an Indianophile by any stretch of the imagination, and indeed, there are several individual Native Canadians that I personally do not give a damn about. But none of that changes the situation.

Name any category—employment, teenage suicide, income, single-parent homes—and I can tell you with confidence who makes up the lowest rung. I can also predict that if you ask 100 Canadians whether or not we have a caste system in Canada, 99 will say no. The 100th will be an Indian.

The creation of Canada, no matter how we look at it, was above all an act of imperialism. A nation-state annexed land inhabited by many other nations and then made them second-class citizens. This is a textbook definition of imperialism. We were colonizers every bit as much as we were colonized. We sent in troops to put down uprisings, and we created a paramilitary police force—the Mounties—to enforce our laws. Today, there are more than 2,200 reserves still existing in Canada, the remnants of First Nations scattered thinly across the land. They are small indeed; the average reserve is just over four square miles, and the average population is less than 1,000. More than half the reserves are so remote they are only accessible by boat, plane or footpath. Indians in the United States, by comparison, have a much larger land base—over nine times more land allotted per status Indian than in Canada.

American Indians have also been recognized as having "domestic dependent nation" status.

Apologists will tell you that Canadians are still Nicer Than Most. This should be our National Embroidered Catch Phrase, alongside "Home, Sweet Home." We are so nice, in fact, that some people even argue that our treatment of Aboriginals is *exemplary*. You run into this bizarre assertion now and then. Just look, the argument goes, at all we have done for Them.

Well, we certainly have spent an awful lot of money. Between 1968 and 1988 alone, a period of just twenty years, Canada spent well over $26 *billion* "helping" the Indians. Unfortunately, the priorities were a little odd at times. One chief noted that while his welfare budget was presently $2.7 million, his economic development budget was $52,000.

What better way to destroy a man, asked the poet Felix Leclerc, than to pay him to do nothing?

While in Japan I attended a dinner party where I made the mistake of describing Canada's treatment of Natives as "effectively a system of apartheid." A fellow Canadian overheard this and became outraged. How, she wanted to know, could I say such a thing? "What kind of image is that to give to the Japanese? We most certainly do not have apartheid in Canada! We don't have separate laws for Indians. We don't. So how can you call it apartheid? How can you say such a thing?" And on and on she went, her voice getting shriller and shriller until only dogs and nationalists could hear it.

I was dumbfounded by her logic as much as by her outburst. We have *always* had separate laws for Indians. Stranger still, this toadlike woman was from Winnipeg, home of one of Canada's largest Native ghettoes, where our caste system is a daily, visual slap in the face. But none of that mattered to her. She believed in a storybook Canada, one of tolerance and kindness and big fuzzy hugs, and the facts—like the First Nations to our forefathers—just got in the way.

Instead, our past *and continuing* sins are written off as ancient history. Once the woman from Winnipeg ran out of air, another man, also an expatriate Canadian and clearly college-trained in the art of thoughtful nodding, said "Come now, Will. We can't be held hostage to our past."

Terrific slogan, that. It absolves us of responsibility in a neat turn of phrase. But replace "hostage" with "responsible" and it reveals itself for what it is: ethical dodge-ball.

We keep wishing the problem away. This pattern was well established as far back as 1876, when the Indian Act was first drafted. Reserves were designed to be temporary holding cells, where, it was confidently assumed, Indians would be fully assimilated within three generations. They would be kept segregated and accounted for until they were deemed morally worthy of Canadian citizenship.

This is not editorializing on my part, these were the explicit objectives of the Indian Act. If you were good, if you were very good, you could graduate from being an Indian. All you had to do was to give up your identity, move into the mainstream, lose your language, forswear your culture, and you too would be allowed to vote and own your own land. This was called "enfranchisement."

To be enfranchised, you had to (A) abandon all tribal customs, (B) be judged of good character, (C) be fluent in either French or English, and (D) have passed a three-year probation (just to make sure you didn't lapse back into savage custom or language). Only then would you be allowed the privilege of not being an Indian. In Canada, the only Good Indian was an Assimilated Indian, and as very few of them accepted assimilation, we had very few Good Indians.

Enfranchisement remained policy until—*when?* 1900? 1910? 1920? No. The government did not concede defeat and remove enfranchisement from the Indian Act until 1985. Ancient history, that.

In 1990, Desmond Tutu, the Archbishop of Cape Town and a leading figure in the anti-apartheid movement in South Africa, saw clear parallels between the homelands of his nation and the reserves of ours. Of Canada's Native people, he said: "They have been treated less than justly. They have the right to be human and Indian. Their culture must be recognized as having integrity and must not be subverted."

Ours is an apartheid that runs deeper than geography. It is the apartheid of the heart, a marginalization—social, economic, historical—of a people. We have segregated and subdivided and sought to swallow cultures prior to ours and nations older than our own. And we have failed.

You see, a funny thing happened on the way to assimilation. The two goals of Indian policy, separation and assimilation, were contradictory: they cancelled each other out. The reserves that were meant to segregate Native Canadians gave them a land base that now acts both as a focal point of political activism and a refuge—however shaken, however poverty-stricken. The resurgent Native culture and explosive Native pride come directly from the reserves,

and it is from the reserves that Natives Canadians are leading a full-scale counterattack. Apartheid has backfired.

The Native groups that are now calling for self-government are on sound legal footing. Their case, poetically,
hangs upon the very technique used against them: the
treaty. We broke our agreements, we signed invalid contracts, we did not negotiate in good faith—we were too
clever by half. Our Conquest by Memo has come back to
haunt us, for it has shown itself to be just that: victory on
paper alone. As Professor Harry S. LaForme points out in
The Canadian Journal of Native Studies:

> Contrary to popular myth, Aboriginal people in Can-
> ada are not people who were militarily defeated or con-
> quered by those European nations attempting to settle
> the country.
>
> I believe it is with that background that one must
> begin to examine the Aboriginal meaning of sovereignty.
> It is simply the right of self-government or self-rule
> which the Aboriginal people neither surrendered nor
> lost by way of conquest.

One of the most common objections to all of this—and
one that has been faithfully repeated for well over two
hundred years—is that Indians can't go back to hunting
buffalos and living in longhouses; those days are over. Indians, it is implied, are living in a fantasy world and would
be better off if they just gave up and assimilated.

In his book *The Imaginary Indian,* historian Daniel
Francis notes the term "Modern Indian" has always been
seen as an oxymoron. This dogma tells us that Indians are

a people of the past, not the present, and certainly *not* the future. This insistence that Indians, *real* Indians, exist only in history books, has been maintained for centuries.

Native Canadians do not live in a fantasy world. They know reality up close, warts and all. It is the rest of the nation that needs to adjust its thinking. In *A Long and Terrible Shadow*, Thomas Berger, a lawyer specializing in constitutional law and Native rights, explains:

> Native people do not want to recreate a world that has vanished. They do, however, want to find a secure place in the world that we have forced upon them. Indian treaties, Indian reserves, Indian Acts—these are all institutions that Europeans have devised to manage Native people primarily for the convenience of the dominant society. Now, Native people want to develop institutions of their own fashioning; they are eager to see their cultures grow and change in directions they have chosen for themselves. They do not want to be subjects of sentimentality. They do not want to return to life in tipis and igloos. They are citizens of the twentieth century.

It isn't a matter of being lost in the past, it is a matter of claiming the future. It is the opposite of the Québec separatist movement. The First Nations do not want to separate from Canadian society, they want to join it—but on their terms.

You will still hear stubborn souls repeating, like a mantra, that it is too late, that the only option left is assimilation. Well, I hate to break the bad news, but this isn't going to happen. We have thrown everything we had at them:

treaties, sentimentality, contempt, Christianity, government studies and—may God forgive us—social workers. And all for naught.

Remember Vietnam? How the Americans just kept frantically pounding away because they were convinced that the larger arsenal eventually had to win? Same principle.

After five hundred years of disease, reserves and poverty, they have refused to vanish. Of our three national themes—keeping the Americans out, keeping the French in, and trying to make the Indians somehow disappear—we won the first, tied the second and failed in the third.

I REMEMBER AS a child complaining to my mother about how my friends were always getting cheques from the Department of Indian Affairs. We were just as poor and just as downtrodden, but we didn't we get any cheques. It wasn't *fair*. (I was young and still believed in such words.) Why can't we get cheques as well, I wanted to know. After I wheedled and whined, my mother finally turned and said in a firm voice, "You should be grateful we are *not* receiving cheques." I didn't understand at the time, but I do now. It was like envying a crippled worker his compensation payments.

Whenever I hear people grumble over the fact that Natives living on reserves don't pay taxes, or that there are special funds available for Natives who make it to university, I feel like stapling the following message from Chief Dan George to their foreheads (from his essay "My Very Good Friends"):

[W]e are a people with special rights guaranteed to us by promises and treaties. We do not beg for these rights,

nor do we thank you... we do not thank you for them
because we paid for them... and God help us the price
we paid was exorbitant. We paid for them with our culture, our dignity, and our self-respect. We paid and paid
and paid...

Canada is our native land, in every sense of the word.
We have claimed it as our own. Half a continent for ourselves. But we are neither as pure nor as unsullied as we
would like to believe. Neither are we as insipid. Canada *is*
a wonderful country—there is much to celebrate and honour, much to laugh about and much to puzzle over—but we
get nowhere by denying the past or by avoiding the present.

We are as much defined by our sins as by our heroics,
by our foibles as by our virtues. Beneath the surface shine,
we are a nation of opposing forces and deep contradiction.
French and English. European and First Nations. History
and Forgetting. City and Forest. Garrisons and Shopping
Malls. Somewhere in the synthesis of all these elements is
who we are. Do we contradict ourselves? Fine, we contradict ourselves. We are large, we contain multitudes.

And that's what Canada is.

A FEW
CHOICE WORDS

. . . .

*P*AMELA LEVI is beautiful. She is nineteen years old and her hair tumbles
down her shoulders to waist length. She fidgets, smiles,
shrugs. Every now and then she sweeps back her hair and
laughs. It makes it hard to conduct an interview. I keep
losing my train of thought.

Pamela is a Micmac dancer featured in a musical production called *Spirit of a Nation.*

"How do you feel when you dance? What goes through
your mind?"

"I feel proud," she says. "Proud to be an Indian."

I sit smiling at her for a few moments until she says, "I
think your tape stopped."

Oh. I hit eject, flip over the mini-cassette and press record. "Sorry. Now then, you were saying that when you dance you feel proud to be a Native Canadian."

But that is not what she said. She gives me a puzzled and slightly annoyed look. "I said, I feel proud to be an *Indian*."

Later, I play the tape back, both sides, and discover that she is right. I also discover that during the entire interview I have twisted and contorted my syntax to avoid using the word Indian at all. I say "Native North American." I say "Aboriginal." I say "People of the First Nations." But nowhere do I say, simply, "Indian." (When it came time to write this book, I made a point of including the term Indian as well as the others.)

Words, like ideas, can fall out of fashion. Others become tainted. The error made by the Politically Correct movement was in trying to hurry the process along. It isn't something that can be dictated by committee, it just happens. For a long time, the word *squaw* was used simply to mean any Native woman. Today it has a crude, offensive sound to it. An example of how words evolve: Gordon Donaldson's popular book *The Prime Ministers of Canada* was first published in 1969, but has been added to several times since then, most recently in 1994. Although it has been expanded, the book's original core material has not been altered. Mr. Donaldson makes several references to *squaws*:

- He describes Fort Whoop-up as being "deserted but for one old man and a few squaws."
- He speaks of American marauders who "raped the squaws."

- He labels George Carmack, one of the founders of the Klondike Gold Rush, as a "squaw man." [Carmack was married to a Native woman.]
- Mr. Donaldson even repeats a joke made by John A. about how protectionism is "like a drunken squaw's view of liquor—a little too much is just enough."

This may have been funny in 1875, and it may still have been funny in 1969, but is anyone laughing now? When I read Mr. Donaldson's book, I cringed when I came across such passages. (Mr. Donaldson also defines *métis* as "a half-breed Indian." Surely half-breed and Indian are mutually exclusive terms, no?)

When I was in Britain I was astounded to find the term *Red Indian* still in common use. Astounded, but not surprised. After all, this is the same country whose tabloids regularly use the word *Jap* in their headlines.

What of the word *Indian* itself? For one thing, it isn't accurate. Columbus was convinced to his dying day that he had reached Asia and that the people he had encountered were honest-to-God Indians. That doesn't necessarily make the word an insult. After all, the name *Canada* itself is a case of mistaken identity (derived from a Native word for "village"), but no one would find the term *Canadian* demeaning.

Legally, *Indian* is a slippery term. The official definition seems to include the Inuit of the far north, but in practice it does not.[1] Depending on whether you take a cultural,

1. Incidentally, the Inuit vs. Eskimo debate is over. Inuit won, and the term Eskimo is slowly fading away, lingering mainly in the work of uninformed writers and in the names of professional sports teams.

racial or legal viewpoint—and whether you count treaty status, nontreaty status, off-reserve or on-reserve—the number of Indians in Canada ranges anywhere from under 200,000 to over 1,000,000.

The United States is just as confused about definitions, but the Americans appear far more sensitive to the nuance of words. I was publicly scolded after one of my lectures on Canadian culture by an American woman who said, with a sniff, "In the United States we don't use the word Indian. We say Native American." And where was this lady from? Which haven of racial and ethnic harmony? Los Angeles.

The word *Indian* may have become unfashionable in academic and liberal circles, but on reserves you will still see bumper stickers and T-shirts proudly proclaiming "Indian Power!" Which is it, a slur or a badge of honour?

There is often a process of reclamation and then rejection in cases like this. Consider the word *nigger*. It began as slave-era slang, but during the 1970s and 1980s black activists claimed it as their own and neatly subverted its meaning. Having sucked the power out of it, they then spit it back out. It is now considered so offensive that the media has begun referring to it as "the N-word." The spell-checker in my computer won't even acknowledge its existence. Even when I spell the N-word correctly, it insists that I am wrong, offering instead: *nagger, Niger, niggler* and *nudger*. Somehow, having Mark Fuhrman refer to O.J. as a "dirty nudger" loses its impact. My how times have changed. I defy anyone to sit through Mel Brook's *Blazing Saddles,* a film we once thought was hysterically funny, and *not* squirm every time Mel says something hilarious like "The new sheriff is a nigger!"

But my spell-checker is not consistent. The terms *red-skin* and *squaw* are acceptable. Injun is not. Will the day come that the word Indian will evoke the same revulsion as nigger? Will we start referring to it as "the I-word"?

I decided to call Gary Abbott.

I met Gary the same way I met Pamela, through the musical theatre of *Spirit of a Nation*. Gary is a member of the Thompson Nation of British Columbia. He is the president of NAPA (the North American Pow-Wow Association) and has been a pow-wow dancer since the age of two. He specializes in the Hoop Dance, an intricate ritual involving twenty-nine separate hoops, which he pulls in and around his body to reveal woven moons, wombs and animal shapes.

Gary is very much aware of the nuance of words. When I referred to the various, spectacular costumes he wears during his dances, he said, "They aren't costumes. The correct term is regalia." I also notice, when I replay my interviews with Gary, that he avoids the word Indian as well. He refers instead to Natives and non-Natives.

Gary Abbott has been active in Native society as a social worker and as a crisis prevention caseworker. He is also the head of his own Vancouver-based software development company, and he is now planning to enter medical school in Vancouver, where his long-term goal is to combine modern medical techniques with older, herbal and meditative treatments. All this, and he is still in his twenties.

No one would ever accuse Gary Abbott of being one-dimensional. He straddles several worlds, from the art of the dance to the competition of the pow-wow to the intricacies of cyberspace.

I once asked Gary, "Who are you? Are you a dancer? A businessman? A computer developer? A social worker? A doctor? A medicine man?"

He shrugged. "I am whatever I am doing—at that moment. If I'm dancing, I'm a dancer. If I'm doing software development, I'm a software developer."

What began as a minor semantic quest had taken a new turn. We were no longer talking about mere labels, we were talking about identity. This is what I had been chasing ever since I returned from Asia, my own definition of self, that tenuous connection between the abstract and the specific, between a concept—*Canadian*—and the concrete—*me*.

We are defined by multiple layers, beginning with Canadian and working our way down, peeling the onion—and at the core?

"Are you an Indian?"

It's a stupid question. Of course Gary is an Indian. I rephrase the question. "Is the word Indian offensive?"

He thinks a moment. "It isn't offensive. But it is outdated. We aren't Indians. We are Native Canadians. The proper term is First Nations."

Words matter. *In Our Home or Native Land?* Melvin H. Smith bristles at the use of the term First Nations, insisting that there is "little support in law for the view that the tribal societies that *may* have existed before the arrival of the white man constituted nationhood." (Italics mine.)

Mr. Smith hit a nerve with his attack on the corrupt, multibillion-dollar lawyer/advisor/bureaucrat "rights industry" that has sprung up around Native issues. But with all due respect, it seems that Mr. Smith has confused *state* with *nation*. A *state* is a legal entity. A *nation* is a group of people sharing the same language, customs and heritage, usually in a common geographic area.

The First Nations lived, hunted, planted, sowed, loved, laughed, raised children, spun legends, sung of heroes, worshipped gods, made alliances, warred with their neighbours, took slaves, formed intricate alliances and trading patterns, and practised art and intrigue for thousands of years before the arrival of Europeans.

I have come across the term *nation* to describe Native societies in references dating back to 1779. When George Washington's Continental Army went on a rampage against Iroquois settlements, the commanding officer noted with no small amount of pride, "I flatter myself that the orders with which I was entrusted are fully executed, as we have not left a single settlement or field of corn in the country of the Nations."

By any standard, the complex societies that existed in Canada prior to European contact were nations. In fact, the Iroquois Confederacy, with its delineated territories, longhouse laws and binding pacts was (arguably) a union of political *states* as well as ethnic *nations*.

Québec nationalists claim that they too constitute a nation. And they do. But whether ethnic nations are automatically entitled to statehood—be it Native self-government or Québec sovereignty—is another question entirely. (Pierre Trudeau, for one, fought long and hard against the insistence that every ethnic nation must be given a political state.) The reason Smith avoids using the term First Nations when referring to Native societies is that he doesn't want to acknowledge their prior claims—legal, moral or otherwise. When Smith is forced to use the term, he makes a point of adding editorial quotation marks: "First Nations."

Mr. Smith is fascinated with the minutiae of Native/provincial/federal negotiations. I am interested more in human feelings.

So I called my sister.

Darla is my youngest sister—the Quiet Ferguson, they call her—and she is Cree.

"Is the word Indian offensive?" I ask her.

"No."

I wait, but that's it. "Come on, help me out here. I'm trying to write a book. Give me something pithy and insightful."

She sighs. Darla is a very practical-minded woman and such hairsplitting annoys her. I would love to see Darla and Professor Smith go head to head. I don't imagine the good professor would come out in one piece.

"Well," she says. "It's like anything. It depends on how it's used. I don't find it offensive, but there are some people who will take offence at anything, I suppose. *Native* sounds better, but most Indians don't really care." Then, as an afterthought. "The volleyball team I play with is called the Hobbema Indians. I helped pick the name."

Words are empty vessels. They take on whatever meaning we give them, good or bad. The single, multisyllable word *Canadian* carries enough weight and context to fill an entire book. The word *Indian* is even more complex, more ambiguous, more problematic.

Will *Indian* ever become socially taboo? Perhaps. But somehow I doubt it. For one thing, the Politically Correct Wave seems to have peaked. For another, the Indians themselves don't seem overly concerned. But most importantly, Pamela Levi of Big Cove, New Brunswick, is proud. Proud to be a dancer. Proud to be an Indian. But above all, proud of herself.

In the end, words fail us.

Jimmy Cardinal, raconteur and general ne'er-do-well from my home town, put it best. "Personally," he says. "I prefer to call myself a First Nations Aboriginal North American Native Indigenous Canadian Person. But it doesn't fit on the forms."

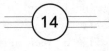

14

GOD BLESS THE QUEEN
(AND ALL HER ASSORTED INBRED,
DYSFUNCTIONAL OFFSPRING)

. . . .

/ ONCE CAME across an article in a science journal about a certain ant colony in a university lab. The ants had expanded their elaborate network of tunnels and decided (insomuch as an ant can be said to "decide" anything) to move their bloated queen to a new lair. Worker ants clamoured around her, hoisted her up on their shoulders (insomuch as ants can be said to have shoulders) and carried her down the tunnels.

But when they arrived at the designated spot, the ants found themselves jammed into a narrow bottleneck. They shoved and pushed and shoved some more, until finally they succeeded in ramming their queen through the entrance. Unfortunately, in the process, they decapitated her. The mob didn't notice. And so, the headless queen was carried in and a nest was built around her. The queen, you see, still *smelled* like a queen and so the colony continued on, blithely unaware. The worker ants piled offerings of food before the slowly decaying shell of what had once been their sovereign. The smell of royalty became the stench of royalty, but did the ants care? Not at all. They had their queen and the colony was happy.

That's a true story, but the parable is implicit.

The Third Millennium is at hand, democracy is breaking out all over, the Cold War has ended, and the Baby Boomers are finally starting to die off. Things couldn't be better. And yet, for all these modern progressive forces blowing around us, Canada still has her Queen: Elizabeth II, Her Most Excellent Majesty and Sovereign of the United Kingdom of Great Britain and Northern Ireland and Her Other Realms, Head of the Commonwealth, Supreme Governor of the Church of England and Defender of the Faith.

Long Live the Queen! Long Live the Queen! Until she croaks, that is, then it's *Long Live the King! Long Live the King!* Yes, Charles will soon be our sovereign lord and our coins will have to be cut with two extra Mickey Mouse circles to accommodate his ears, which will cause havoc with vending machines across this great land—but no matter! Long live the monarchy! Huzzah, huzzah.

Here is what my Laotian friend Bouthien had to vow when he became a Canadian citizen:

I swear that I will be faithful and bear true allegiance to Her Majesty Queen Elizabeth the Second, Queen of Canada, Her Heirs and Successors, and I will faithfully observe the laws of Canada and fulfil my duties as a Canadian citizen.

Queen, law and then duty: in that order. What's wrong with this picture? Could it be that Canada—a multicultural mélange of Native, French, Scottish, Scandinavian, Chinese, German, Irish, Italian and African people (to name but a few)—is still under the figurehead rule of a dowdy Englishwoman in a funny hat? Is it just me, or does anyone else find it odd that a modern, pluralistic, democratic society—the very antithesis of Royal Rule, figurehead or otherwise—still clings to the shopworn remnants of its colonial past?

True, the Queen also symbolizes our membership in that most vital of organizations, the Commonwealth. Through it, Canada reaps untold benefits from having close ties with such economic powerhouse nations as Belize, Botswana, Western Samoa, Guyana, Gambia, Papua New Guinea, Swaziland, Brunei Darussalam, Lesotho, Tuvalu, Zimbabwe and, of course, Tonga. Critics may scoff at the usefulness of being a member of the Commonwealth (which, I should point out, has little in common and not a lot of wealth), but I say *pshaw!* Pshaw, I say! As any Canadian nationalist knows, the real advantage of being a member of the Commonwealth is that we get to simply clean up in medals at the Commonwealth Games—a kind of By Invitation Only Olympics, to which nations like China, Russia and the U.S. are not invited, allowing Canadian athletes to stomp all over those pesky little Papua New Guineans. At the Commonwealth Games, Canada rules!

Of course the Commonwealth also includes India, New Zealand and Australia, but Australia itself is now moving away from the monarchy and seems on the brink of declaring itself a republic. The Australians apparently woke up one morning—with a hangover no doubt—looked at a world map and said, "Hey, w'ya look at this! We're in Asia. We are an Asian nation. Instead of tying ourselves to a defunct ex-Empire, maybe we should think about integrating ourselves more into the Pacific Rim."

The Commonwealth is just another name for detritus. It is made up primarily of ex-possessions, like a group of emancipated slaves still hangin' around the plantation owner's dilapidated mansion.

Here is a hard fact for monarchists and nationalists alike to face: other than the Native caste, Canada has no class. This is a salient feature, a defining trait and a fine selling point. Canadians live in a land of unfolding opportunities, where the sperm of your great-great-grandfather doesn't necessarily dictate your own position in life; and if this is callow, it is also invigorating.

Britain, in sharp contrast, has a deeply entrenched, anachronistic system of Lords and Ladies and Dukes and Consorts and Doubloons and Purple Knights of the Royal Potty. Even today, Britain has titled absentee landlords who have crofters working their land like latter-day peasants.

Canada does not. The only Duchesses and Lords you will meet in Canada are in the psychiatric ward alongside Napoleon. People made noble simply by a quirk of birth—rather than any actual *achievement* or *ability* (foreign words in any class system)—have no place in a country like Canada. And what is the Royal Family but the highest point in a social hierarchy built on bloodlines: status by breeding, like show dogs. And the gene pool has been getting mighty shallow lately. Charles, with his Mr. Potato Head facial features, is like a poster boy of inbreeding, a laboratory experiment gone mad.

The incestuous aristocracy that lingers on in Britain and other European countries is part of their heritage, perhaps, but it is no longer a part of ours. We flirted with aristocracy, but fortunately it never took root. New France was established around a seigneurial system of landowners, Prince Edward Island was divided into feudalistic lots and auctioned off to absentee proprietors, and the Canadian Senate was originally meant to be reserved along bloodlines, like the British House of Lords. Being short on landed gentry, Canadians opted instead for patronage appointments. And patronage has been a proud a part of our heritage ever since.

We are a classless society and yet, on our coins and stamps and coat of arms, we still display the potentate symbols of Crown and Queen. If this were mere history, there would be little reason to object. But it isn't. The Royal Family is still with us, living breathing reminders of a predemocratic belief in hereditary rule.

It is little more than borrowed grandeur, but Canadians lap it up anyway. The Royals are a big hit in Canada. Indeed, I was warned that with this essay I would probably alienate 80 per cent of my readers—and that includes my Grandma, who will not hear a word spoken against the Queen and may never forgive me for my stance. Clearly then, with even our grandmothers against us, sullen-faced antimonarchists such as myself are vastly outnumbered.

The emperor may have no clothes, but in Canada it is considered very rude to point this out.

(I'll give you all a moment to try to mentally wipe out the image of the Queen without Her clothes on. A shot of whisky ought to help.)

As one might anticipate, the only ethnic group to oppose the notion of British Royalty is the francophone community. And rightly so. For more than 130 years, the French in Canada have been told that they are part of a new land, that they belong in Canada and should think of themselves as being a part of Canada. And all the while, our symbols of statehood are plastered with the benign image (in the sense that a tumour can also be benign) of a British ruler—a *foreign* ruler, a reminder not of Confederation but of conquest.

When Montréal hosted the Summer Olympics in 1976, the Queen showed up to officially open the Games—by pitching a javelin and then chugging a bottle of Molson's and belching out the national anthem. She finished with a lap around the stadium. It was all very exciting. But the Québécois were not amused.

The Queen faced assassination threats during a 1964 tour of Québec. Andrew and Sarah got booed by a handful of antimonarchists while in Québec City—until they started speaking French, a talent that few Canadian nationalists have mastered. And when the Queen planned a Canada Day tour of Hull in 1990, the mayor sent word that she was not welcome. Some PQ supporters turned their backs on Her Majesty's motorcade, but other than that not much happened. The visit went off fairly smoothly. More than a few francophone Canadians are actually in favour of the monarchy, seduced as they are by the glitz, glamour and sex scandals. As we all are.

Nothing diminishes Canadians more, and nothing re-asserts our self-abnegating colonial complex better, than our gawking, stumble-bum approach to a Royal Visit. On a recent tour by the Duke and Duchess of York, the ironi-cally named George Proud—a Liberal MP from Prince Edward Island—explained the subtle social intricacies of the elusive Royal Appeal. "We're the commoners," he said, "and they're the royalty, and I think that people in a strange way must secretly like that." *Strange* being the operative word. (Incidentally, I *am* related to Sarah Ferguson, past Duchess of York—but only in a "distant" way. Meaning, close enough to claim kinship, but not enough to be able to call her up and ask for money. Alas.)

Now, you would think that Canadians would have got-ten used to all the archaic rituals and taboos and demean-ing curtseys and snooty protocol surrounding a visit by the Royals—such as the quaint rule that allows only those officially designated to address Her Royal Highness. There have been well over 150 Royal Freeloader Tours through Canada since the end of World War II (the fight for democ-racy, remember?), but Canadians still get all goose-bumpily and tongue-tied whenever the Royal Dog and Pony Show comes to town. This often results in minor but amusing gaffes, such as during a 1992 jaunt through the Vancouver Aquarium when Diana was welcomed as "The Princess of Whales!" (Diana was later stripped of her royal title, HRH, by personal order of the Queen. It was a petty move on the Queen's part. Keep that in mind next time someone tells you how innately nice the Royal Family is.)

We aren't the only ones. When the wife of Australian Prime Minister Paul Keating refused to curtsey, and
then Keating himself actually dared to touch the small of
the Queen's back as he led her through a series of greet-
ings, the British press was outraged. "The Queen was not
amused last night after Australia's prime minister and his
wife subjected her to a new barrage of insults!" *Barrage of
insults?* Off with their heads, I say.

But, I hear you protest, the Royals are so Very Nice.
And well-mannered. To which I reply, they had damn well
better be. The Queen is the richest woman in the world—
in the world—with assets tallied at $13 billion U.S., miles
ahead of even Imelda Marcos, who weighs in at a paltry
$3 billion, poor dear. Prince Andrew, on top of all the
other perks and bonuses, gets a $300,000 allowance from
Mummy every year. Not bad for cutting ribbons and waving to the proles.

Of course, the Queen. Herself is a very hard-working
woman and is kept dreadfully busy what with her duties as
the Head of the Church of England, the Commonwealth
and various charity groups aimed at helping the great
unwashed. How about dishing out some of yer billions and
billions worth of loot, M'Lady? Until just a few years ago,
the Queen didn't even pay taxes. That's right, make $13
billion and never pay taxes! Call now!

The Royals do generate big bucks both at home and
abroad. Indeed, without them the entire Commemorative
Plate Industry would collapse overnight. But however Nice
they are and however many plates and gossip magazines
they sell, and however many worthwhile projects Charles
dabbles in, is all utterly irrelevant. The Royals represent
an idea whose time has long since passed. They are like

walking corpses, the standard-bearers—or rather, the pall-bearers—of a world view preserved in pickle brine and withered elitism.

Royalty is just crime with a pedigree. As Mark Twain pointed out, every crown and every kingdom was won through deceit, war, theft and bloodshed. Their descendants are no more worthy of respect than are the grandchildren of pirates and privateers. Royal tales are filled with swashbuckling adventures, eccentric villains and dashing heroes. But so are tales of piracy. I would sooner have the Jolly Roger fly over Canada than the Crown.

So why not give these Royal Leeches a good kick up the backside and make Canada Canada, and not a nation caught in stunted evolution somewhere between colony and country?

Arguments for Royalty usually hinge on history and tradition: Loyalist tradition and British history. Never mind that many of the Loyalists who fled the American Revolution to what is now Canada were not British but German, Italian and African, it is nonetheless true that the decisive aspect of Canadian history is that we resisted revolution and preserved ties with Mother Britain. A good deal of that, however, was more an abhorrence of extremist rhetoric and violence than it was undying loyalty to Crazy King George.

Canada does owe Britain an enormous cultural debt. Canada's British heritage has shaped the national character and has given us almost all of our national institutions, from representative parliamentary democracy to bad complexions and bland cuisine. Britain once had a magnificent, epic Empire and Canada was a part of it. But surely we can honour our British cousins in other less regressive ways. Isn't saying *zed* and writing *cheque* enough? Must we also accept the institution of Royalty and all the insidious assumptions about class and human values that it entails?

To make matters worse, many a Canadian nationalist harbours the bizarre fear that should we ever reject royalty, we would instantly mutate into Americans, as though the Canadian sense of self is so frail and delicate a bud that the only thing stopping it from being swallowed whole by the U.S. is an English lady in a funny hat. It is breathtaking how much importance Canadian nationalists pin on the Royals. Breathtaking, and in a way, sad.

In *The Canadian Forum,* columnist Heather Robertson goes even further:

> Without a hereditary queen, we would be prey to all the tacky pretenders who inflict their egomania on other nations of the world, and cause a lot of trouble until they are assassinated or deposed.

Never mind that a good many of the egomaniacs and tyrants who were assassinated or deposed were in fact the proud forebears of our current Queen. Robertson is only warming up. She goes on to assert that, although the Queen has no personal power, "the Crown is the foundation of Canadian political, legal and social practice, and the guarantor of our rights and freedoms."

Gosh. And you thought the Queen was just a figurehead. So the next time you have a run in with the power company, give Liz a call. She's your guarantor.

Because they are forced to defend something that is purely irrational, monarchists in Canada often do an amusing flip-flop of logic. On the one hand, they assert that the Queen is absolutely vital to our national institutions, as Heather Robertson did earlier. But then, when pressed on the issue of why Canadians should concede any rights of authority to someone based purely on heredity, they quickly say, "But the Queen is just a figurehead. Royalty doesn't have any real power or influence in Canada." So why keep it? If it has no power and no authority, why should we maintain it? Like a dog in pursuit of its own tail, monarchists will loop back to the "vital foundation of Canadian society" argument. In other words, the Queen is not important but she is. It's enough to make your head spin.

Let's get one thing straight. Royalty exists only through an act of wilful ignorance on the part of their subjects. Call it suspension of common sense. In the land of the blind, the one-eyed man is not king—he's an antimonarchist.

With or without the Royals, we are not Americans. Nor are we British. Or French. Or void. We are something else. And the sooner we define this, the better.

MY GRANDMOTHER PASSED away while I was in Japan. I miss her very much.

Grandma and I used wrangle endlessly over the monarchy, in free-wheeling discussions that were as much kinetic as they were verbal. After one of my more venomous diatribes, she shook her head in exasperation.

"There is no reason to get so angry about the monarchy," she said. "The Queen is just a symbol. And symbols are very important."

I couldn't agree more. Symbols *are* important. We must choose them with care.

DEATH
BY NICENESS

· · · · · ·

*A*S REPORTER Alan Freeman and con-
sultant Patrick Grady point out in
their book *Dividing the House,* the time to stop the separatist movement in Québec was thirty years ago. It was then
that Canada still had the option of "declaring the unity of
the Canadian federation inviolable, by outlawing the Parti
Québécois and never allowing a referendum on the issue."
But this could easily have provoked the kind of sectarian
violence seen in Northern Ireland or among the Basques
in France and Spain. "Whether deliberately or not, our
government has admitted that Québec can go if it decides
democratically to do so." In other words, we have been too
civil, too democratic, too *nice.*

Consider this: the separatists of the Bloc Québécois are all on the federal payroll. For three and a half years, they enjoyed the perks and frills of being a member of Her Majesty's Loyal Opposition, including the promise of a fat bloated pension once they retire. Take Jean Lapierre, who resigned from the Bloc Québécois in 1992, having worked long and hard to break up Canada. The Canadian government rewarded him for his efforts with a $40,000 a year pension until he dies. If he lives out his existence according to the average human life span, he will receive from the Canadian taxpayer, in salary, perks and pension, the equivalent of $4,000,000. Talk about chutzpah. I don't how Mr. Lapierre gets his pants on in the morning, he must have balls the size of ham-hocks.

That separatists are allowed to feed at the national trough, where in other countries they would have been arrested for sedition, is further proof that Canadians have pushed tolerance to the point of self-destruction. Indeed, it is a testament to Canadian tolerance that separatist leader Lucien Bouchard has been allowed to drag his sorry carcass across the political landscape for as long as he has. The fact that the separatists have not been rounded up and thrown in jail reflects well on Canadians.

Which brings us to the heart of the matter. Right up until the moment of actual secession, the separatists have all the advantages. They have a knife at Canada's throat and they know it. But their strength is drawn only from the *threat* of separation. At the very moment that separation becomes a fact, they will lose their power.

This simple truth is something that separatists refuse to accept. They believe that even after separation they will still enjoy the power and influence they had while in Confederation. Polls routinely show that 80 per cent of Québécois favour—and *expect*—an economic and monetary union with Canada in the wake of separation.

They used to call it Sovereignty Association, now it's just called sovereignty, but the intent is the same: separation by half steps. Why? Because most Québécois do not want outright separation. Just like the Bloc Québecois, they want all the perks and frills of Confederation with none of the responsibilities. Pandering to this desire, the separatists camouflage the truth of what will happen, promising that although everything will change, nothing will really change. Through common currency, passports and continued access to Ottawa's largesse, the separatists want a minimum of trauma. That is, not only do they want to split up the nation, they expect Canada to help make it is as painless and as safe as possible—*for Québec*. For us to agree to this would be like telling Québec "O.K. You can sodomize us, but only if you agree to wear a condom." They should call it for what it is. Sodomy Association.

Jacques Parizeau, the once would-be future Glorious President of the Free Republic of Québec, insists, common sense to the contrary, that "If Québec wants to keep the Canadian dollar, it will do so." And not only that, "The decision is Québec's to make." Yes, he assures his fellow Québécois, "We'll keep the Canadian dollar, even if the Canadians don't agree."

Many separatists also expect to continue receiving equalization payments as well. And why not? If you're going to make up a wish list, you might as well ask for the stars.

All this talk of money. Always money. The PQ is still convinced that the only reason they lost the referendum in 1980 and then again in 1995 was because the average Québécois was worried that his standard of living would drop should Québec leave Confederation. So the separatists now go to great pains to paint a rosy, prosperous future.

I am not so sure. I have always suspected that the reason the PQ keeps losing referendums has less to do with filthy lucre and more to do with a certain contrariness of character on the part of Québécois. Call it a survival skill. The Québécois have kept their language and culture alive through some dark times. It is a contrariness that is easily mobilized by separatists, but it also works against them. Quebeckers will not be stampeded into either assimilation *or* isolation. End result: stalemate.

The separatists' mistake was in wording The Question in the affirmative. They asked the people of Québec to say *oui!* to separation. Had they asked them instead to say *non!* to Canada, they might have gotten somewhere. It is easier to get Québécois to resist than agree. They voted *non* to sovereignty association in 1980, *non* to the Charlottetown Accord in 1992 and *non* to sovereignty-plus-passport-and-currency in 1995.

It is a stubbornness that I find wholly admirable. They survive better than they surrender. This is their greatest strength and, perhaps, their greatest single flaw. Either way, they deserve our respect as a people "that know not how to die." But the separatist leaders, as far as I'm concerned, deserve no such respect. They have misrepresented the consequences of their actions.

Separation means separation. No Canadian pensions, no Canadian currency, no Canadian passport, no automatic inclusion in NAFTA. (Such inclusion depends upon Canada's approval.)

Québec will also have to accept its share of the national debt, and when each percentage point equals roughly $4 billion, the stakes are high. Depending on the criteria used and whether you take a pragmatic or legalistic stance, Québec would be responsible for anywhere from $196.7 billion to $0. (Legally, Québec could refuse to accept any debt on the grounds that it was incurred in the name of Canada by the federal government, but this would damage Québec's credibility beyond repair.)

And then there are the Cree and Inuit of northern Québec, who claim a sparsely populated, wind-swept hinterland twice the size of France—and which also happens to include the James Bay hydro plants that supply almost half of Québec's energy. This gives the Cree and Inuit enormous leverage in any negotiation with Québec. Canada has been accused of fighting its battles through a Native proxy, and there is some truth to this. Let's face it, the only reason Canadians are suddenly fervently defending Native rights in the northern half of Québec is because it will piss off the separatists.

It is a lot of fun watching Québécois nationalists trying to grapple with their own sovereignty-minded ethnic minority. Here is separatist firebrand Pierre Bourgault in *Now or Never!* wrestling with the subtleties of this issue. His lack of perception borders on the breathtaking. (Try substituting "Québécois" for "Aboriginal," and see how far you get with Mr. Bourgault.)

[Aboriginal people] have abandoned all sense of reality, especially when they start calling upon ancestral rights that take them back to a bygone era, denying contemporary history in the process. They have a habit of forgetting that a lot of things have happened in the last 300 years . . .

No matter how the territory was conquered, the sons of the conquerors will never agree to being pushed into the sea. The aboriginal people will have to live with them whether they like them or not.

Arguing with separatists, Senator Jacques Hébert once observed, is like trying to talk politics with a Marxist-Leninist or religion with a Jehovah's Witness. It's a waste of energy. Separatism has indeed become a religion in Québec, one of black-and-white morality, uncompromising principles, crusades, enemies and a messianic future. It is also based largely on a call to race. *Québec pour les Québécois!*

The initial draft of Bill 101, Québec's first language law, defined Québécois as being *francophone* Quebeckers only, thereby stripping of citizenship the over half-million non-francophone residents of the province. The passage was eventually dropped, but the sentiment remains the same. My niece Aidan, though born and raised in Québec, will never be considered a *pure* Québécois.

Having thus defined the Chosen People, Québec nationalists must now define the enemy. This is easy: *les anglais,* that mythical, monolithic English presence looming in Montréal mansions and in wastelands beyond the provincial borders. With the birth rate of the "dyed in the wool" *pures laines* dropping, the siege is on. Of course, demographics also demonstrate that the drop in birth rates is a fluctuation and that French is not threatened within Québec, but none of that fits the dogma of fear, so it is discarded. Québec *could* replenish its population with French-speaking immigrants, say Haitians, Vietnamese, Lebanese, North Africans and Syrians, but these people aren't, ahem, *real* francophones. Remember, language is a smoke screen. The real issue is ethnic and racial identity.

Although capable of whipping themselves into a frenzy, the separatists have had trouble igniting the same hatred of *les anglais* among the general population. So the enemy has become, instead, the federal government. That is, Ottawa.

For those of you just joining the program: Canada has two levels of government, provincial and national, which act as counterweights. The federal government redistributes income among regions (the beloved equalization payments) and controls the military, foreign policy, monetary regulations, etc. etc. etc. yawn. Provincial governments control education, health care and something else that I forget but can't be bothered to look up. In many cases jurisdiction between federal and provincial matters overlaps. This is called "duplication of services" and is branded as something akin to the anti-Christ by separatist "thinkers." And that's about it. (There is more, but it's too boring to get into.)

The main point is that federalism is a system, not an ideology; it can be adjusted, it can be tinkered with. Albertans and Québécois may rant and rave that Ottawa is a tyrant, but the fact remains that among industrial nations, Canada is one of the most decentralized in existence. Attacking the federal system is like putting on a suit of armour and attacking a dessert tray. It's like mugging Santa Claus.

In a pluralistic society, federalism is a safeguard against the abuse of power. Canadian federalism has kept the French fact alive in North America. This is why Québec did not become another quaint Louisiana, folkloric and anglicized. Separatists go into apoplectic fits if you point this out to them. It's blasphemy. But true.

History, you see, is used selectively by Québec nationalists. The Conquest is, of course, their favourite lament, and make no mistake, French Canadians have suffered from callous Anglo arrogance for years. But Canada is no longer a British nation trying to impose its will on a French minority. *Les anglais* as a united ethnic tribe doesn't exist any more. But Québec nationalists are as obsessive as they are compulsive. Like someone home from the office, still remembering insults his boss made, livid with rage and coming up with endless comebacks and should-have-saids, the separatists carry their list of humiliations with them at all times, close to their hearts. The failures of Meech Lake and the Charlottetown Accord were only the latest in a long line of humiliations.

Separatists live in a strange world indeed, one of conspiracies and perpetual grievances. Examples abound, and for lovers of the absurd, there are many cases to choose from. One of the strangest occurred in November 1991, after Greenpeace protested the proposed flooding of huge tracts of Native hunting grounds by Québec Hydro, an act that would have created an artificial swamp/lake larger than Northern Ireland. The first phase of the project had already contaminated fish with mercury, and Greenpeace decided to launch a protest.

Yves Beauchemin, author and avowed intellectual nationalist, was indignant over an advertisement Greenpeace placed in the *New York Times,* and he wrote them an open letter that is so bizarre it is worth quoting at length. (In the passage, *Warriors* refers to the Mohawks who blocked construction of a golf course, and *Richler* is Mordecai Richler, the non-francophone Québec author who has been disowned by Québécois nationalists for refusing to take them seriously.) Here goes:

> Is this advertisement part of the smear campaign that has been unleashed over the past year, and which gathers momentum as the national liberation movement deepens here at home?
>
> Has Greenpeace signed on with the Trudeaus, the Richlers, and other Warriors whose goal seems to be to relegate Québec culture to the history books? In joining this great symphony of slander, have you taken the trouble to inform yourself about the conductor of that symphony? Some curious forces converge in these fanatical and widespread attacks, forces that seem to serve the interests of English Canada.
>
> You know as well as I do that certain parties are working ferociously hard to ensure that Québec independence dies in the delivery room so that the unity of this artificial and heterogenous Canada, which for Quebeckers has always proved to be more of an iron collar than a cradle, might be preserved. In this affair, the environment and the constitution make a suspicious blend.

Gosh. Iron collars. Symphonies of slander. Liberation movements. Who would have thunk it? Another chasm in perception is worth noting. For Beauchemin, a "heterogenous" nation is by definition a bad thing—gotta keep that blood pure—whereas for the rest of Canada it is something to be proud of. (For the record, Mr. Beauchemin is the same man who dismissed "French Canadians outside of Québec" as "still-warm corpses," thus rejecting the vibrant Acadian and Brayon cultures as well as francophone communities in Manitoba and northern Ontario. It reveals how utterly uniformed and profoundly stupid most separatists are.)

Where the separatists get positively hilarious, however, is when it comes to actually negotiating the terms of their departure. Here are the hard facts: Canada's population after separation would be 22 million to Québec's 7 million, a ratio of more than 3 to 1. The Canadian economy after separation would also outnumber Québec's 3 to 1. It is also more diversified and growing faster than the Québec economy. Furthermore, international law does not recognize the right of internal secession. Members of the United Nations, many of which face secessionist threats of their own, offer absolutely no support for Québec independence. There would be no rush to welcome Québec on board. Everything would depend on how negotiations go with the RC. For the first time in thirty years, Canada would have the upper hand.

Not that I am suggesting Canadians should be spiteful or vindictive or mean-spirited when negotiating with—fuck it. Let's be vindictive. Freeman and Grady argue that "a scorched earth policy between Canada and Québec won't help anyone," but I say, scorch the earth! Salt the fields! Unleash the hounds! If we have to negotiate the breakup of our nation, let's go kicking and screaming all the way. Let's make the separatist bastards pay. Let's go out with a bang, not a whimper.

But wait! What is that I hear? Could it be the timid worries of a post-separation Canada? Well, let's just hammer those fears down like a game of whack-a-mole. The big worry is that separation will make orphans out of Atlantic Canada. With this, comes a fear of annexation: that somehow the Atlantic provinces would be absorbed into America *against their will*. But the people of Newfoundland and the Maritimes are not separatists, nor are they pro-American. They are Canadians and they wish to remain Canadians. That is all there is to it. When commentators in Toronto fret over the breakup of Canada following the loss of Québec, they usually begin with the Atlantic provinces, as though Québec were some kind of glue holding them onto the rest of the nation. To make this assumption is to disparage the loyalties of Canadians in the Atlantic region. Nothing is more insulting to a Maritimer than to hear some central Canadian yutz predicting that Atlantic Canadians will be as quick to sell Canada short as the separatists of Québec.

And anyway, it's not like they'd be able to jump the queue. The Atlantic provinces would have to get in line behind Puerto Rico, Guam and the District of Columbia, all of whom have prior claims on statehood. So it looks like our Maritime brothers and sisters are stuck with us. Sorry. As for a Canada divided, a Canada cleaved down the middle, pessimists say it can't work. But Alaska, also separated by geography but still very much a part of the U.S., suggests otherwise.

Canada would be torn asunder only on *maps*. In real terms of loyalties, government and transregional identity, Canada would remain a nation. If anything, separation would bring the regions of Canada closer together, like a trauma survivors' support group. Remember, most trade routes now go through New England anyway, air travel is impervious to geographic anomalies and the trade rules of GATT—which Québec desperately wants to be a part of—guarantees freedom of transit.

Other alarmists ask, "What about the St. Lawrence?" Well, what about it? The St. Lawrence Seaway is an international passage. Québec cannot block the St. Lawrence, because the Americans, God bless them, would not stand for it.

A point that most Canadians and virtually every separatist misses is this: it is *Québec* which will be cut off from the outside world by separation, not Canada. At almost every turn, Québec trade routes would have to pass through Canadian territory. In the words of political scientist Albert Lagault, the Republic of Québec would be "nothing but a simple enclave within the much larger Canadian federation."

The only question remaining is this: Given that we could survive without Québec, is it really worth all the anxiety, all the concessions, all the heart-rending, hand-wringing pain just to keep them in Canada? *Absolutely*. Québec is worth all that and more. It is always better to be united than apart, always better to rise above divisions, always better to transcend differences. Separation would be the end of a grand and noble experiment. It would be a reversion to tribal thinking, and Canada would be poorer for it. Make no mistake, once they are gone, they are gone, and it will get us nowhere to pine over their departure, like a spurned lover driving past a window late at night and wondering if he still has a chance.

At times the surface tension of the separatist threat seems like a pressure cooker. High-stakes poker, eyeball to eyeball. *Are they bluffing? Should we call it?* Sometimes it seems that the threat of impending breakup is the only thing that gives Canadian politics a pulse. But at other times, as we sweep up the ticker-tape and campaign buttons of yet another rally/march/referendum/forum, it seems like the stalest game in town.

And so, onward we teeter, not so much walking as sustaining a fall. A country cursed by kindness.

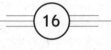

GIVING CANADA A GOOSE:
ASTUTE PREDICTIONS
AND ALTERNATIVE ENDINGS

. . . .

*A*s WELL as having a deep sensitivity to Native issues (see previous chapter), Pierre Bourgault also demonstrates a certain flair for prophecy. In his 1990 separatist manifesto *Now or Never!*, Bourgault assures us that "Jean Chrétien is finished." (Two years later Chrétien was elected prime minister with one of the largest majorities in Canadian history, including solid support in Québec.) Bourgault also tells us that Québec may very well have separated by the time his book goes to print, such is the acceleration of events. That was in 1990. Well, Mr. Bourgault, it's been more than seven years, and if not *Now!* then . . .

A sense of pre-orgasmic urgency shapes *Now or Never!* and it seems to have shaken Mr. Bourgault to near incoherence. He ends his manifesto thusly:

NOW!

NOW!

NOW!

When I was growing up, we used to have a little, highstrung dog named Meeko. If you got Meeko too excited—petted him too much, that kind of thing—he would start peeing uncontrollably. I imagine many separatist writers in a similar way; their legs crossed, bodies shaking, hands trembling, as they peck away at their typewriters. (If I mock the separatists, it is only because they are so very mockable.)

Political economist Georges Mathews, meanwhile, closes his book *Quiet Resolution* with his own insightful predictions. It runs like this: Québec's leaders declare independence unilaterally and coolly out-negotiate the bumbling Canadian federalists. Congratulations pour in from France and America.

Mathews's fantasy continues. Chrétien is dismissed as "the wrong man at the wrong place at the wrong time" and leaves the House of Commons with "tears in his eyes." The premier of Québec, meanwhile, "is lavished with praise."

Not only does Mathews see Canada allowing Québec to take possession of all federal assets in Québec, he also imagines Canada permitting the Republic of Québec to continue using Canadian money. He mentions this something like four times.

Mr. Mathews's mystic vision of *Quiet Resolution* (published in 1990) is set far ahead in the future, in 1991. As always, Separatist Logic imagines that Québec will stride onto the world stage having completely humbled and out-manoeuvred the RC, after which a glorious New Day will dawn. Separatist books are always so much *fun* to read. They're like the old pulp science-fiction stories. "And we'll all live in cities on the moon!"

Let me counter with a different scenario:

- A province outlaws one of Canada's accepted languages, restricting schools and denying children education in their mother tongue.
- The prime minister, a Quebecker considered "too English" by the French and "too French" by the English, struggles to defuse the situation. It goes to court, but this only inflames the issue. French-Canadian nationalism grows.
- Just three years earlier, provincial premiers met to demand (A) Senate reform to better represent the regions, (B) larger federal subsidies, and (C) expanded provincial powers.
- Some Québécois consider Confederation a safeguard and argue in favour of a bilingual nation "united in a feeling of brotherhood." Others, however, consider federalism a dead issue, washed up and wasted.
- A book written by a francophone Quebecker espouses separation and envisions a future with an independent Québec.

Sound familiar?

The year was 1896. The oppressive language laws were not enacted by Québec, but by Manitoba, denying Franco-Manitobans fair access to education in their own language.

This violated the spirit of Confederation as well as the explicit provisions of the Manitoba Act, which was meant to protect the French language.

Faced with growing provincial powers, Ottawa stalls. The language issue goes to the Supreme Court, which declares the anti-French laws unconstitutional, but Manitoba merely ignores the ruling.

Earlier, the provincial premiers had outlined their demands for greater autonomy, led by Honoré Mercier, the premier of Québec. Confederation is deemed a failed experiment. Canada is too big, too diverse, too unwieldy.

Wilfrid Laurier is elected prime minister, but the Manitoba School issue is still unresolved. A weak compromise is reached, but it pleases no one.

Editor Henri Bourassa, meanwhile, is demanding that Canada accept its bilingual nature and respect its diversity. English Canadians, considering themselves an ethnic nation, see the French as merely the refuse of a nation whose time has passed, condemned to be assimilated. Bourassa's vision of the nation as a unifying force seems doomed by petty regionalism and the call for a homogeneous nation-state—in this case, by English Canadians.

At around this time, author Jules-Paul Tardivel writes a futuristic novel, *Pour la patrie* (1895), about a separate French homeland. The two strains of French-Canadian national thought, still with us today, are thus defined by Bourassa and Tardivel: one federalist and outward looking, the other separatist and inward looking.

This all occurred a hundred years ago.

Remember that the next time separatists tell us, "Whether we like it or not, Canada is bound to split up." Or when they tell us that for Québec, "Confederation by itself, as far as our national interests are concerned, has been nothing but a miserable bankruptcy, a bitter, humiliating deception." Remember it too when they assure us that "Canadians are at a crossroads" and that the separation of the provinces is the best alternative.

Oh, yes. Just in passing, those first two quotations are from Jean-Marie-Rodrigue Villeneuve, an intellectual nationalist writing in 1922. The last observation, that Canada is at a crossroads and separation is imminent, was made by Antonio Perrault in 1924, more than seventy years ago.

It would seem, like Mark Twain's famous response on seeing his own obituary, that reports of our death have been greatly exaggerated.

MORE SCIENCE FICTION. In the aftermath of Referendum '95, I was rummaging around in a secondhand bookstore when I came across a faded paperback by Richard Rohmer. Written back in 1981 and entitled *Separation Two,* it promised a "chilling and plausible vision of a future that may await this nation." Figuring it might be good for a laugh, I bought the book and spent the afternoon reading through its yellowed, pulp-fiction pages. This book had everything: evil Calgary oil tycoons, Italian hit-men, PLO terrorists, Arab sheiks and—of course—a referendum on Québec sovereignty. (What action-packed thriller would be without one?) The book was pure fiction, but the ending was not. In it, Québec separatists are narrowly defeated by a tally of 51.7 per cent to 48.3 per cent. The real results of a referendum held fourteen years later? 50.6 per cent to 49.4 per cent. Rohmer was only off by 1.1 per cent. Is that creepy, or what? Mind you, this was the same man who wrote a novel set in the near future about Canada and the United States going to war—and Canada winning!

So clearly, prophecy is a tricky business, especially for anyone writing about something as volatile as Québec. If, for example, I predict that Lucien Bouchard will lead Québec to separation and that Canada will fall apart, I risk sounding hopelessly out of date if—instead of breaking up Canada—Bouchard, say, gets hit by a meteor from Mars and is squashed flat. In which case, you might very well be reading this book amid wild public celebrations across Canada, and I'll look like an idiot.

As Bloc-Head Québécois leader Gilles Duceppe so memorably put it during the 1997 federal election, "I don't want to predict anything—especially the future." (A statement that ranks right up there with the best of Yogi Berra.)

That's the problem with the future: it hasn't happened yet.

And no matter how many times people like Bouchard assure us that separation is inevitable, or people like Preston Manning insist that it's all a big bluff, they do not have any better idea than the rest of us. We are all walking into this thing called tomorrow blindfolded.

How then to transcend the very boundaries of space and time? How can I avoid having my own nationally acclaimed best seller become hopelessly out of date, like some half-empty carton of eggnog two months after Christmas?

Faced with this formidable challenge, faced with the explosive and highly unpredictable nature of Canada's future, I have come up with an inspired solution: *multiple endings.*

Here's how it works. Say you are reading this in the middle of February 1999. Or 2008. Or whatever, the date doesn't matter. Just look down the list of options presented below and find the one which best suits the situation that Canada is now facing at the very moment that you are reading this book. Having made your selection, you may then refer to my uncannily accurate and remarkably prescient observations.

That's right, *Why I Hate Canadians* will *never* go out of date. It's foolproof!

Ending A: Québec separates and Canada is plunged into panic and Constitutional crisis. *Uncannily Accurate and Remarkably Prescient Observations:* "See! I told you Canada was doomed. Doomed, I tell you! We should have outlawed separatism and imprisoned Bouchard when we had the chance."

Ending B: The PQ are ousted, separatism is defeated, and Canada enters a Golden Age of tolerance and bilingual unity. *Uncannily Accurate and Remarkably Prescient Observations:* "See! I told you the separatists were a spent force, all bark and no bite. *Vive le Québec!* Québec is the greatest!"

Ending C: Nothing is resolved, the separatists are still lurking in the wings, and Canada muddles through. *Uncannily Accurate and Remarkably Prescient Observations:* "See! I told you! Canada is a self-sustaining conundrum, unworkable and unsolvable."

Ending D: Lucien Bouchard is struck by a meteor from Mars and is squashed flat. By amazing coincidence, a second meteor takes out Preston Manning. *Uncannily Accurate and Remarkably Prescient Observations:* "Champagne for everyone!"

Part Four

SEX IN A CANOE

AND OTHER DELUSIONS

. . . .

ON BEING CANADIAN:

AN INVENTORY

· · · · · · · ·

*P*IERRE BERTON once defined a Canadian as "someone who knows how to make love in a canoe." But John Robert Colombo was quick to correct him: "A Canadian is someone who *thinks* he knows how to make love in a canoe."

So far we have dealt with some of the larger delusions and fixations that define us, and what do we have?

1. Oh, those Americans! They make me so mad.
2. The Queen rah, rah.
3. French on our Cheerio boxes.
4. _____

  (in reference to Native Canadians.)

This is, of course, only the short list. We could also add Mounties, Moose and Molson's. Hockey brawls. Using steroids. Being really smug about the fact that Red Rose Tea is available only in Canada. And getting heart palpitations by drinking thirty-seven cups of Tim Hortons coffee a day (plus doughnuts). We can also add Kraft Dinner, baby pablum and frozen food to our list of Canadian accomplishments. Our symbols are equally as varied: Maple Leaves. Maple Trees. Maple Sap. Maple Syrup. Maple Sugar. Maple Pie. Maple Soup. Maple Cheese. And just all-round Mapleness.

Consider the following a test of nationality then, a check list to see how Canadian you truly are. There is the Group of Seven. Cirque du Soleil. Lacrosse. Harlequin Romance. Anne of Green Gables. Sunshine Girls (Canada's chaste version of Britain's Page Three Girls). Totem poles. Bonhomme Carnaval. The Calgary Stampede. The Big Owe. Casa Loma. The Confederation Bridge. The Centennial Everything. Mainstream "fringe" festivals. Inuit art. Trivial Pursuit. Pissing off the French. Maria Chapdelaine. Stompin' Tom. And Marc Garneau (who brought a hockey puck with him into outer space; is that Canadian or what?).

There is also screech. Poutine. Saying "eh?" a lot. Mumbling the words to "O Canada" (but in a proud way). Harbouring Nazi war criminals. Pretending to enjoy Cape Breton fiddle music. Going over Niagara Falls in a barrel. Showing up at the U.S. border in December wearing Bermuda shorts and shades, asking "Where is all the sun?" Being baffled by Marshall McLuhan. Being baffled by Leonard Cohen. Being baffled by Red Green. Being generally baffled. Hating Toronto. Moving to Toronto. Wishing you could move to Vancouver. Staying in Toronto. Hating Vancouver.

You know you are Canadian when someone says "Elvis" and you think "figure skating." If you get most of your current events by watching *This Hour Has 22 Minutes* (remove the punch lines and you have a pretty good news broadcast), you are a Canadian. And that's not all.

There is also clubbing baby seals. Discovering insulin. Drinking Canada Dry. Knowing how to spell Gzowski. Knowing how to *pronounce* Gzowski. Knowing who the hell Gzowski is in the first place. Worshipping Donovan Bailey. Taking credit for absolutely everything: the telephone, basketball, the airplane, the wheel, Big Bird, *Saturday Night Live*. Wearing tuques at a jaunty angle. Being really proud of the CN Tower. Understanding Celsius. Using the loonie. Being secretly fascinated by the twonie. Having a passionate but doomed crush on Dini Petty. Having an equally doomed crush on Valerie Pringle (the Mary Tyler Moore of Canadian broadcast journalism). Attending Royal Commissions. Wearing wool socks during sex—not because it's cold but just because it's chic. Getting all sentimental over Robert Munsch. Missing *The Beachcombers*. Knowing almost all the words to the *King of Kensington* theme song. Feeling a deep affinity with snow. Owning at least one book by Pierre Berton. Riding toboggans. Sharpening skates. Freezing pucks. And more: The Sasquatch. The Ogopogo. The Canadarm. The Guess Who.

As you can see, the list of Canadian cultural touchstones is endless. Why, you would need a book, an entire book, just to skim the surface of the vast and fascinating field of Things Canadian. What follows then is the meagrest of samplings, a cross section of Canadian icons and delusions, from Beavers to Superheroes, from Shopping Malls to the Myth of the Natural Canadian and our Obsession With Size.

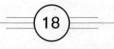

THE MIGHTY BEAVER

. . . .

*L*ET'S BEGIN our assault on Canadian icons with the easiest target we can find: the slow-moving, dimwitted *Castor canadensis,* Canada's largest rodent and furriest national icon.[1]

Could Canadians have chosen a *less* inspiring emblem? The Russians have a bear, the Americans a bald eagle, the British a lion rampant—and Canada? Canada has a beaver. If you want to play a round of Could'a Had, the list is long. We *could'a had* a timber wolf. Or a polar bear. Or a bison. Or a lynx. Or even the conveniently named Canada goose. But no, we got stuck with a 30-kilogram, bucktoothed rodent whose most heroic trait is that he thinks to slap his tail to warn his buddies before he runs away.

---

1.   With the possible exception of Farley Mowat.

I suppose beavers are kind of cute in their own water-logged, rodentesque way, but they certainly aren't up for any Rin Tin Tin Animal Aptitude Awards either. Here is a creature that lives in Canada and does not have the good sense to hibernate during winter. Instead, beavers stock up on branches and tree bark and huddle inside their lodges until spring, when they reappear—fat as ever—blinking into the sunlight and stretching. Sound familiar? Just add beer and cable TV to the equation and you have the average Canadian approach to winter survival. In this, then, the beaver does exude a certain Canadian-like charm, but appearances to the contrary, this is *not* why he is our National Rodent.

Nor was he chosen because of his industriousness. This is the Great Canadian Beaver Lie, and it is usually first encountered in elementary school, when impressionable young waifs are taught that the beaver is our national symbol because he is "hard-working, peaceful, honest and kind." (No kidding, I once had a teacher tell me that beavers were "honest.")

The myth of the industrious beaver has a long lineage. A 1715 map of British North America portrays an entire work crew of beavers, complete with foremen, labourers, medics and carpenters. The beavers walk erect and in single file, carrying stacked wood in their armlike forepaws and dragging rocks on their tails.

In 1820, Joseph Sansom, a member of the American Philosophical Society, published a book entitled *Travels in Lower Canada*. In it, he writes at great length about the social habits of the beaver. Sansom had a definite "republican bias."

He [the beaver] is a pattern of conjugal fidelity and paternal care. Laborious, thrifty, frugal, watchful, and ingenious. He submits to government in the republican form for the benefits of political association; but is never known, in the most powerful communities, to make depredations upon his weaker neighbours... Wherever a number of these animals come together, they immediately combine, in society, to perform the common business of constructing their habitations; apparently acting under the most intelligent design.

No one today would take these descriptions literally, but the basic premise lives on in the notion that the beaver is a symbol—and an ideal—of Canadian industriousness.

It's sad, really, that a nation would try to emulate a fat, flat-tailed rodent. Sadder still that we don't measure up. Canadians, after all, are not exactly renowned for being as busy as the proverbial beaver. (*Esquire* magazine once asked the question, "Are you dead, or just Canadian?") Beavers, in contrast, hurry about all autumn long, chewing trees, damming streams and building nifty lodges with secret James Bond–type underwater entrances. Canadians simply cannot relate to that kind of work ethic.

Our national anthem may describe Canada as "a land of hope for all who toil," but others have not been quite so generous. In *Oh Canada! Oh Québec!*, novelist Mordecai Richler, never one to pull a punch, made the following observation:

[F]or the most part Canadians, a notoriously lazy bunch, still live off the riches we were fortunate enough to stumble on here in the first place. Our prosperity, such as it is, is based on what we can dig or pump out of the ground or harvest from its surface or the surrounding seas.

Interestingly enough, Adolph Hitler expressed similar sentiments about Canada. In a 1940 Berlin address, der Führer noted:

In Canada... there are 2.6 persons per square mile; in other countries perhaps 16, 18, 20, or 26 persons. Well, no matter how stupidly one managed one's affairs in such a country, a decent living would still be possible.

Hitler and Richler are about as far apart as any two people could possibly be, yet on this they agree: Canadians are not so much "busy beavers" as they are "lucky bastards."

This discrepancy between the reality and the myth was best captured in the Montréal Beaver Club, a society founded in 1785 and dedicated to drinking, carousing and general debauchery. Its motto? *Industry and Perseverance*. Members of the club honoured said Industry and Perseverance by awarding themselves large gold medals and then getting drunk, pausing every now and then to raise a toast to the king and to the beaver and to the mother of all the saints and to their children and wives and absent friends and—well, you get the idea. Laborious, thrifty, frugal and watchful they were not.

The beaver has had his share of detractors as well. Not everyone found him honest and hard-working. When the ultra-right wing of the Québec Conservative Party adopted the name "Castors" in the 1870s, their opponents mocked them in the House of Commons:

> What then is a Castor?. . . In the country those little black beasts who live in bands upon the surface of stagnant waters spreading an odour which there is nothing less agreeable, the water skunks, are also called Castors.

Black beasts? *Water skunks?* How did such a creature ascend the heady heights of glory and national pride, especially considering the fact that he has webbed toes?

The beaver has even entered the realm of the mystical. Canada's Parliament Buildings are said to be home to the phantom Great Beaver. The Great Beaver has never actually been seen, but his existence in folklore is firmly established. Visitors often ask to see the Keeper of the Beaver during tours of the House of Commons. This drives tour guides right up the wall.

Enshrined in urban legends such as these, its likeness pressed into pocket change and used to sell everything from athletic wear to two-by-fours, the beaver is an all-Canadian, all-purpose icon. And in 1975, the beaver's place was finally, officially honoured, when the Parliament of Canada recognized the furry creature as "a symbol of the Sovereignty of the nation."

But the question remains: If not for their industriousness, why did *Castor canadensis* come to embody the spirit and esteem of an entire nation?

Well, at the risk of sounding melodramatic, the beaver paid for his fame with his skin. Or rather, his pelt. He was a victim of fashion, you see. Fashion and biology. The beaver has a two-layered coat: a coarse and oily outer one to keep the water out, and a soft and thick underpelt to keep the warmth in. It was the soft underpelt of the Canadian beaver that caught on with the hat-makers of Europe in the early 1600s, and beaver hats became all the rage. Because the finest pelts were culled from colder climates where they were naturally thicker, traders and trappers were motivated to push deeper and deeper into the wild expanses of the Northwest, away from the warmer climes of the American colonies and into the heartland of what would one day be Canada.

It was neither Aztec gold, nor Asian opium, nor Arabian spices that *our* explorers and adventurers pursued. It was a giant aquatic rat, the largest rodent on the continent, the second largest in the world. The mighty, majestic beaver.

So eager were these early Europeans that they willingly paid top dollar for the old, secondhand coats that Indians had been wearing. As the pelts were worn and slept on, the outer hair fell off, making them useless in the rain. Instead of tossing them away, the Indians quickly discovered that they could sell them for huge profits to white traders. The Indians thought this was hilarious.

As the demand grew, traders began buying new pelts and in larger and larger quantities, which drew Native trappers into a market relationship. And, like the rustic, intuitive conservationists that these early traders and their Native suppliers were, they trapped the beaver right to the brink of extinction. By 1820 the beaver was almost gone.

Fortunately, it was not the fate of the beaver to end up like Ecuador's condor or America's bald eagle—poignant national symbols struggling to survive. If nothing else, the beaver was still a rodent, and rodents die hard. Throughout the dark years of the fur trade, the beaver valiantly hung on (honest *and* valiant!) and at last, just when things were at their bleakest, like some glorious *deus ex machina,* fashion changed. Around 1830, silk hats became popular, and the hat-makers of Europe sent traders scrambling to the Orient as the price for beaver pelts plummeted. But by then, the hinterland had been opened up and the beaver was already a part of Canadian folklore. (The Chinese, showing considerably more restraint than Canadians, resisted the temptation to designate the silkworm larva as *their* national emblem.)

As the fur trade went into a long, slow decline, settlers moved in and pushed back the already diminishing habitats of the wolf, the lynx and the black bear, the beaver's only natural enemies—other than hat-makers.

Beavers began to repopulate and eventually *over*populate their environs. And later, when the Europeans—suddenly all remorseful and mushy and Greenpeacefully aware—decided that fur wasn't fashionable *at all,* the price per pelt toppled to the point where it was hardly worth the effort to trap them. Even global warming has played a part in saving the beaver, as Canadians themselves are buying fewer and fewer fur coats, and even fewer hats.

Today, beavers have overpopulated to such an extent that they now skirt the streams and waterways of Greater Suburbia itself, wreaking havoc with city water supplies and sewer lines, damming rivers, and flooding forests and farmers' fields. They have gnawed down rows of poplar trees that were planted to protect topsoil from wind and rain erosion, and they have even managed to wash out the

Trans-Canada Highway in Manitoba—a province where the beaver population may soon surpass the dwindling number of *human* inhabitants.

In 1991 alone—the last year for which I could find figures—the Manitoba government spent over $200,000 on its war against the beaver, most of it going towards dynamite to blow up dams in an unapologetic Kill-a-Beaver Pogrom which has, naturally, raised some ethical questions.

Ed "Just Doin' My Job" Engen of the Manitoba Department of Natural Resources is caught in the middle. After all, the beaver is not just *any* pest. "The animal-rights people get emotional and say we're killing Canada's national symbol," says Ed in an interview with the *Christian Science Monitor.*

"Beavers," writes columnist Stewart Macleod in *Maclean's,* "are the only members of the animal kingdom with the capacity to pit environmentalist against environmentalist. Just how do you deal with a fur-bearing creature whose Protestant work ethic is totally dedicated to the destruction of trees—with nothing better in mind than perhaps washing away the odd cottage?"

Yes, the Emblem of Canada has become a pain in the ass. A fat, furry, bucktoothed, waddle-happy, tree-gnawin', tail-slappin', dimwitted, hard-workin', web-toed, no-longer-in-fashion, right royal pain in the ass.

And you just gotta love him for it.

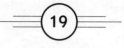

SUPERMAN VS.
CAPTAIN CANUCK

. . . .

*L*ET'S LAY one myth to rest right now: Superman is *not* a Canadian. He's from the planet Krypton.

We have got to stop claiming the Man of Steel as a Canadian icon. It's embarrassing. He is not "a part of our heritage," no matter how much we insist. Marsha Boulton's otherwise excellent book, *Just a Minute: Glimpses of Our Great Canadian Heritage,* devotes an entire chapter to Superman and even features him on the cover right alongside Jacques Cartier and Laura Secord. I repeat: Superman is not a Canadian.

One of his creators, Joe Shuster, was born in Toronto, but he moved to Cleveland, Ohio, at the age of nine, and it was there, years later, that he developed the Man of Steel with writer Jerry Siegal. Superman's mild-mannered alter ego, Clark Kent, originally worked at a newspaper called the *Daily Star,* an allusion to the *Toronto Daily Star.* But one of Shuster's editors changed it to the *Daily Planet,* and that was the last of any Canadian content to be found in Superman. Since his debut in 1938, Superman has been the "defender of Truth, Justice, and the *American* Way."

When *Superman: The Movie* was filmed in 1978, the Canadian connection resurfaced. Lois Lane was played by Margot Kidder, an actress originally from Yellowknife, and Superman's father was played by Québec-born Glenn Ford. The city of Calgary, with its shiny towers and lack of graffiti, became Metropolis. And Smallville, Superman's boyhood home, was in fact High River, Alberta, the real-life home town of Joe Clark. Joe, as you may recall, was Prime Minister of Canada in the late '70s and early '80s. (That is, from June 1979 to March 1980, a grand total of nine months. Pregnancies have lasted longer than Joe Clark's Reign of Power.) *Clark* Kent. Joe *Clark.* The same home town. Coincidence? I think not.

I have this theory that Canadians elected Joe Clark because they were convinced his bumbling, awkward manner was but a ruse. We secretly believed that one day Joe would rip open his shirt, scattering buttons, and reveal his true super-identity! With baited breath, we waited for the moment to arrive. And waited. And waited... And waited...

Alas, poor Joe never did transform himself, and we had to face the fact that we had no Superman to defend us. We were heroless. Hopeless. Alone. *But wait!* What's that sound? Faster than a speeding ballet, stronger than a local motif, able to leap Royal Commissioners in a single bound, could it be? *Yes!* It's Johnny Canuck, Canada's very own action guy!

Johnny Canuck personified Canada in much the same way that Uncle Sam represented the U.S. and John Bull, Britain. But where John Bull was fat and Uncle Sam lanky and old, Johnny Canuck was barrel-chested, fit and youthful, symbolizing the promise and purity of a new land.

Johnny Canuck first appeared in a political cartoon, kicking Uncle Sam in the ass. (More correctly, a *forerunner* of Johnny Canuck, labelled "Young Canada.") The year was 1869 and Canada, only two years after Confederation, had just finished repelling the American-backed Fenian Raids, so feelings were riding high. Later Johnny Canuck and Uncle Sam would become fine friends. "Bend over, Johnny," Uncle Sam would say, "I want to tell you about Free Trade."

Johnny Canuck evolved into a strong-jawed, trim-moustached he-man who wore a khaki uniform and a wide-brimmed stetson, much like the hat worn by the Mounties. He was a pioneer—pious, proud and just about as bland as you can imagine. He was also clearly meant to be an *English*-Canadian. (The French equivalent was Jean Baptiste, named in reference to the patron saint of Québec.)

"The heyday of Johnny Canuck was a long one," writes author Ken Lefolii in *The Canadian Look,* "from the 1870s until World War I."

But then came the roaring twenties. With the rise of Hollywood, prohibition, gangsters and flappers, dependable ol' Johnny was beginning to look rather out of date.

In the United States, the comics were coming of age with the advent of full-length, colour comic "books": Buck Rogers, Prince Valiant, Dick Tracy, and, of course, Superman. Heroes were bursting out all over the U.S., yet very few were being produced in Canada. Convinced perhaps that all the exciting stuff happened south of the border, Canadians preferred their adventures imported from the U.S.A. Their heroes became our heroes.

The American comic boom was at its peak when World War II began, so the shock was great when the Canadian government included comic books in its ban on all non-essential imports from the U.S. Early in 1941, American comic books disappeared from our nation's shelves and stayed off until 1945. This short four-year period would prove to be Canada's one and only Golden Age of Comics.

Canadian artists and publishers rushed to fill the demand. A former sign-painter named Cyril Bell hired more than sixty young artists to crank out seven different titles featuring dozens of heroes every month. Gallant Canadians like Ace Barton, Spanner Preston, Captain Red Thorton, Thunderfist, The Brain and The Invisible Commando bravely battled the forces of evil as represented in crude, racial caricatures of our wartime enemies, the Germans and the Japanese.

The comics were called "Canadian whites" because, unlike American comics, they were printed in black and white, with only the covers in colour. Many of the heroes and story lines were lifted directly from American comic books, but most—like *Dixon of the Mounted!*—used distinctly Canadian themes and imagery. One of the most imaginative was Canada's answer to Wonder Woman:

Nelvana of the Northern Lights, Daughter of Koliak, King of the North. Nelvana protected Canada's Inuit from the evil encroachments of the Kablunets (from the Inuktitut word *kabluna,* meaning "white man"). Adrian Dingle, the young illustrator who created Nelvana, based his heroine on an Inuit legend told to him by Franz Johnston, one of the Group of Seven painters. In Inuit tradition, Nelvana is a shamaness who commands the Northern Lights and can make herself invisible. Dingle, of course, added some embellishments, such as putting Nelvana in a miniskirt and having her fight Nazis on occasion.

But best of all, the ban on American comics brought back Johnny Canuck. Liberated from editorial cartoons and immigration poster propaganda, Johnny was now "Canada's answer to Nazi oppression!" With no secret powers save pluck and a masculine physique, Johnny punched his way across Axis Europe, wreaking havoc and justice wherever he went. "Fools," cries der Führer, "You promise arrest but dot svine Canuck goes on destroying our war machine!"

Our Johnny was pure of heart, deft of hand, and rakish as well. He never punched a bad guy without saying something pithy beforehand. Face to face with Hitler, Johnny says coolly, "I guess it's time to pull up stakes, but I'll leave this with you Adolph old pal." And *pow!* he wallops der Führer right in the kisser. Captured by the Gestapo, Johnny bursts free in an instant, and the caption reads, "The Germans had better start making stronger rope if they want to hold Canadians captive!"

The man behind Johnny Canuck's resurrection was a fifteen-year-old high school student from Toronto named Leo Bachle. Leo modelled Johnny's face on his own and drew some of the Nazi henchmen to resemble his less popular teachers. Talk about wish fulfilment. "Give me a D in geography will you?! *Pow!*"

Seen through the eyes of a Canadian comic-book aficionado, the Armistice was a disaster. With the end of the war, Canada's short-lived pantheon of heroes and heroines was unceremoniously dumped. In *Comic Relief,* popular historian John Herd Thompson writes: "Profit, not patriotism, had inspired their publishers to produce them. When wartime exchange controls were eased to allow printing mats to be imported from the U.S., Canadian comic book publishers laid off their artists and simply reprinted American comics."

Bell Features tried to keep Johnny Canuck and some of their more popular comic books going, even importing colour presses to compete head-on with the Americans, but the Wartime Prices and Trade Board that was still in operation refused to renew Bell's newsprint quota. So Johnny Canuck faded away, not the victim of Hitler or Goebbels but of Canadian bureaucrats. Such an ignoble, yet somehow appropriate, end to a Canadian hero.

For thirty years Canada was left unprotected. And as you know, a nation without superheroes is a nation vulnerable to the whim of every mad scientist and alien overlord who shows up. Those were dark days indeed. But then, suddenly, in the summer of 1975, Johnny Canuck burst back on the scene. It had been a long time alright, but Johnny was spry as ever. In the interim he had acquired a mask, a new name and even a promotion; he was now *Captain* Canuck, "Canada's superagent of the future!" and the stories were set in those heady, futuristic days of 1993 when everyone drives hovercars and Canada has become an "essential world power."

"Rest assured," wrote the publishers, "Captain Canuck will be as heroic defending the Canada of the future as Johnny Canuck was defending the Canada of the past."

They weren't kidding, either. Captain Canuck was locked into a 1940s morality. Just like Johnny, he had no superpowers, but relied instead on clean living and large biceps to save the day. In the second issue, they tell us, "Captain Canuck's tremendous strength and endurance comes from a good wholesome diet and lots of exercise. His alertness and determination come from having a strong, clean mind." But then, in issue five, they decided that really the Captain's strength came from space aliens. It was all very confusing to a twelve-year-old like myself, but at least it was Canadian.

And Canadian it was! Together with his trusty partners Kebec and Redcoat, Captain Canuck helped put down insurrections in northern Saskatchewan and an attempted invasion of Canada's Arctic. In the very first issue (which I am hoping will become a collector's item some day so that I can sell it), Captain Canuck rides a dog sled across the frozen arctic wastelands, leading hundreds of young readers to ask, "What, no hoversleds in 1993?"

When a villainous mastermind captures Captain Canuck and tells him about his secret plan to take over Canada by inciting civil war, Captain Canuck defiantly replies, "Not in Canada! The worst we'd have is the War Measures Act! Then the Army would be every where!" So the evil mastermind hatches Plan B: forming a new political party. (Is this Canadian, or what?)

Comely Comix, which produced Captain Canuck, was the brain child of Richard Comely, who drew, edited, inked and wrote the early issues. Richard Comely was also a Mormon, and the religious undercurrents tended to get in the way of the action, if you know what I mean. Here is an excerpt from Issue #2, The Brain Machine:

> *General:* This assignment begins now! Have you anything to add before you go Captain?
> *Captain Canuck:* Just one, General: Permission to have a word of prayer, before we start.
> *General:* Permission granted!

It was just what we needed, an action comic written by the Moral Majority. In moments of stress, Captain Canuck would say things like, "Dear God, give me the strength!" It didn't make for good pacing, and I know what I'm talking about, I've got almost every issue. (A large part of my research for this chapter consisted of going through my boxes of old comic books, looking for *Captain Canucks* in among the *Spidermans* and *Jonah Hexes*. I did find a first edition of *Conan the Barbarian* by Barry Windsor Smith that would probably be worth just about a zillion dollars by now if my little sister hadn't scribbled all over it with her crayons. Not that I am still bitter after all these years, but if my sister ever gets married, I plan on sneaking in the night before the ceremony and scribbling with crayons all over her wedding dress and then laughing hysterically.)

In looking through all those dusty back issues of *Captain Canuck,* I realized that Richard Comely was truly a man of great optimism. It must have been all that praying.

He really expected *Captain Canuck* to take off. Every issue was crammed full of ads for Captain Canuck T-shirts, Captain Canuck posters, Captain Canuck fan clubs, Captain Canuck 3-D dioramas, Captain Canuck decorative plaques ("In Your Choice of Magnesium, Brass, or Copper"), Captain Canuck sparkling doodle posters, Captain Canuck ball-point pens, Captain Canuck note-pads, and of course those indispensable Captain Canuck sun visors that were all the rage back when I was a kid.

At one point Comely even drove a yellow Pacer around Winnipeg with the Captain Canuck logo emblazoned on the sides to promote his hero, but to no avail. After struggling financially for years, Comely Comix finally folded after putting out just a dozen or so issues of *Captain Canuck*. Once again, Canada was without a superhero to protect her from aliens, monsters and new political parties. And boy, couldn't we have used the good Captain round about the time the Reform Party and the Bloc Québécois came into being.

Ironically, the next great generation of Canadian superheroes was created not by a Canadian company but by Marvel, an American company. In 1983, *Alpha Flight*—a band of mutant Canadian superheroes—arrived on the stands. They were very, very, Canadian. They had Canadian names, Canadian superpowers, and many of the storylines involved snow.

The cast of Alpha Flight includes *Aurora,* who controls the Northern Lights and speaks with a comical accent because she is supposed to be French Canadian. She says things like, "Eef some of zee magic zat once made me whole still exists zen maybe zere ees 'ope after all, oui?"

A genuine quote, that. Aurora has a twin brother named *Northstar* whose real name is—and the boys at Marvel have done their research—Jean-Paul Baptiste. *Shaman* is the token Indian, wise and at one with nature and mystic and all that. *Snowbird* is a shape-changing Mountie. *Box* is a kind of transformer robot or something. And *Sasquatch* is, well, a sasquatch. Sasquatch also has a secret identity; he is a Jewish physics professor at McGill University who goes by the name of Walter Langkowski. (I'm not making up any of this.)

In keeping with the Canadian name motif, there is also a member of Alpha Flight named *Windshear* and even one named *Puck,* a muscle-bound half pint. His secret name is Eugene. Eugene is, I believe, the first superhero ever to hail from Moose Jaw, Saskatchewan.

The leader of Alpha Flight, meanwhile, is *Vindicator,* who I swear had a sex change, because in the first issues he's a man and then later he's a woman. Or maybe I'm just confused. Comics have become so complicated lately; they're like soap operas. No one can just beat up a bad guy any more, they have to go through deep emotional turmoil first.

Alpha Flight all wear ridiculously skintight uniforms, still *de rigueur* among the superhero set. (You never see Batman or Catwoman fighting crime in baggy sweats and running shoes, even though that would be far more comfortable and allow for greater movement.) Alpha Flight's uniforms are bedecked with stylized maple leaves just in case you forget they are Canadian.

Although basically a branch-plant brigade, it is still nice to know that they are out there protecting us from evil:

Aurora, Northstar, Walter, Eugene. If only they weren't, you know, run by Americans. It's like NATO all over again.

Even then, the members of Alpha Flight weren't the first Canadians to appear in American comics, they were just the first to warrant their own book. The *X-Men* had a token Canadian of their own, a short, borderline-psychopath with claws named Wolverine. He came from Calgary, appropriately enough. On his first outing he took on the Incredible Hulk, amid the usual mayhem and pithy pre-punch dialogue.

It gets even weirder. My older brother Dan, a Vancouver-based media junkie, tells me that during Expo '67, DC Comics presented a commemorative "imaginary story" in which *two* Supermen are created, one the usual U.S. version and the other a clone who takes up a new life in Canada as a *Canadian* superhero, complete with a secret identity as LeBlanc, a mild-mannered reporter with a Montréal daily. So in a way, Superman did come home. Except, of course, that no one has heard of LeBlanc or the Canadian Superman ever since. Such is the fate of celebrities who choose to remain in Canada.

In the end, I put away my boxes of bittersweet boyhood dreams and went down to the Silver Snail Comic Store, where they laughed outrageously at my scribbled-on *Conan* and offered me two bucks for my first edition of *Captain Canuck*. I took it.

On the way out, just as I was going to exit sadly from the stage, the clerk remarked, "He's back, you know." My heart skipped a beat. A tingle ran down my spine. Could it be true? Dare I hope? I spun around and there on the wall was a poster: *Captain Canuck—Reborn*. It was true. It was!

Comely Comix renewed production in 1994, and the Captain is back. He has even become kind of hip in a retro, postmodern kitsch sort of way. A few alternative newspapers and arts magazines have picked him up, and a recent issue of *Time* magazine featured the Captain on its cover as a symbol of the Great White North, under the heading "Canada is the new superhero of global trade (and even Superman is being produced in Winnipeg these days)," in reference to the fact that a Winnipeg-based company now produces the colour-digitization for the *Superman* comic books.

And in 1995 Captain Canuck was awarded his very own postage stamp, as were Johnny Canuck, Nelvana and a modern Québécois Wonder Woman named, what else, Fleur de Lys. Unfortunately, Canada Post also issued a Superman stamp, as once again we appropriated this American icon as our own. David Williams, columnist with the *Saint John Telegraph-Journal,* enthused "Yes, Superman is a Canadian."

No. He isn't. For the last time, Superman is from Krypton. Captain Canuck is from Canada. And he's back, fighting evil separatists and a long-haired stubble-chinned villain named The Quebecer. Captain Canuck, defender not of Truth, Justice and the American Way, but "peace, order and good government." Order your sun-visors now, while stocks last.

AN INORDINATE PRIDE
IN MOUNTAINS: THE MYTH OF
THE NATURAL CANADIAN

. . . .

*W*HAT IS IT about the Rocky Mountains? Why are Canadians so damn proud of them? It's not like we *earned* them, right? It's not as though we built them ourselves. They were already there. We just showed up. So why this inordinate, proprietorial sense of pride?

When I travel through the North or through the Rockies, I am awed by the sheer majesty and scope of Canada. But I don't revel in personal glory and I certainly don't feel *proud* of them. Bragging to the world about your landscape is a little like bragging about your spouse's cooking. It's pride by proxy, reflected glory. And yet, Canadians are obsessed with geography and size.

Personally, I blame Mercator.

Gerardus Mercator was a sixteenth-century Flemish cartographer and mathematician. His great claim to fame is that he solved one of map-making's most persistent problems: how to reproduce a lumpy, spherical, three-dimensional world on a flat sheet of paper. The Mercator Projection, as it is known, stretches the world at either end, keeping the shapes accurate, but wildly exaggerating the scale—especially as you go further north.

The Mercator Projection has warped our view of the world. On a Mercator map, Greenland looks larger than South America, and Alaska looks larger than Mexico. The Mercator method is only now being abandoned—or at least tinkered with—but in Canada this four-hundred-year-old mathematical solution to a cartographical conundrum still has a certain nostalgic, nationalistic charm. It is a bit like looking at a fun-house mirror that expands your biceps or bust-line to cartoonlike proportions: it's an ego stroke. Using Mercator's method, Canada looms across the northern hemisphere like some large looming thing. A behemoth or something. On the old maps, the Commonwealth countries were always shown in pink, and Canada looked positively huge, especially when compared to—you guessed it—the U.S. of A. *Ha ha!* They might have more guns and larger penises, but just look at all that pink we own!

Make no mistake: maps are works of interpretive fiction. They are subjective and selective, and they colour our outlook more than we realize. I saw this first-hand while living in Japan, where world maps are divided not down the Pacific but down the Atlantic—a technique which just happens to place Japan in the very centre. Fair enough.

Putting Japan smack dab in the heart of everything shows the nation's relation to the rest of the world much better. Harder to explain, however, is why Japan is the only country coloured red on Japanese maps. It creates this warped perception of the world, where Japan is utterly unique and central—and small. By positioning itself in the centre, Japan is surrounded by the largest nations on earth: China, Russia, Australia, the United States and Canada. This has a desirable effect in Japan, where the citizens prefer to see themselves as a "tiny put powerful" nation, outgunned and outsized, yet still succeeding through sheer will power and racial purity. Japan is, in fact, *not* a small country. The main island of Japan alone is larger than "Great" Britain. If Japan were in Europe, it would dominate the continent.

Canada is just the opposite. Because of Mercator's optical illusion, Canada appears much larger than it actually is. True, we are—and if you say it fast enough, you can get it out in one breath—*thesecondbiggestcountryintheworld*. Or, even more straw-graspingly, *thelargestcountryintheWestern-Hemisphere*. The message being, What we lack in depth we make up in sheer size.

It is very adolescent, this fixation we have on size. What is the *third* largest country in the world? Canadians don't have a clue. All that matters is that we are number two. And for the record, number three is not the United States. It's China, which is virtually the same size as Canada. But here's the kicker: so is the United States. Forget Mercator. Canada and the U.S. are—for all intents and purposes— the same size. Canada covers 9,976,139 km² and the U.S. 9,372,614 km², a difference of 6 per cent. That's right, Canada is a whopping 6 per cent bigger than the United States. *Yeeehaw!*

On Mercator it looks like this:

In real life, like this:

Depressing, isn't it? We looked so large on those Fun-House Maps that we started to believe they were accurate in their portrayal. It gets worse. When you consider that almost 50 per cent of Canada is permanently frozen, and that there are approximately 225,000,000 more Americans than there are Canadians, we are left with little to celebrate. Even now I can hear your chests deflate like leaky balloons. It may be hard to face, but the truth must come out! We are, effectively, a much, much smaller nation than the United States.

Not that we are a small country in general. No sir. We have geography coming out the wazoo, we have vast reaches of tundra, trees and muskeg, and more empty land than those namby-pamby mamma's-boys over in Europe can ever hope for, but what's the point, right? It is only the U.S. we are really interested in beating. The fact that New Brunswick is larger than Ireland, or that you could drop the U.K. into Alberta with room to spare is hardly cause for a flush of national pride.

So why this obsession with geography? Mainly, I suppose, it's because we do have a lot of it, and as noted earlier, people tend to glorify whatever their particular specialty happens to be. The Scots are dead proud of the moors and the Highlands, rejoicing in what is in essence a large deforested midge-infested bog. In Canada it is the Rocky Mountains, "the snow-capped Rockies, shiny white in the setting sun!" The Rockies are *the* definitive image of Canada, both abroad and at home, and they have a powerful effect. Jean Chrétien, for one, is especially fond of appealing to the Rockies in the name of national unity. "Da Rockies dey are my Rockies and everybuddy's Rockies!" This may be a bit embarrassing, but it's not unusual. Landscape has long been used as a tool of nationalism.

Classically, there are two ways in which landscapes are exploited by nationalists, but I have added a third way—one more common among Canadians:

1. as a sacred "homeland"
2. as source of communion
3. as an object of personal pride.

In his study, *National Identity,* Professor Anthony D. Smith of the London School of Economics outlines the appeal of the homeland as the cradle of a culture, "the repository of historic memories and associations."

> Its rivers, coasts, lakes, mountains and cities become "sacred"—places of veneration and exaltation whose inner meanings can be fathomed only by the initiated, that is, the self-aware members of the nation.

"Nationalism is about *land,*" writes Smith. "Both in terms of possessing and of belonging."

This mystical, profound attachment to one's homeland is a powerful force indeed. But this is not what inspires the average Hoser's pride in the Rockies. The key element, "self-aware," is usually missing.

The second method is more private: landscape as source of personal communion. The classic example of this is Pierre "Still Virile After These Years" Trudeau, last seen sliding out of the mist in his canoe and buckskin jacket. When he was just twenty-five years old, Trudeau penned a stirring essay entitled *Exhaustion and Fulfilment:*

The Ascetic in a Canoe, which ends with the following observation:

> I know a man whose school could never teach him patriotism, but who acquired that virtue when he felt in his bones the vastness of his land, and the greatness of those who founded it.

This is certainly the type of relationship that most Canadian nationalists allude to: an immediate and sublime connection between the individual and the land he or she inhabits. This is landscape as an extension of self. This is the spirit of the voyageur—and Trudeau was undoubtedly the Last of the Voyageurs. But let's face it, Trudeau is a cut above the rest of us mere mortals. He haunts us still, *yaddah-yaddah-yaddah.*

The average Canadian isn't delving as deep as Pierre Trudeau when he or she boasts about the Rockies. Canadians like to think they have a special affinity with nature, but statistics show otherwise. Canada is a hopelessly urban society whose average citizen couldn't pick a moose out of a police line-up. Yet still we wax poetic about majestic forests and open tundra. This has nothing to do with communion; it has everything to do with ego.

Here's a test: when was the last time you, a noble and natural Canadian, really communed with nature? (Riding a bicycle through Stanley Park does not count.)

In days of yore, it was the Canadian frontier that drew our hearty pioneer forefathers (and foremothers and forecousins and foreoxen) westward, ever westward, inveigled as they were with promises of free land and open space.

And it is the frontier—be it the Rockies or the Arctic or the Canadian Shield—that is still being trumpeted as a cause for Canadian patriotism. But "frontier" is just another word for colony. Frontiers are invented solely to be tamed.

So why the love of frontier? Partly, I suppose, it comes back to that tin-can allure of potential. The promise of future greatness. Partly too, it comes from patterns embedded deep in the Canadian psyche. Commentators call it "the garrison mentality," bred in the bone as we huddled in small pockets of civilization, surrounded by forests primeval thick with Windigos and wolves and Wacoustas and all the rest. But that is far too heroic. What we have today is not a Garrison Mentality but a Mall Mentality, a climate-controlled, consumer-oriented cocoon.

The Natural Canadian no longer exists. We no longer experience the Canadian wilderness as pioneers but as spectators. At best, we are backwoods dilettantes, spending the long weekend in our cottages in Kenora before scurrying back to the sanctity of the suburbs and the safety of shopping malls. I do not claim to be any better than this, but at least I am upfront about it. I don't take any personal pride from our rugged outdoors. The Rockies are a magnificent range of mountains, but they would be magnificent no matter who was living here. We are merely tenants.

It was that great grey blob of a prime minister, Mackenzie King, who made the oft-repeated quip: "If some countries have too much history, we have too much geography." I don't mean to suggest that His Royal Blandness was wrong, but here in Canada we have plenty of history. Tons. We have history to spare. It is just vastly underappreciated, in much the same way that our geography is vastly *over*appreciated. We have elevated real estate at the expense of history. We are proud for all the wrong reasons.

The flaw is this: By predicating national pride on our landscape, we remove Canadians from the equation. I grew up in northern Canada and trust me—tundra is overrated. Instead of boasting about our landscape, we should be asking ourselves what we, as Canadians, have achieved. What difference would it make to the world if we had never existed? What do we have to show for ourselves?

I prefer my landscapes inhabited.

It is in the cities and towns and villages of Canada that I feel most Canadian. It is there that Canadians have shaped a culture and a way of life: in Old Québec, in ramshackle St. John's, in Ragged Ass Road, in impossibly twee Victoria, in my own dear Loyalist town of St. Andrews.

Not far from where I live is a Loyalist graveyard, lying quiet among the autumn leaves and bracketed on either side by noisy schoolyards: an elementary school on one side, a high school on the other. This quiet Loyalist burial ground contains memories, ghosts and small personal epics. That graveyard, with its tangled tales of love and betrayal, with its collection of lives lived, surrounded on both sides by unruly schoolchildren—that is a landscape that stirs my soul. I am proud to be part of a country that created St. Andrews. I am proud of both our graves and our schoolyards. This too is pride by proxy—all nationalism is—but it is at least a pride in humanity, not geography. We must not forget the critical part of Trudeau's epiphany, "the vastness of his land, and *the greatness of those who founded it.*" As Canadians, our true connection to Canada is primarily with the people who came before us and those who will come after, and not the wild indifferent landscape against which those human epics were set.

The Rockies are magnificent, but far more stirring to me *as a Canadian* are the rolling hills and small villages of Prince Edward Island. Here is the interplay of people and land: the cliffs of Cavendish, blood-red in the sunset, the winding lanes, the vermilion roads, the farms, the endless procession of churches, the lighthouse on the far cape.

Writing-on-Stone National Park in southern Alberta is the site of ancient Blackfoot pictographs that delineate tribal territory and call forth great events of the past. It is the writing and not the stone that gives this landscape resonance. And the challenge for Canadians is to decipher and learn to appreciate not the stone, but the writing—faded, half-lost, evocative.

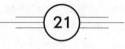

THE SUDBURY
SYNDROME

. . . . .

SO FAR WE HAVE been discussing Canada largely in the abstract. Let's now take a closer look at some of the places and spaces we occupy. Canada on the street corner of a specific town or city is far different from the Canada of the imagination. With that in mind, I give you the city of Sudbury. And remember as you read this that (A) I love Sudbury, and (B) our scars define us every bit as much as our smiles, and our collective scars define us even further. Plastic surgery is *not* the answer.

ENGLAND MAY HAVE the White Cliffs of Dover, but Canada has the Black Cliffs of Sudbury. And unlike the cliffs of Dover, which are really more of an *off*-white, the cliffs of Sudbury are black. Even better, they are man-made.

You see the cliffs as you drive into town, Sudbury's slag-pile glaciers, the scorched tailings of the city's infamous nickel mines. Rail-cars roll up to the edge, then pause, tilt and pour out the molten slag, casting an orange echo against the sky, like the castle defences of a medieval siege. The slag cools into a crust, then blackens, and is in turn covered.

No animal can live off its own waste. This is a basic rule of biology, and yet Sudbury, a city of 90,000 in the scrub-backed land of the Canadian Shield, seems to defy this. Folk singer Murray McLaughlin called it a "hard-rock town." Others have been less charitable. But if Sudbury has a bad reputation, it came by it honestly. It may be ugly, but it was a damn sight uglier and nastier just a few years ago. (*Suggested town motto:* You think it stinks now, you should have seen it before!)

Sudbury started in 1883 as a muddy, backwoods rail town at the junction of two main lines. With the discovery of the world's richest nickel deposits came an economic boom. Two companies blasted their way to the top of the slag pile and stayed there: Falconbridge Mines and the almighty American-based International Nickel Company, now known simply as INCO.

INCO ruled Sudbury for almost eighty years. As final courts of appeal, there was God, Ottawa and INCO, but not necessarily in that order. As late as 1964, the mayor of Sudbury was cheerfully informing newcomers to the city "INCO calls the shots around here, and don't ever forget it."

Oh the girls are out to bingo,
and the boys are gettin' stink-o,

And we'll think no more of INCO
on a Sudbury Saturday night.

So sang Stompin' Tom Connors, and the words ring
true of a company town that ate its own. The pollution was
horrific. Every dollar earned was wrestled from the earth,
carved, blasted, crushed, melted down and skimmed off.
For miles around the vegetation was dead, the land was
barren and sullied. Lung cancer, acid rain, lakes turned
to vinegar, bedrock torched bare: Sudbury had it all. It
was—and still is—a hard-drinking, blue-collar place, with
a rowdy mix of French and English. An archetypal mining
town, a sorrowful and sickly place.

And yet never were a people so proud of their town.
The good citizens of Sudbury will defend their rocky home
amid the smokestacks with the same fierce stubbornness
that a parent defends a particularly ugly child. It's a town
with a chip on its shoulder, and so it should. If you were
the brunt of innumerable jokes, if in high school you were
always voted most likely to die of industrial disease, you
too would get pissed off at writers like me who come into
town, shake their heads and declare it a "sorrowful and
sickly place."

Later, INCO built Superstack, the tallest chimney in
the world, to throw the emissions out higher and over a
larger area. This massive, spewing smokestack is a symbol of Sudbury as much as the Giant Nickel on the road
into town. (In his travel book *Last Train to Toronto,* Terry
Pindell recalls meeting Miss Nude Canada, the amply
endowed Kathy Stack, in her home town of Sudbury. Her
stage name was XTC, but everyone around town called her

Superstack, though I believe this nickname may not have been in reference to the INCO chimney.)

The glory of nude dancing aside, Sudbury went into free-fall sometime around 1980 and just kept tumbling. A series of bitter strikes and layoffs was followed hard by recession and terminal unemployment and the apocalyptic INCO strike. The picket lines, the cutbacks, the false mini-booms that came and went like death spasms, all weighed heavy on the City That Nickel Built.

The story of Sudbury doesn't end there, though by all logic it should; it was a one-industry town and its time had run out. But then, like a minor miracle, the clouds broke and the Sudbury Renaissance began. A streak of civic pride, as deep as any nickel core, saved them. (That and millions of dollars in federal and corporate aid.) The strategy was simple, the mantra short: diversify or die.

And what do you think they decided to base their recovery on? You'll never guess. Never. They decided to make Sudbury a centre for *tourism*. That's right, tourism. "I don't know, honey, this year it's either Paris or Sudbury, I just can't decide." The crazy thing is, it worked. Tourism is now a major, multimillion-dollar industry in Sudbury and one of the cornerstones of the city's recovery plan.

INCO donated $5 million towards the construction of Science North, a tourist-oriented interactive centre. It was the biggest single corporate donation to a community project in Canadian history—something which INCO never tires of pointing out.

Science North is "science beyond the classroom." The buildings are designed in the shape of snowflakes, *stainless steel* snowflakes, that are connected via bedrock tunnels.

And how do they entice you to come to the complex? With the promise that you will *"Pet a tarantula! Hold a porcupine! and lie on a bed of nails!"* Tarantulas? Bed of nails? Just how does this tour end? Do they poke you in the eye with a stick and set your hair on fire? In fact, Science North is a lot of fun. And yes, as I discovered, you *can* pet a porcupine. His name is Ralf, he likes to have his belly rubbed, and no, his quills don't come off. Unless he's angry. So you should try to stay on his good side.

Sudbury has reinvented itself, and with tourism now booming, people are actually ending up in Sudbury *on purpose!* The city's concentrated tree-planting and beautification project finally paid off when *Chatelaine* magazine—that purveyor of good taste—ranked Sudbury as one of the ten best Canadian cities to live in. *Crowds cheer! Balloons fly! Parades parade!*

Now then, let's not go overboard. Sudbury, no matter how many trees you plant is still, well, Sudbury. Many of the newly built and much ballyhooed residential complexes were really just the generic Canadian Suburb transplanted whole into what was once, and still is, a rough northern town. All the trees by the side of the road are not going to hide the rock and refineries. (*Suggested motto:* As far as industrial wastelands go, we're not that bad!)

It's true, the United Nations Environment Committee has applauded Sudbury's urban renewal efforts. (*Crowds cheer, balloons fly,* etc. etc.) Do you remember back in grade school, when the teacher used to give special silver stars to that slow kid who tried really, really hard but was still a bit thick? They called the award Most Improved. Well, Sudbury is that student, and she wears her star proudly.

From the top of the hill, beside the giant stainless steel nickel, she proclaims, like Scarlett O'Hara in *Gone with the Wind,* "As God as my witness, I will never be ugly again!"

And on the other side, across the hill, the slag cars rumble and roll, pouring the fire that slides down like lava and cools into blackness on the edge of town.

TUCKED IN WITHIN Sudbury's Copper Cliff townsite is a place called Little Italy. Built by migrant workers to resemble the mountain villages of their native land, it is a small enclave of narrow random streets and oddly angled houses. From Little Italy to the Giant Nickel, from the Black Cliffs to the Superstack itself, Sudbury has stories to tell. Love her or hate her, there is no place quite like her. Sudbury *is* ugly. It is a city with a past, a city covered with scars, but it is also a city with that elusive quality we call *character,* and character is not something you can buy. But it is something you can lose.

Every time you pass through Sudbury, you will notice the encroaching sameness of suburbia. It is happening across Canada. I call it the Sudbury Syndrome: the desire to eradicate the scars and birthmarks of a place and import instead the shiny surfaces and retail clones of a common urban/suburban culture. It is nothing short of the Blanding of Canada. Local character and diversity is slowly being watered down, and our cities and towns are fast becoming as interchangeable as shopping malls.

The town of Sudbury, with its gritty working-class roots and nickel-plated pride, epitomizes this. A campaign has been under way since the early 1990s to change Sudbury's image, to make it more like every other town, to make it as innocuous as possible. To make it as nice as everybody else.

LET ME TAKE YOU now to Saint John, New Brunswick, or, as I like to call it, Sudbury-by-the-sea. Living as I do in the fey little town of St. Andrews, I have come to rely on Saint John (population: 79,000) as my pipeline to consumer goods, import foods, cinemas, and adult sex shoppes (*sic*).

St. Andrews, with a population less than 1,300, has a mind-boggling variety all its own, a riffraff collection of greying hippies, faded back-to-the-landers, imported salmon researchers, restless college kids, price-gouging landlords, wealthy elders and assorted craftspeople. The town has also, wisely and with more than a little smugness, decided to resist the drift towards mass commercialization. The town stewards have kept fast-food chains and discount department stores at bay and the result is an expensive but largely unspoiled town. Quaint. Historic. Narcoleptic.

The city of Saint John, an hour and a half down the road, is a world away from St. Andrews, and the two coexist like a dowager aunt and a tattooed dock-worker: uneasily.

Let's be frank. Saint John is a functionally illiterate city. Trying to find a decent used bookstore in Saint John is like trying to find a decent restaurant in Regina. Much like Sudbury, Saint John is a blue-collar, gaseous, foul-smelling, knocked-about town. And just as Sudbury has been cursed and blessed—but to my mind, mostly cursed—by the presence of INCO, so has Saint John suffered at the hands of its own capitalist overlords: the Clan Irving.

To me, the Irvings have always seemed to be old-school caricatures: cigar-smoking, round-bellied, union-busting capitalists of nineteenth-century America. Except it isn't the nineteenth century any more (a fact which no one has had the nerve to tell the Irvings) and Saint John remains a city in thrall.

Have you ever started packing to move, and you start out by boxing and labelling everything and then arranging them carefully by content and size, but by the time you are done you are throwing things into boxes and shoving them wherever the hell they can fit? Well, it's the same with Saint John. There may have been a plan way back when, but the city is now a stack of random boxes jumbled along the bedrock, wedged in among highway overpasses and Irving shipyards. With its one-way streets and sadistic bypasses, Saint John is an unforgiving city; take a wrong turn and it's *Hello Moncton!*

And yet, for all that—because of that—I love Saint John. It's a great place. The Old City is filled with surprises and the people are as raw and real as they come. Whether you're eating the meatloaf sandwich and spicy fries at Reggie's Diner or waiting for the Reversing (yawn) Falls to do their stench-side trick, it is hard not to feel a begrudging admiration for Saint John. Like Sudbury, it has a character all its own. Which makes it all the more depressing that it was in Saint John that I experienced my worse case of Urban Amnesia ever.

FREDERICTON, MEANWHILE, is a government town. Inhabited largely by bureaucrats, poets and students, Fredericton can't quite make up its mind if it wants to be eccentric or snooty and has settled on a kind of eccentric snootiness that puzzles as much as it captivates. Like most Canadian cities, Fredericton (population: 45,000) is inflicted with a perimeter rim of shopping malls and fast-food emporiums. Like Saint John, Fredericton is about an hour and a half from St. Andrews.

Where Saint John is pure grit, Fredericton is pampered and refined. Where Saint John is masculine, Fredericton is feminine. Where Saint John is dark, Fredericton is light. It's yin, it's yang. It's the fiddle vs. the violin. It's diner coffee vs. cappuccino. Saint John is unforgiving, Fredericton is welcoming.

The two cities are as different as any two could be, and yet, during a grey winter outing as I wandered down a hermetically sealed shopping mall corridor, I suddenly lost all sense of place. I couldn't remember if I was in Saint John or Fredericton. Everything was completely familiar—and yet I had absolutely no idea where I was. It must be the way a victim of amnesia feels.

Which city was I in? Fredericton? Saint John? There was nothing to distinguish it either way. Shopping malls, like suburbs, have no real character. They are, by their very nature, generic.

It turned out I was in Saint John, which I discovered only after I stopped someone and asked. (And boy, did I get a funny look.) It was a heart-sinking moment to realize just how standardized modern Canadian culture has become. It is cheerful and clean and comfortable. And empty.

What this country needs is more Sudburys and fewer shopping malls.

SUCCESS WITHOUT RISK:
THE CANADIAN DREAM

. . . .

*I*F THE ultimate Japanese career is that of salaryman, and the American one is that of entrepreneur, what then is the ultimate *Canadian* career?

Lumberjack? Synchronized Swimmer? Civil Servant? No. The ultimate Canadian career is that of Associate Professor. Why? Because a career in academia has all of the elements that Canadians love best: it is very earnest, it is publicly funded, it is nonprofit, and—best of all—it promises success without risk. From this comes the highly scientific and amazingly insightful Ferguson Formula for Determining the Suitability of Canadian Aspirations:

$$CD = S-R$$

(Canadian Dream equals Success without Risk)

A career in higher education fits this formula perfectly. It involves hard work, perhaps. Talent, optional. But risk? Hardly.

CD = S−R. By using this carefully crafted formula, you can now determine the suitability of any given job. Lumberjack, for example: high risk, small financial reward. It is definitely excluded from the Canadian Dream. Voyageur? Same thing. Farmer? Well, there are government subsidies and there is the fringe benefit of Incessant High-Horsedness ("We farmers are the salt of the earth, I tell you. The salt of the earth!"), but anything dependent upon rainfall in southern Saskatchewan can only be described as risky.

Hockey Player? Certainly there is High Success (to be in the NHL is to be a god among men in Canada), but there is also heavy risk, by which I mean "brain damage." You think boxers have it bad, try getting slammed into the boards by Mark Messier every night and see how many brain synapses you retain at the end of it all. Prior to repeated encounters with the Number 11 Bus (i.e., Mark Messier), hockey great Joey Sloboka was once a trained nuclear physicist conversant in several Indo-European languages, and now look at him. The guy can barely tie his shoes, let alone lace up a pair of skates. They just wheel him out like Frankenstein at the start of every game.

A career in hockey is not a dream, it's a *wet* dream, a fantasy; for the true Canadian Dream we have to look elsewhere. So how about Synchronized Swimmer? Once again the prestige factor is high. (In Canada, synchronized swimmers are second only to hockey players in the awe and deference they command.) But once again there is the risk of brain damage. Being underwater for hours on end with the consequent lack of oxygen to the frontal lobes explains the blank grins they are always wearing during performances, nose-plugs and waterproof mascara intact. Truth is, they never *stop* grinning. (Kidding! I love synchronized swimmers. Not like lumberjacks. Those guys piss me off.)

Well then, what about that much-coveted position of Civil Servant? (Heavy sarcasm on both the "civil" and the "servant.") True, this was once the very pinnacle of the Canadian Dream, but not, alas, any more. Mass firings and retroactive patronage have taken their toll. In Ontario, civil servants have actually started getting violent—or at least, very, very peeved. The police responded with their truncheons and the civil servants expected the rest of us to care. Is that hilarious or what? They actually expected us to care. "Look, honey, that lemon-pussed witch from the Department of Motor Vehicles is getting clobbered on the head on national television! That is so sad."

Speaking of slack jobs, what about road crews? You know the ones I'm talking about, the human signposts and five-men-one-shovel projects you see loitering beside construction zones across this great, pothole bedeviled land. Other than the occasional ten-car pile-up, there isn't a lot of risk—or even thought—involved. Surely this too must rank as a "Canadian Dream." Ah, but you are forgetting the second part of the equation, you poor, helpless fool you: *success*. Road crews are dangerously close to being A Real Job, requiring long hours, low wages and a serf-like relationship to the boss. So road crews too must be rejected, as must Wal-Mart Greeters, television announcers and standup comedians. And I don't even want to talk about journalists.

How about Editor? Certainly you have a high Power Factor, wielding large pruning shears, emasculating the prose of betrodden writers, and enjoying the fast-paced jet-setting lifestyle that comes with it, but the risk factor is also very high. When you are an editor, you are always just one step away from being gunned down by a disgruntled author—and I speak as an often-disgruntled author myself. Let's not forget what happened to George Brown, Father of Confederation and senior editor. It wasn't because he was a Father of Confederation that he got shot. So I'm afraid the much-coveted, despotic position of editor must be disqualified as well.

By now you must be asking in despair, "Will, oh wise and reportedly well-endowed one, having eliminated lumberjacks, hockey players, synchronized swimmers, road crews, civil servants and editors, what else is there?" Well, there is always Being An Offspring of Wealthy Hong Kong Émigrés. It's a great job if you can get it. Or you could try Being Married to Conrad Black, but I do believe the position has already been filled.

Having slowly and meticulously eliminated all other jobs, what are we left with? Academia, that's what. Academia in all its glory. Being on the public tit has never been better than in the echelons of higher education. This is the ultimate low-risk, high-reward, pseudo-prestigious job as far removed from the real world as possible. Risk? Think tenure.

Canada was called into being by fur traders and pioneers, by teachers in one-room schools and railroad barons in pursuit of a vision, by bastards and boneheads, by sinners and saints. We have been militaristic and chauvinistic.

We have been heroic and inventive, wild and introspective. We have been many things, but until just a few decades ago, we were never boring. Then came the slow slide into the welfare state and the culture of victimhood, the cult of collective rights, the lure of the consumer society and the ascendancy of the career bureaucrat. And from all of this, climbing atop the heap in a perverted reverse-Darwinian process, came the Associate Professor. The Canadian Ideal. $CD = S-R$. And the rest is history. (Sorry, *hisandher*story.) Yup, you are stuck on an elevator with Grandpa. You didn't know I was just another neoconservative muttonhead when you bought this book, did you?

The truth is, I'm not. I am wary of any ideology, left or right, that seeks to replace good ol' everyday cynicism. (And there is a crucial distinction to be made between *cynicism* and *pessimism*: cynicism denotes a scathing, critical outlook on life; pessimism is a form of despair, which is to say, cowardice.)

Whatever the benefits, Canadians have created a coddled society built on equality rather than ambition. We accept equalization payments and subsidies and UI and EI and welfare and government grants as a natural right—or at least inevitable. And we are nicer for it. We truly are. But like every compromise, there has been a price to pay.

What of the original Canadian Dream, of being more than who we are? Of reaching for the sky—not to surrender, but to succeed.

Canadians are nice: we tell ourselves this all the time. We, the children of giants, the heirs to half a continent, insist on defining ourselves in the most inoffensive, innocuous way possible. We tread water. We wring our hands.

We write adolescent love letters to Québec separatists. We attend National Action Unity Committees. And we aspire—to what? A house in the suburbs, a cabin in the country.

We are the luckiest, most spoiled people on earth. We have it all, with virtually none of the usual negative side effects. Being a Canadian is like winning the lottery—and then blowing it all on RRSPs. It's like wearing triple condoms, it's like taking a bath with your socks on. We have become cautious to the point of cowardice, comfortable to the point of coma. Forget the suburbs and forget security. With all the possibilities open to us, shouldn't we aspire to something more? Shouldn't we aspire to greatness? Or at least something more exciting than Associate Professor?

Part Five

CANADA REMADE

. . . .

IN PRAISE OF HYPHENS:
LESSONS FROM
KENSINGTON MARKET

. . . .

*S*ATURDAY MORNING. The streets are humming. You catch the beat and walk with it. Augusta Avenue. Kensington Place. Conversations caught and lost. A shopkeeper haggles with a poker-faced patron. A young mother frowns at some cheese. Unbelievably beautiful eyes appear and are gone. Music and Mediterranean hand gestures. The smell of spice and roti.

Tables overspill with produce and a thousand kinds of beans. Earth-tone shades of beige and brown. Herbal medicines. Dusty smells. The unexpected scent of cinnamon, so sharp you taste it on your tongue. Rabbis and fishwives and polite punk rockers. "Excuse me, spare change?" Carved cows strung up like tackling dummies. Pakistani video shops. Religious kitsch. Pressed-wood furniture. And everyone hustling to make a buck.

Piñatas hang in the windows—explosions waiting to happen. Kensington Market. Toronto.

I stop for coffee at the Trivoli Billiards, where they serve espresso as it was meant to be, in chipped cups and with a lack of pretension—or even good manners. Moroccan coffee sold by Moroccans.

Toronto is a city of neighbourhoods; you are always on the cusp of cultures, and Kensington is the city's Khyber Pass. Shoe stores and discount bins have replaced camel caravans, and credit cards have replaced barter, but the song is the same. If anything, history has taught us this: the greatest ideas and the most vibrant cultures flourish not in the serene courts of the capital but at the crossroads. In the market.

I toss back the espresso like a tequila shooter and I feel my pulse begin to flutter. Kensington. It's been too long. Five years in an ethnically pure nation, where everybody was one of two things: Japanese or Not Japanese, and now back into the bumper-car culture of an immigrant nation. I want to dance like a dervish, I want to argue in Hebrew, I want to eat pigeons and yell at merchants. After such a long and lonely exile, I want to be Canadian again.

Maybe it's the caffeine count in my blood stream—an espresso epiphany—but suddenly I see it: that elusive snow leopard of Canadian identity. We have been going about it all wrong. We have been standing in our own light. Canada does not exist on some higher plane, it is site specific.

We won't discover Canada by stepping back, because there is no Grand Vision, no teleology of design, no phrase that sums it all up. We will find Canada only by stepping *closer,* when we lose sight of the picture frame and see the texture of each brushstroke. We have been looking for Canadian identity through the wrong end of the telescope. Canada slips into view like faces in a crowd—it is caught and lost and carried forward. Not a destination, but an activity. Not a noun, but a verb.

That was some strong espresso. You wouldn't want to operate heavy equipment after drinking a Trivoli special.

I walk through Kensington and once the initial caffeine rush of enthusiasm subsides, I notice something else. Wet, dank garbage clotted in the gutters. Cigarette butts. Rotting produce. Fish-heads. Mangy alley cats . . . Markets are messy. They are not for tidy minds. They are messy and they exhaust you. They are filled with cultures in conflict, nations in conflux. They ricochet. They crowd the senses. The signs shout in capital letters and command phrases: BUY! SELL! SALE! Polyglot persuasions—flowing Arabic, angular Korean—circles and slashes that translated would read: BUY! SELL! SALE! Junk shops and sewing centres, yams and pita bread. Crowds that collide, arguments that overlap. Seedy, smelly. Tattered. Kensington Market is on the make and in your face. And everywhere, if you look for it, punctuating the collage like a question mark, is the red leaf flag of the Canadian nation.

CANADA WAS THE first country in the world to pass a national Multicultural Act and the first to establish a Department of Multiculturalism. The word "multiculturalism" itself was coined in Canada, and it might well have been coined to describe Toronto. Visible minorities make up almost half the population of this great city, and tax notices are routinely sent out in six different languages: English, French, Chinese, Italian, Greek and Portuguese. None of this has turned the city into a seething cesspool of racial violence and cultural anarchy. Quite the opposite. There are tensions to be sure, but a life without tension is not a life at all; it's a coma.

Forget the mosaic; our national metaphor is the market. Multiculturalism is our new ideal, and we chose it because we had no choice. Almost 40 per cent of Canadians now claim origins other than purely British or French. As sociologist Reginald Bibby notes in *Mosaic Madness,* "Canada has decided to enshrine a demographic reality into a national virtue."

We were not always so eager to accept differences. Immigration policy once routinely barred Blacks ("too cold for them"), Asians ("yellow menace, that") and right up to the end of World War II, Jews. The Department of Immigration had a list of desirables that neatly fit the Vertical Mosaic, with Anglo-Saxons at the top.

Even with all the immigration regulations and lists, problems arose. The "undesirables" kept trying to get in. In 1914 a passenger ship with 376 British citizens on board steamed into Vancouver harbour. The passengers were excited. They had arrived to begin a new life in Canada and they were dressed in their finest clothes for the occasion. They smiled and waved at the crowds along the piers. "Nobody," notes author Walter Stewart in *But Not in Canada!,* "waved back." The passengers were British citizens, but they were *Indian* British citizens. Sikhs.

The ship was the *Komagata Maru,* carrying legal emigrants who had paid their own way. Police turned the ship back, forcing it to anchor offshore. Ignoring the Sikhs' British citizenship, an editorial in *British Columbia Magazine* declared, "We must keep this country a white man's country at any cost, and a British country if possible." The ship sat in harbour for two months before a Canadian cruiser, the ironically named *Rainbow,* arrived and chased the *Komagata Maru* away. The good citizens of Vancouver cheered from the docks.

Most Canadians have never heard of the *Komagata Maru.* It doesn't gibe with the nice image we have of ourselves. It is also a reminder of who we were before we were converted to the cause of multiculturalism. Walter Stewart writes:

> Whenever I hear an immigration minister expand on the friendly welcome that awaits the foreigner in Canada, whenever an after-dinner speaker leans across the remains of his chicken-a-la-king to warble the usual malarkey about our open hearts and open doors, I think about the *Komagata Maru,* and the poor, dumb bastards who thought they could ride her into Canada.

Fortunately, times have changed. It is true that multiculturalism is often derided as being a facile 3-D approach: dress, diet and dance. But this does not give due credit to government strategies that have helped Canada avoid the incendiary race riots of Britain, the economic disparities of the U.S., the xenophobia of Japan and the violent racial undertones of the newly united Germany.

Like the city of Toronto itself, multiculturalism has its share of detractors, and the number seems to be growing. The most compelling objection comes from francophone

Canadians who argue that multiculturalism reduces the French in Canada to the status of just one ethnic group among many. René Lévesque dismissed multiculturalism as mere folklore, a "red herring" used to deny Québec its special status. When Manitoba premier Gary Filmon declared "Canada has an aboriginal past, a bilingual present and a multicultural future," he may have warmed the cockles of the politically correct, but he chilled the hearts of the Québécois.

The rules have changed. The binary code of English-French has been replaced with Chaos Theory, and the Québécois fear this new turn. The fear is visceral, and it is based on a misconception: that somehow multiethnic groups form a unified "bloc" that will diminish the role of francophones in Canada. But at an ethnic level, the influx of so many non-Anglo culture groups actually *strengthens* the position of French Canadians within Canada. Soon, Canadians of French background may very well be the largest single segment of Canadian society. If we are all going to be reduced to ethnic factors, the Québécois will make up the most united and largest factor of all.

For other people, pluralism itself is the problem. We now have Aboriginal rights and women's rights and men's rights and left-handed albino lesbian rights. "Where will it end?" cry the critics as they pull out handfuls of hair.

The syllogism goes something like this:

A. Multiculturalism is a form of pluralism.
B. Pluralism leads to ethical relativism—that is, the belief that all opinions are equally valid and that right and wrong are merely conventions.

C. Relativism (in theory) undermines social cohesion, destroys national unity, worships choice as an end in itself, rejects moral truths, causes acne, and is just generally distasteful.

Of course, cults such as fascism, communism and religious fundamentalism are about as far from ethical relativism as you can possibly go, and we all know how much they did for social cohesion.

Several fallacies are operating in the condemnation of multiculturalism. One is an overextended metaphor. Mosaics are shards imbedded separately: thousands of solitudes with no common identity or loyalty. Multiculturalism, it is argued, splinters and alienates us from one another because it segregates us into separate solitudes.

But ethnic groups do not exist in a vacuum; they jostle, interact and come to terms with one another. The Vietnamese grocer, his Lebanese supplier and their Anglo customer do not—*cannot*—operate in any Old World context; they must meet on common ground. That common ground is Canada, and it is defined and reinvented daily, in a thousand neighbourhoods in a thousand contexts. "Multiculturalism must be viewed as an ongoing process, not a state to be achieved," notes John W. Friesen, a specialist in multicultural issues, in *When Cultures Clash*.

The critics of multiculturalism assume that ethnic identity and national values are incompatible. They are wrong. A lively mix of imperial archetypes, working-class roots, linguistic tensions, suppressed guilt (i.e., Aboriginal Canadians), American ambivalence and a vast indifferent landscape has shaped the Canadian value system into one that is based on tolerance, caution and—dare I say it—integrity.

Yet, more than one commentator has fretted over a lack of overriding Canadianism. This is often worded in the form of a question, like a riddle without a punch line: What do an outport Newfoundland fisherman, a Saskatchewan farmer, an Acadian businesswoman and an avant-garde artist from Montréal have in common? The insinuation being that they have nothing in common whatsoever, that their regional identities automatically exclude any sense of being united as Canadians. I'm sorry, but this is one of the biggest nonissues in Canada today, and it ranks right up there as an example of Stupidity By Consensus. That is, the more people repeat something, the more accepted it becomes.

What do the people listed above share? They share a nationality. They are united by a common context and a common frame of reference. To treat regional character as if it is incompatible with national unity is to employ the crudest kind of either/or thinking. You could apply this same argument to any country. What does an urban Edinburgh junkie have in common with a rural Highlands crofter? Or an Okinawan fisherman with a Tokyo punk rocker?

A Canadian living in Alberta is different from a Canadian living in Cape Breton: therefore, there is no such thing as Canadian. What kind of logic is that? And why stop at provincial or regional identities? You can make the same specious claim based on a given city. Take Vancouver, for example. What, you may ask, can the stockbrokers in Yaletown have in common with the refried hippies and crunchy granola crowd in Kitsilano? What can a devout Marxist from the Downtown Eastside possibly have in common with the rich folk in Point Grey or the drug addicts and runaways of East Hastings? And why not go even further and divide it along a single street? After all, what could a third-generation Italian shopowner on Commercial Drive have in common with the lesbians at Joe's Cafe? Or what about Granville Street? There's a magic carpet ride for you. It starts as a bus mall then transforms into the tenderloin strip, filled with triple X cinemas, body-piercing salons and tattoo parlours. Cross the bridge and you transverse Granville Island, a sort of Disneyland for the Politically Correct centred around a public market thoroughly infested with tourists. You then arrive in South Granville, home of art galleries, shoe stores and overpriced apartments, and then blocks and blocks of ritzy houses until, finally, you enter the suburban ennui of Richmond. And that's just a single street. What could any of these people have in common? Clearly there is no such thing as Vancouver, because there is no such thing as a common "Vancouver identity." *Voilà,* we have made a street and a city and a country disappear. Impressive, wouldn't you say?

You can perform this same exercise in any community. You could divide Kensington Market block by block, or even stall by stall. Applied to Canada's multicultural demographics, the same alarmist rhetoric kicks in, bemoaning the lack of some homogeneous ethnic sense of what it means to be Canadian.

Which now brings us to the Great Canadian Hyphen Lament.

This lament is based on a very shaky premise: it assumes that we will never be a real nation until everyone stops qualifying who they are with prefixes like Italian- or Ukrainian- or Dutch-. For the blessedly short period of time he was prime minister, John Diefenbaker often rallied support for the "unhyphenated Canadian." (In fact, he never shut up about it. Would that he had spent as much time fretting over the economy.)

Critics of multiculturalism are always pounding their chests and "refusing to be hyphenated" as though it were some heroic stance and not simply an overblown declaration of self-importance. The Hyphen Lament has become as automatic a reflex as the anti-Toronto gag. You can't lose by raging against hyphens. Here is journalist Laura Sabia in an address to the Empire Club of Canada, taking up Diefenbaker's crusade: "A dastardly deed has been perpetuated upon Canadians by politicians whose motto is 'divide and rule.' I, for one, refuse to be hyphenated. I am a Canadian, first and foremost. Don't hyphenate me."

In *Selling Illusions,* author Neil Bissoondath also rages at length against hyphens, saying he refuses to be categorized as an East-Indian-Trinidadian-Canadian living in Québec. Well, bully for him. As far as I'm concerned, he can call himself whatever he likes. He can call himself Sergeant for all I care. But when he accuses supporters of multiculturalism of being "zealots" intent on perpetuating "cultural apartheid," he enters the land of hyperbole. It's like calling traffic cops "Nazis." It doesn't get you out of a ticket and all it does is make you look a bit hysterical.

Can anyone explain to me—without lapsing into hysteria and hyperbole—how the term Chinese-Canadian or Italian-Canadian is subversive to national unity? I could understand if we were using simply the terms Chinese or

Italian when speaking of Canadian citizens, but how does acknowledging different origins threaten us? Are we really so frail a nation that we tremble in fear of punctuation?

I refer to myself simply as "Canadian," but only because I do not personally identify with my Scottish, Irish or Norwegian roots. This is my prerogative. I have other friends, and even family members, who get misty-eyed over the moors and heather of the Old Country. That is their prerogative.

How we identify ourselves is an intensely personal matter. The cry of "no hyphens!" asks that we induce amnesia, that we exorcise the memory of who we are and where we came from. Virtually every Canadian is here because of adventure, either personal or ancestral. Hardship, dreams, greed and sadness: we are the children of adventure. Why wipe the slate clean and say we must now forget all of that and strive to be as similar to one another as possible? We can only be poorer for this.

Literary critic Northrop Frye made a key distinction between *identity* and *unity*. Identity differs with each individual. It involves layers: family, gender, upbringing, ethnic background, personal values, religious inclination. Whatever shapes us, *is* us. The state is only one part of this. Our identity is a personal collage, our unity is a public fact.

To identify yourself solely with the state gives us the facile nationalism mentioned earlier. The other extreme, identifying yourself exclusively with an ethnic collective, gives us racial segregation, separatist dogma and almost inevitably, intolerance. But we do have a *third* choice: to unite our personal background with that of the nation. Hyphens allow us to straddle separate worlds. Hyphens enlarge us, and in enlarging us, they enlarge Canada. The antihyphen crusade, in contrast, is the nationalism of suburbs and shopping malls. Suburbs and shopping malls have no hyphens. They also have no depth, because they lack two key ingredients: variety and a past.

Whoever we are and however we define ourselves, we *are* Canadians. Canada is the one category we all share. Rick Leung runs Friends and Neighbours Café in the Old Strathcona neighbourhood of Edmonton. He came to Edmonton from Hong Kong; this defines him in ways that I can never understand, just as my own northern Alberta, small-town roots are beyond his frame of reference. Rick and I, however, are united in more ways than we are separated. We are united by friendship, by our common nationality, by a Charter of Rights, by a Constitution, by a name: Canada.

Hyphens identify us: on the left side is our private story, on the right side is our public story. Together they encompass who we are, and as a nation our point of contact lies in our common denominator. A Hungarian-Canadian and an Irish-Canadian share neither Hungary nor Ireland. But they do share Canada. In any adjective-noun arrangement, the noun takes precedence, whether it be radical-Canadian, urban-Canadian, or Dutch-Canadian.

As Canadians, we have an overriding identity and overriding values. What we don't have any more is an overriding racial or ethnic identity—if we ever really did. Critics of multiculturalism confuse the two, assuming that if we lose ethnic homogeneity, we also lose our sense of common values.

In *Stand Up for Canada!* Professor Robert J. Jackson and his wife, Doreen, write that multiculturalism "is an attractive concept in the abstract, but in practice it is extremely divisive." But all of my experiences tell me they are wrong, as absolutely wrong as they can be. It is only in the *abstract* that the idea of multiculturalism seems fraught with danger. In working everyday practice, out in the market and on the streets, it is an exhilarating experience. Even Jackson and Jackson acknowledge this, noting that "positive attitudes toward multiculturalism have been shown to be strongest in areas where 'other' ethnic groups are most concentrated." In other words, multiculturalism works best where it is most apparent. It creates its own supporters.

Unfortunately, these *supporters* can descend to extremism as well, labelling anyone who dares question multiculturalism as racist. In *Sex in the Snow,* pollster Michael Adams takes a Baby Boomer look at social values, putting people into such specially coined categories as Cosmopolitan Modernists, Disengaged Darwinists, Extroverted Traditionalists and Autonomous Postmaterialists. Although purporting to be objective, Adams's bias appears when he describes the opposition many Canadians have to multiculturalism as being "of course . . . a form of racism, if much more polite than that of the Ku Klux Klan or the Aryan Nations." But to say that Canadians who are worried about multiculturalism differ from neo-Nazi Klansmen only by a degree of "politeness" is a ridiculous statement. Opponents of multiculturalism are not automatically racist. Not by any stretch of the imagination.

Laurie Snow teaches French immersion. She lives in Charlottetown, P.E.I., with her husband, Chuck, who is with the RCMP. I spent a few weeks with them in the autumn of 1996 and I enjoyed their company immensely. A French teacher and a Mountie and their last name is Snow:

could you get more Canadian than that? Were a contest ever held for All-Canadian Family, the Snows would win hands down. And yet Laurie, a European-educated, well-spoken cosmopolitan woman, has some legitimate concerns about the gung-ho commitment Canada has made to multiculturalism. Laurie strives to see both sides of the issue, but an unrestrained surge in new, often conflicting cultures has her worried that we will begin to see growing racial and ethnic clashes in Canada.

"Cultures have limits," she says. "You can't swamp a society and expect everything to be fine. I believe very much in creating a tolerant nation, but there are limits to what any society can absorb. We have to accept that these limits do exist. Societies change slowly, and I'm afraid we are moving too far, too fast. This can lead to serious trouble. I have seen it happen in other countries, and I don't want to see it happen here."

Laurie is right. There are limits to the changes a society can absorb. The tensions sparked by the recent mass migration of the Hong Kong elite to Vancouver is a case in point. But limits are made to be pushed and stretched and expanded, and I have confidence in Canada's adaptability. Laurie and I disagree only in a matter of intensity. Laurie is worried about a backlash, but I say "full steam ahead!"

Walk through Kensington. Look around. We are not tottering on the edge of anarchy. We are tottering on the edge of greatness. Earlier, I described Canada as being on the edge of a cliff. This is true. We are clinging to a vine at the edge of a cliff. But if we let go, we will not fall. We will fly.

Canada is a grand experiment and it is up to individual Canadians to carry it out. History has made us multiethnic *whether we accept this fact or not, whether we rage, whether we weep.* Let the record show that Canadians rose to the challenge, that we turned it to our advantage. Of all the national touchstones we have examined—our pride in landscapes, our adolescent anti-Americanism, our self-congratulatory modesty—multiculturalism is the one element that deserves the acclaim it has received.

KENSINGTON MARKET ON A Monday morning in late September. It is as quiet as a boulevard after a parade has passed. Now that the weekend crowds and commotion have dispersed, you see the backdrop, the stage that holds Kensington together. Not much, really, just a couple of streets, some houses, a neighbourhood. You cannot isolate any one shop or house and say *this,* this is Kensington, for Kensington is contained in every building, every brick. It is everywhere—and it is nowhere. This is what's known as "the paradox of identity." This is also the paradox of Canada.

And paradoxes, by definition, are unanswerable.

There are no more epiphanies, but one, and it is a simple lesson indeed: in the market that is our world, variety is its own reward. *Saturday morning, the streets are humming. You catch the beat and walk with it.*

THE RETURN
OF PETER PAN

· · · · · · · ·

*H*AVING SUCCESSFULLY squandered all my Japanese savings in the span of one winter, I ended up on Prince Edward Island desperately seeking gainful employment. The opportunity for respectable work denied me, I became a journalist, although when my parents asked, I told them I was a piano player at a whorehouse to avoid bringing excessive shame on the family.

Even then, I couldn't escape Japan. The managing editor at the local paper (*stirring masthead motto: "Covers Prince Edward Island Like the Dew"*) gave me my own newspaper column. The focus was to be, roughly: *What is it with all these Japanese anyway?* P.E.I. is one of Japan's most romanticized tourist destinations, and the growing flood of Japanese visitors has left many an Islander perplexed. My column, cleverly titled "East Meets West," was going to help cross this cultural gap. It was replete with handy, inside tips on doing business with the wily Japanese. The fact that I had done business with them myself for five years and was now flat broke was not something I liked to call attention to.

So when I heard there was an opening with Tourism P.E.I. for a job handling Japanese promotions, I leapt at the chance. The interview consisted of me barging in to the Tourism P.E.I. office, armed with my truthful but highly embellished résumé and a collection of "East Meets West" columns, which I assumed would qualify me as a sort of minicelebrity in their eyes.

Sadly, it didn't work.

As you can deduce from the fact that I am now a hack writer living on paltry publishing advances and not a highly overpaid globetrotting civil servant drinking *saké* and flirting with Japanese hostesses on taxpayers' money, I didn't get the job. Tourism P.E.I. rejected my application. Not that I'm bitter. True, I have taken to driving by the personnel director's home late at night and peering through his bedroom window with a pair of infrared sniper goggles. But I am not bitter.

I'm not sure why I didn't get the job. I did everything they tell you to do at an interview. I was inquisitive: *So how big is my government expense account?* I asked lots of questions: *How many free trips to Japan will I get?* And I showed initiative: *When I go on my free trips to Japan, is it okay to pad my government expense account? Or is it already fat enough?*

Unable to find a position with the government, I had to look elsewhere. My weekly newspaper column wasn't exactly making me rich, but fortunately I was able to find a second job. It was with a tour company selling Anne of Green Gables to Japanese tourists, and I didn't feel like a pimp at all. No sir.

Selling Anne to the Japanese is about as difficult as selling a glass of water to someone whose hair is on fire. The Japanese love Anne. She's cute, she's innocent, and she has a youthful spirit: all things the Japanese admire, though rarely attain. The company I worked for was Avonlea Tours, which was owned and operated by Roger Doiron, a man of infinite stamina. Roger also ran a taxi company and an apple-shipping business, and before that he owned a zoo. As he manoeuvred deeper into the tourist trade, he must have longed at times for the tranquillity and calm of zoo-keeping. Roger hired me to plan a revitalized attack on the Japanese market, and we did all right. I spent a lot of Roger's money, and a few of my devilishly clever plans blew up in my face, but in the end we more than doubled our Japanese business from the previous year.

Roger was a true entrepreneur, the kind of self-driven independent businessman that Canada is not usually renowned for producing. It was my first real contact with this world, and I found it all very exhausting and confusing, yet somehow *redeeming*.

Roger can trace his roots in Prince Edward Island all the way back to 1763 and the arrival of Acadian settlers who escaped the Great Expulsion. The Doiron family name has a long lineage on the Island; the equivalent of having come over on the *Mayflower*. At Avonlea Tours, eighteenth-century Acadia and twentieth-century entrepreneurship came smack up against a wave of Japanese tourists, and my two worlds—Japan and Canada—came crashing together.

I spent my evenings wandering the mean streets of Charlottetown (population: 16,000). Having long since outgrown my teenage fascination with jazz and hashish, or cigarettes for that matter—and isn't it funny how much jazz relies on hallucinogens to keep our interest?—I was feeling somewhat adrift.

Charlottetown is a city of fiddle music and Irish *ceilidh,* not smoky jazz halls. I spent my evenings drinking beer at the Dublin Pub and watching young Richard Wood saw his fiddle with such heat and intensity that I expected him to burst into flames at any moment. It was the musical equivalent of spontaneous combustion. Richard was still in his teens and filled with fire.

Somewhere along the way, amid my beer-soaked wanderings, I fell in with a group of Japanese expatriates who had collected in Charlottetown like so much driftwood. They reminded me a lot of the expatriate Americans, Brits and Canadians I had known in Japan. They drank too much, they made fun of the locals, and they didn't seem to fit in anywhere, at home or abroad. It is a strange world view, that of the expatriate, one caught in a state of limbo, halfway between escape and surrender.

"The trouble with Canadians..." was how most of the sentences began, and it brought back memories of my own circle of disgruntled outsiders in Japan, where the sentences inevitably began, *"The trouble with the Japanese..."* It was all very familiar.

Most of us have a stereotyped view of the Japanese as "corporate ants," but here—in various degrees of alienation—was a truly bohemian circle of misfits. For them, Prince Edward Island, and by extension Canada, had once been a dream, a dream of Shangri-La. But the problem with any Shangri-La is that once you get there, the dream seldom lives up to expectations. *Welcome to Paradise.*

Down and out in Charlottetown, and hangin' with the ex-pats. We drank ourselves into numbness in the sidewalk cafés of Victoria Row, we argued passionately about things we didn't understand, and we talked and talked and talked about future plans. It was an incestuous little circle, filled with malicious gossip and random, almost lethargic, love affairs. One of the Japanese ex-pats was a young man from Okinawa named Yukio. He had ended up in Charlottetown because he made the mistake of falling in love with a Canadian girl. He met her on holiday in Banff and, after a whirlwind romance, they pulled up stakes and relocated to P.E.I. It didn't last long. Within a few months she had taken all his stuff, cleared out his bank account and moved back to Banff. She even snatched his family's Buddhist altar, a spirit house that contains the dignity of one's ancestors, an heirloom Yukio had shipped over to Canada at great expense—both financial and emotional.

As a mutual friend of ours asked, "What kind of sick person would steal a spirit house?"

It was very hard convincing Yukio that Canadians were particularly "nice."

One night, bored and sad, Yukio and I walked the streets of Old Charlottetown for hours. As the dawn washed pale and pink across the city, we sat on the steps of Province

House and compared our tales of woe. The streets were empty and the early morning air had an autumn chill.

"Canada," said Yukio, sleepily, drunkenly. "Canada. Why? I don't understand."

"It's Canada," I said. "Canada is Canada. You can't understand it. Don't try."

IT WAS HERE in Charlottetown that our nation was born. Born from an idea put forth at a conference in 1864, an event commemorated annually in the city's quirky Festival of the Fathers. At first the Islanders rejected Confederation, but after running themselves into near bankruptcy with a railway that was as crooked in intent as it was in design, they were forced to reconsider. With a sigh, they agreed to become a province. A perfunctory, lacklustre proclamation was read to a crowd of three (who just happened to be passing by), and that was it. Prince Edward Island belonged to Canada, or vice versa, depending on your point of view. There were no parades, no celebrations.

Today, all of that has changed and P.E.I. now glories in its fleeting but pivotal role in Canadian history. Indeed, Charlottetown remains the only place in Canada willing to accept responsibility for Confederation. The Japanese and American visitors who now file through Province House have a hard time grasping the significance of the conference tables and chairs they are shown. An historic *board room?* A country created by bureaucrats? A country arranged like some minor corporate merger? No revolution, no Declaration of Independence, no samurai armies uniting rival clans, no nuclear bomb signalling one's entry into the modern world. Nothing. Just a collection of relatively anonymous delegates, some champagne, a waltz or two, some closed-door meetings and *bingo,* this vast enterprise we call Canada was somehow conjured into existence.

Right beside historic Province House is the Confederation Centre of the Arts, one of the greatest unprosecuted crimes of urban planning in Canadian history. Built in those madcap days of the '60s, this squat, oversized chunk of architectural contempt is completely out of proportion and out of place with its surroundings—although the architect apparently was making some kind of heavy-handed gesture towards imitating the shape and texture of Province House. Across the street from the Confederation Centre's backside are the beautiful red brick shop-fronts of Victoria Row, hedged in claustrophobically by this looming ode to centralized government. It reminded me of the Stalinist architecture you see in Russia, impressive only in its sheer mass. And in a certain, nagging way, it *is* a symbol of Confederation, this unnatural ill-suited presence wedged in and overpowering the local character. Or maybe it's just a really ugly building.

The Confederation Centre contains a theatre (home of "Anne the Never-Ending Musical"), a gift shop, an art gallery and a library. (I wrote a good deal of this manuscript at the Charlottetown Public Library, and let me tell you, my heart sank in despair every time I approached its misery-grey, windowless entrance. Libraries shouldn't look like prisons, am I right?)

The Confederation Centre of the Arts is also the proud sponsor of something called the Young Company. And it is here, where I least expected it, that my story takes a surprising turn.

EVERY YEAR, the Confederation Centre brings together young performers between the ages of eighteen and twenty-five, from every province, every territory, every region, and as many ethnic and linguistic groups as possible. They perform an outdoor musical production called *Spirit of a Nation*. They dance, they sing, they emote. It's like Katimavik, but with talent.

I first heard about *Spirit of a Nation* from Midori— lithe, elegant Midori, a former Miss Osaka who now sold expensive sweaters to Japanese tourists at the CP Hotel. The tourist season bustled, but during the long, grey winters Midori would always wonder why she was still on the Island, why she was still in Canada. "But then, in the summer, I watch *Spirit of a Nation* and it convinces me to stay." Her voice was soft, and it almost sounded like she resented the Young Company for making it so hard for her to leave.

Spirit of a Nation is a distinctly Canadian endeavour, painstakingly multiethnic and resolutely upbeat. The show features everything from Acadian step-dancing to Native rhythms, from Caribbean colours to high-leaping Ukrainian bravado. "Come," says the Young Company. "Come celebrate with us."

To which my immediate reaction was: There has got to be a way I can make some money out of this. Maybe it was the newly awakened entrepreneur in me. Maybe it was simple greed, who knows? I arranged interviews with various members of the Young Company and with the director herself, Janis Dunning. My cunning plan was to write an article on the Young Company and then peddle it to daily newspapers across Canada for big bucks. After all, here was a young, upbeat story with both national and regional appeal. It had a "hook," it had an "angle," it had young multiracial Canadians. What more could you ask?

Here is how my business plan broke down (any impressionable young freelancers out there may want to take note): I spent $120 on long-distance charges calling newspapers from the Yukon to Newfoundland, getting the names and addresses of the appropriate editors. From this I narrowed it down to seventy-eight daily newspapers. I then carefully tailored each article to the specific region the newspaper served. For example, if I sent one to Hamilton, I titled it "Young Company Offers National Opportunities to *Hamilton* Youth." If I sent it to Saskatoon, I titled it "Young Company Offers National Opportunities to *Saskatoon* Youth." And so on. Pretty darn clever, eh?

I printed 78 copies of the article (78 articles @ 12 pages an article=just under two reams of paper), and I mailed them off with the required return postage and a self-addressed envelope. Total mailing costs, including SASES: 78 packages x 90-cent stamps + 78 SASES x 45-cent stamps=$105.30. Then, in preparation for what was sure to be an overwhelming flood of requests, I took more than 300 colour slides of the Young Company in action. Total costs for pix: $182.42. I arranged the slides into piles of ten, in advance of orders for the article, and then sat back and waited, practically cackling in anticipation.

Here's what happened. Out of seventy-eight carefully targeted newspapers, three—count 'em *three*—bought the article: the *Sherbrooke Record* ("Voice of the Eastern Townships since 1837"); the *Truro Daily News* ("Serving Central Nova Scotia since 1891"); and the *Nanaimo Free Press* ("We Don't Send Freelance Writers Clips of Their Article

So Who Knows What Our Masthead Slogan Is"). Everyone else, from Sault Ste. Marie to Corner Brook, turned me down. The *Nelson Daily News* in B.C. even sent me a rejection notice that read: "I regret to inform you that the position of Reporter/Photographer has been filled." I was now getting turned down for things I hadn't asked for *before I even asked!* Pre-emptive rejection, surely a low point in any writer's career.

Total income from my three (3) sales: $195. Total expenses, including phone calls, paper, postage, pix and ink: $427.58. (You can see how much entrepreneurial savvy had rubbed off on me during my stint with Avonlea Tours.) So what is the point of this long, .convoluted anecdote? Simply this: you can't make money off of multiculturalism. I tried, and it didn't work.

The hardest thing was convincing Revenue Canada that I was indeed a writer.

"You are a writer, is that correct?"

"Yes!"

And they would look over my income statement and ask, "Why?"

Almost as difficult an experience were the actual interviews I conducted with the young performers themselves. They were impossible to hate. They were the singularly most *inoffensive* group of people I have ever met. They were brimming with enthusiasm, as though they were auditioning for life itself. I kept expecting them to suddenly break into song and dance, like a Hollywood musical. It was the same problem you run into with Canadians in general. When all is said and done, you really can't hate Canadians. *Don't you just hate that?*

The members of the Young Company were chosen to represent a cross section of Canadian society. But did they? Hardly. For one thing, they were all far too good-looking. And young. And energetic. There should have been at least one overweight, unemployed slug slouched in front of the TV, eating potato chips—if only in the interest of accuracy. And the message. So upbeat. So proud. So strong. Where was the self-deprecation? Where was the identity crisis? Where was the lack of confidence? Hell, they were even sexy in their own inoffensive way. And sexy is not a word one usually associates with Canadians. (Pamela Lee Anderson doesn't count: she is an android. No real person looks like that.)

I met with the Young Company on several occasions. They always made time for me and they always answered my questions, no matter how leading. ("Any really big arguments or fist-fights among cast members?") It was hard getting a controversial or even mildly negative quote out of them. They were all so—so damned *nice*.

Stephen Lilly is a show-stopping Ukrainian dancer from Saskatoon. One minute he is making death-defying leaps across the stage, and the next he is hip-hopping through a rap number about the environment, consumerism, nuclear war and, oh, a bunch of other stuff. "I had a great summer," said Stephen. "I hope I can come back next year as well. It was wonderful."

When I asked Twaine Ward of North York, Ontario, if he could sum up the Young Company in three words or less, he thought for a moment and said, "It was a fantastic growth experience." Technically, that's six words, but I understood what he is getting at.

Will he be back?

"I hope so. From now until auditions begin next year, I am going to work my butt off and hopefully they will see that there is such a vast improvement they will *have* to bring me back."

This is the future of Canada? Working hard? Striving to improve?

In search of some undercurrents of tension and—failing that—some good old-fashioned muck, I approached one of the Québécois members: Barbara Alexandre of Montréal. With her family ties to Haiti and Québec, Barbara is very much aware of the show's multicultural and bilingual emphasis. (One of the preferred requirements of the performers is a working ability in a second language.) "I was surprised," said Barbara, laughing. "This summer I wanted to practice my English, but the other performers wanted to talk French with me. I didn't know there is that interest outside of Québec."

Julia Halfyard-Martin of St. John's concurred with the rest of the Young Company. Julia's training includes ballet with the Newfoundland and Labrador School of Dance and six years of piano and ten years of voice. She has a Bachelor of Music degree from Memorial University and is currently studying opera performance.

"The Young Company has made me more confident," she says. "It's opened my eyes to what is out there."

Then, just when I thought I couldn't take any more positive reinforcement, I met Jimmy Le.

Jimmy is from Edmonton. Trained as a hair stylist, he competed in the 1996 Hair Olympics in London, England. He has also studied kung fu and has led the dragon in traditional New Year's celebrations. In *Spirit of a Nation,* he performs a sword dance and sings a solo extolling "highways and industries."

By now I was expecting the usual enthusiasm. And I got it. Jimmy is just as deeply sincere as the rest. "In my life, there are so many colours now. And hopes. And dreams." I asked Jimmy if he had a favourite moment in *Spirit of a Nation,* and he mentioned a scene depicting the arrival of refugees. Jimmy's own family came to Canada from Vietnam.

"I wanted to be in that scene so bad, because I have a personal connection to it. I can step into the character. My sisters and brothers came to Canada in a boat and they told me all these terrible stories. When I am on stage, I am thinking—this is my brother, at this time, at that moment. I am starving. I am very cold because there are not enough clothes to wear. There is no food. There is no hope. It is going to rain soon and there is no place to take cover."

Then, just when all seems lost, a hand reaches out and a voice whispers in song, "Come to my land. My land is a garden. Come to my land and make it your home."

"Here, in Canada, I have so many choices," said Jimmy. "I can be anything I want to be, as long as I work hard for it. I realize now how proud I am to be a Canadian."

I was taken aback by it all.

I also noticed how carefully *Spirit of a Nation* maintained ethnic categories. The Chinese sword dance was performed by someone who *looks* Chinese. The Caribbean dance was performed by someone who *is* black. The Greek dance was performed by someone who is white. And so on. What would happen, I wonder, if you took all of the roles we play in *Spirit of a Nation* and turned them 90 degrees. What then?

I posed this question to Janis Dunning. Together with Creative Director Jacques Lemay, Janis is the driving force behind *Spirit of a Nation*. She has a soothing, almost birdlike voice—and a laserlike intensity in her eyes. Janis Dunning is a sword wrapped in silk. I was a little bit scared of her.

"The spirit of any nation is its youth," she said, her eyes challenging me to say otherwise.

Some people talk in complete sentences. Janis Dunning talks in complete, articulated *paragraphs*.

"It is not a frothy show that says everything is beautiful, there are no problems here. We address issues. We are trying to make people more aware of the many issues going on within Canada: environmentally, racially, separatism, economic issues. But at the core of it, first and foremost, is the fact that we are proud to be Canada, proud to be Canadian. We allow, within that, flexibility about what Canada is and will be."

When she mentioned flexibility, I leaned forward. "Let me ask you something, then. Jimmy Le is from Vietnam. Barbara's family is from Haiti. Pamela is Native. In *Spirit of a Nation,* Jimmy performs a Chinese sword dance, Barbara performs an Afro-Caribbean dance, and Pamela a Micmac dance. Now, I realize that on one level this is strictly a casting decision. If someone is going to portray a Chinese dancer, they had better look Chinese. But my question is this: would it work the same if, using the same cast, you moved everyone over one position. If you had Jimmy Le perform the Caribbean dance, if you had Barbara perform the Native dance, and Pamela perform a Chinese sword dance?"

Janis sat back a moment and considered the question and its implications. "I don't think Canada is quite ready for that. When Jacques Lemay and I present authentic ethnic culture, it is very important not to give offence. If you are from that ethnic culture, and particularly if you are first generation, you want it done well. You don't want it to be made light of. At the same time, though, we are always interweaving cultures. For example, in *Spirit of a Nation,* everyone does the Greek dance together, to show that all Canadians can celebrate and participate. The same with the Micmac dance. And everyone takes part in the dragon dance at the end, again to show that in Canada we can all share in the heritage of our various peoples. In the future, perhaps, we can mix it up even more, but Canada hasn't got that far—*yet.*"

There was only one question left to ask. "Can the Young Company save Canada?"

Janice didn't laugh or smile or brush the question off. It was clearly something she had thought about. "Can the Young Company save Canada? No. It is a gradual process of opening minds that will save Canada. But by exchanges like this—and this is an exchange—by working side by side with people from different regions and different perspectives, we *are* opening minds. By seeing this show, it is amazing how many people relax and allow their minds to be opened to the greater possibilities of Canada."

The greater possibilities of Canada. I had heard this kind of thing before, but I had forgotten the power of such sentiments. Janis Dunning believes. She truly believes. She reminded me of a younger, more intense version of Jacques Hébert, and talking with her brought back a flood of memories from my own youth. Katimavik. Project Megapôle. Canada World Youth. I was suddenly very uncomfortable in Janis's presence, in much the same way that an apostate feels uncomfortable when the bishop drops by for a cup of tea.

CANADA DAY. Flags are all aflutter. Crowds are milling about. Children are laughing and playing (or screaming and crying, as the case may be). The government is rewarding us for being Canadian by handing out little pieces of birthday cake and Dixie cups of coca-cola, and we are going crazy. We are so ecstatic to be receiving this largesse that we go through the line four more times in our enthusiasm until we are informed that, really, it is only one little piece of frosted cake per person.

No matter. It is Canada Day. Canada Day. My first in six years.

Canada Day. Canada Day. Everyone is happy, the rain has stopped and the sun is up where it belongs. Canada Day. Canada Day. God, I'm bored.

My expatriate Japanese friends are all in bed nursing hangovers, Yukio has long since returned to Okinawa, and I am wandering about among strangers. Canadians. Fellow citizens. I listen to long interchangeable speeches and I eavesdrop on bits of mundane repartee. "The pieces of cake are much bigger this year, aren't they?" "Oh, yes. Much bigger." The sound of people agreeing: Canadians in conversation.

Canada Day in Charlottetown, the Cradle of Confederation, the symbolic epicentre of the nation. And suddenly, the crowd surges forward. People fill the amphitheatre seats, balancing serviettes and cake on their knees, shading their eyes with paper flags.

And now everyone is cheering as the Young Company takes the stage in a swirl of colour and good intentions. The music rocks the crowd as the performers sing out in relentless, rhyming multisyllables:

We're the generation
that's got the inspiration
Take this declaration
all around the world!

The crowd loves it, and I begin composing lines of my own: *"We will ease the inflammation / of constant constipation / and compulsive masturbation / all around the world."*

But the momentum is theirs. The Young Company is flying and their energy is infectious. These kids are *wired.*

With pride and dedication
We're moving in formation
Let's get this body shakin'
With the Spirit of a Nation!

Next up are the Hearty Pioneers, smiling away to beat the band. Jimmy Le is in a suit and tie, Barbara is in a bonnet and apron. Distant sounds of war begin—and the mood shifts. A ragtag band of refugees enters, stage right. Smoke rolls across the scene like a tableau from the French Revolution. A young woman slowly stands, reaching out. Reaching out.

There is a land
I believe
where you can dream
and see your dreams come true.

The emotion begins to build anew, and I sit back in bewilderment as the show soars, colours burst back onto stage, and *Spirit of a Nation* comes crashing to a climax with the entire Young Company, arms linked, singing: *"I want to be / free to travel any road / I want to see / all there is to see."*

And something happens.

A chill, faintly discernable, runs like a drop of water down my spine. The music crests and the roar of the crowd rolls like thunder, as the Young Company sings out with one voice, clearly, loudly, unapologetically:

Given the chance
And given the choice
I want to be—

(and here the background voices rise up in counterpoint, hitting the high note and holding it, holding it, *"I want to be—"*)

Canadian

And the chest tightens. The throat aches. There it is, shining through. There it is, defying the odds and even common sense. That Peter Pan faith. That stubborn, hard-won naivety. That unwavering belief in magical gestures.

Canada. My homeland. It was good to be back.

ACKNOWLEDGEMENTS

But Not in Canada! by Walter Stewart, used by permission of the author. *Canada Inside Out—How We See Ourselves, How Others See Us* by David Olive, used by permission of Doubleday Canada Ltd. "Canada Is" by Steve Hyde and Eric Robertson, © BMG Music Publishing Ltd. for The World, all rights reserved, used by permission. "Captain Canuck" used by permission of Richard Comely. *Dear Canada/Cher Canada* used by permission of Ben Wicks & Associates. "Les douteuses alliances de Greenpeace" by Yves Beauchemin, *Le Devoir*, 5 November 1991, used by permission of *Le Devoir*; English translation by Chris Korchin for *Boundaries of Identity: A Quebec Reader*, edited by William Dodge, Lester Publishing, used by permission. *The Loyalists* by Christopher Moore, used by permission of McClelland & Stewart, Inc. *My Discovery of America* by Farley Mowat, used by permission of McClelland & Stewart, Inc. *Nationalism without Walls* by Richard Gwyn, used by permission of McClelland & Stewart, Inc. *Now or Never! Manifesto for an Independent Quebec* by Pierre Bourgault, translated by David Homel, used by permission of Key Porter Books. "Something To Sing About," words and music by Oscar Brand, TRO—© Copyright 1963 (renewed) 1964 (renewed), Hollis Music, Inc., New York, NY, used by permission. "Spirit of a Nation," used by permission, Janis Dunning, the Canadian Heritage Arts Society. "Sudbury Saturday Night," music and lyrics by Tom Connors, © 1970 by Crown Vetch Music, used by permission; recorded by Stompin' Tom on the album "Bud the Spud" (EMI 92974). "Coureur de Bois" in *The Wounded Prince* by Douglas LePan, used by permission of McClelland & Stewart, Inc.